CW00377018

# IN SEARCH OF THE ASSASSIN

# In Search Of The Assassin

Susie Morgan

BLOOMSBURY

First published 1991


Bloomsbury Publishing Ltd, 2 Soho Square, London W1V 5DE

A CIP catalogue record for this book
is available from the British Library

ISBN 0 7475 0401 6

10 9 8 7 6 5 4 3 2 1

Typeset by Hewer Text Composition Services, Edinburgh
Printed in Great Britain by Butler & Tanner Limited, Frome and London

In 1984 Susie Morgan, an English journalist, was critically injured in a bomb attack at a press conference in Nicaragua, just across the Costa Rican border. The conference had been urgently convened by Edén Pastora, charismatic leader of the anti-Sandinista Contra rebel force, at his jungle headquarters. Seventeen journalists were injured and three killed in the blast. Pastora, the target, miraculously survived.

It took Susie two years and dozens of operations to recover, and, as she did, she became obsessed by a desire to track down the assassin – a man who had passed himself off as a Danish photographer, had travelled with journalists to the press conference and had planted the bomb, concealed in his camera case, only inches from where Susie Morgan stood.

An intensely gripping story which chronicles Susie's own emotional odyssey, it is also a highly dramatic narrative of one woman's tenacious and courageous struggle against the labyrinthine machinations of corrupt governments on every side and of the enormous difficulty she faced as a journalist, with no legal powers, to get to the truth: a truth almost everyone wanted hidden.

This book is dedicated to the victims of La Penca.

# CONTENTS

## ILLUSTRATIONS

# ACKNOWLEDGMENTS

As well as thanking those people mentioned in this book – family, friends, colleagues, contacts, the film-crew, Central TV – who made it possible, I should like to acknowledge my debt to Martha Honey and Tony Avirgan for their *La Penca* report (1985) and to Leslie Cockburn for her book *Out of Control*. I should also like to thank Steve Barclay for his wonderful editing of the documentary; Phil Gunson for his unflagging support, including reading this manuscript; Nicholas Faith, who helped me organise the book and fed me champagne; Don Rowe who got me started; Lyle Prescott, Paul Halloran, Lynne McRitchie, Jill Neville, Nick Wadley and Jasia Reichardt; my agent Xandra Hardie; and my publisher Liz Calder. Finally I should like to thank my editor Alison Mansbridge, who not only did a superb job editing the book, but also cared. Last of all I want to thank Margaret Branch, who helped me more than perhaps even she knows. The views expressed in this book are, however, mine, as are any errors.

Whenever you have eliminated the impossible, whatever remains,
however improbable, must be the truth.
Sir Arthur Conan Doyle, *The Sign of Four*

President Ronald Reagan's 8-year crusade to stop the spread of leftist revolution in Central America was always a two-war Front. The President and his men realised from the start that to carry out their aggressive plans to defeat the Marxist rebels in El Salvador and to oust the Sandinista government in Nicaragua they would need to neutralise the post-Vietnam public opposition to US intervention in the Third World. To win this war at home, the White House created a sophisticated apparatus that mixed propaganda with intimidation, consciously misleading the American people and at times trampling on the right to dissent. In short the Administration set out to reshape perceptions of Central America and the Orwellian methods employed could be one of the most troubling legacies of Reagan's Presidency.
Robert Parry and Peter Kornbluh,
'Iran-Contra's Untold Story', *Foreign Policy* (1988)

Map of Journalists' Route to La Penca Press Conference (Detail)

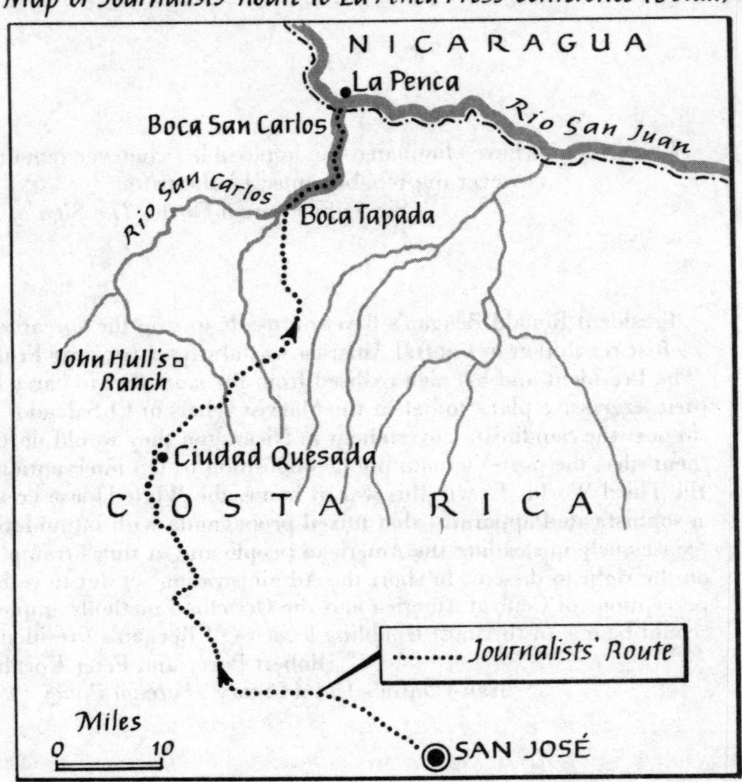


Map of Central America

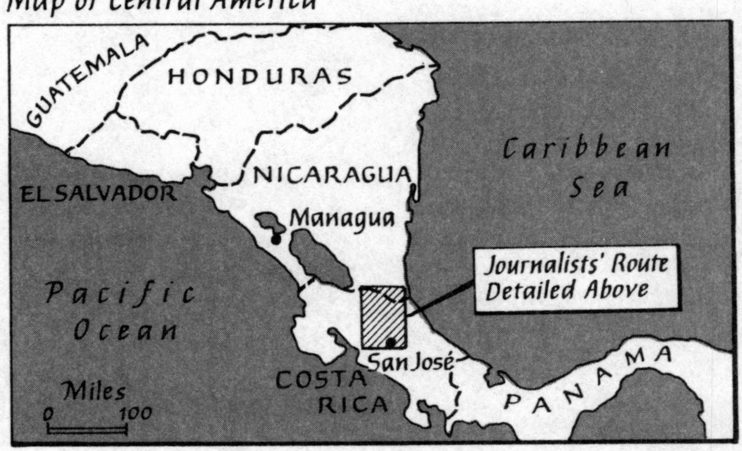

# La Penca

*Shortly after the press conference started I felt a strange sensation of unease, a strong, dreadful premonition of danger. Something was wrong. Some sixth sense was telling me I should move, that everything was too quiet. Colleagues later told me the camera-case at my feet was making fizzing sounds, but I don't remember this.*

*Suddenly, there is a yellow-blue flash, brighter than anything I have ever seen. It lights up the room. My eyes won't open. I can't see. Pieces of live metal are fused to my skin. I don't know what that light was. I think it has burnt me.*

*I find that I am lying on the floor. It is dark. Everyone around me is screaming. I am screaming. My body is convulsed, racked by electric volts. Every few seconds there is a pause: each one exactly the same length, followed inexorably by a new, terrible surge of power. I know this will kill me, that my heart will stop. But I can't move.*

*Something terrible has happened, but it has happened so fast my mind can't comprehend it. It's not like anything I have ever known yet at the same time it's all strangely familiar.*

*I am going down a bright path that I recognise in some dim part of my brain. I feel I have been here before. But still I feel bewildered, disoriented. Why won't my eyes open? Why is everything dark? Why can't I stop screaming? This is like being in hell. Am I dead? I must be dead. Someone, please, help me.*

*I have been lying on my stomach, curled in a foetus-like ball, for I don't know how long, reacting to the shock, the unendurable pain, by screaming, unable to think, unable to move. I know subconsciously that I am desperately hurt. I don't know how I know this. Then I smell my skin and hair burning. I feel I am quite alone.*

*I can hear a gruff voice shouting at me:* 'No grites, no estás muerta' – *'Stop screaming, you aren't dead.' At some point a voice I recognise as Peter's says gently to me, 'Susie, something terrible has happened. We're all hurt. We should get out of here, it's burning in here, too hot, it's not safe.' He tries to help me to my feet, but I know I can't stand. I collapse immediately.*

*I hear the voice of Gilberto comforting me and ordering the guerrillas to get me a stretcher and evacuate me because I am* 'muy, muy mal' – *'very, very bad'. After what seems like hours they lift me on to some kind of stretcher and carry me down some steps. I remember the river. They must be putting me into a canoe.*

*The boat journey seems interminable. I am still screaming, asking if I am going to die. Gilberto is beside me. 'How long to hospital?' I ask, again and again. I know I can't wait long for treatment. Gilberto each time tells me,* 'Otra media hora' – *'Another half-hour.'*

*I start to wonder what is hurt or missing from my body. I try clumsily to check by first feeling my face. But my hands have somehow clenched themselves into tight fists and I can't unclench them. Nonetheless I laboriously and methodically try to check whether my nose, eyes and chin are still in place. I have no recollection of what I discovered.*

*I am starting to think I can't hang on when I hear a doctor explaining that he can't operate on me immediately because there might be others who need life-saving surgery, such as amputations, and there is only one operating theatre. I hear nurses commenting, in some surprise, on how much blood I have lost: over two litres. They say my pulse has virtually disappeared.*

*Two journalists died that night and one soon after. Seventeen were badly hurt and took years to recover from their injuries. I was fortunate to be one of them.*

# 1

# A Terrible Waste of Time

I spent the three years from 1981 to 1984 in the killing fields of Central America. I had wanted to go there ever since I read in the British press that priests in El Salvador had to sleep in different houses every night to stay alive. Then, in June 1980, the Archbishop was assassinated. What kind of hell-hole could El Salvador be, I wondered. I decided I had to go there to find out.

Back then I remember feeling there was nothing more important than the job I was doing: being a witness to the place where history was in the making and telling it to my readers; struggling to find words that could adequately describe the savagery of civil war, the butchery of innocents, the cynicism of US policy; despairing that readers living in comfort and safety in the US and England could grasp the reality behind my reports.

I was still under the spell of the romance of being a war correspondent. Some of us had pictures on our walls of colleagues who had died telling the story, but we all believed our being there could make a difference, even change the world. Equally gripping for many of us was the Hemingwayesque life: the adrenalin rush from danger; the hard drinking late into the night; the passionate romances, soon consummated, soon consumed. The pace was intoxicating. By 1984, however, I was emotionally and physically exhausted – sickened and worn down by the diet of unremitting violence, and frustrated by the sheer intractability of the situation. Far from glamorous, my chosen career now seemed lonely, demanding and draining, the constant travelling unsettling. Sometimes I would wake in a strange bed wondering fearfully, in that eerie moment between sleeping and waking, where I was. I would then resort to deductions along the lines of 'If it's Tuesday, then this must be Guatemala/Honduras/Nicaragua.' Nonetheless, perversely, when I made dutiful annual pilgrimages home to my family, and they, along with my friends, exhorted me to stay, to 'settle down', the idea filled me with horror. I felt trapped. Repelled as I was by my unstable, rackety, unreal existence in Central America, I no longer felt in tune with my former life and friends. I knew several colleagues who were 'burned out', and some were heavily into drugs and booze, kept in these war-zones by a strange compulsion, constantly taking insane risks. Some had a death-wish; others had become 'war-junkies'. Was I becoming like them?

I had, in those three years, become well acquainted with the violence caused by the perennial struggle between the privileged few and the impoverished many, especially in El Salvador and Guatemala, where armed clashes between Left and Right were accompanied by the activities of right-wing death-squads, secretly sanctioned by the armed forces and even by the government. In Guatemala there was a policy of killing Indians that bore a more than passing resemblance to genocide. In El Salvador in 1980 and 1981 over 10,000 civilians a year were being killed in what President Duarte himself grimly described to me as 'industrial quantities'. This wholesale slaughter was not unconnected with a statement made by Al Haig, the US Secretary of State, to the effect that tiny El Salvador, the size of the state of Massachusetts, was the new front-line drawn by the US in its war against communism; the policy declaration was interpreted by the Right throughout the region as an implicit carte blanche. Anything to avoid a second Nicaragua.

Such experiences took a tremendous toll even on Western

reporters. I remember one fellow woman journalist whose tough professionalism I used to admire and try to emulate admitting that when she was by herself after witnessing some particularly harrowing sight she used to break down and weep uncontrollably. I had never been under any illusion about the level of violence I would encounter in this turbulent region, but I soon discovered that knowing about this intellectually was very different from experiencing and living it. I have often felt I have the wrong temperament for a war correspondent, constantly getting far too upset and personally involved. Yet I'm sure that the French colleague who once told me, when I was starting out as a reporter in Africa, that one could not be a good journalist without being sensitive was right; unless you feel the passion you can't convey it. This fact makes burn-out a constant professional hazard.

I encountered horrors daily. Many stick in my mind. Once I was driving through the lush Salvadorean countryside with a colleague when he turned to me and said, 'You see that building?' I looked; there was a long whitewashed shed in ruins, its roof destroyed, the walls still standing with gaping holes. 'Yes,' I said cautiously. 'That,' he explained, 'was a slaughterhouse; but the guerrillas found its lights were burning at night – after curfew; then they remembered that the most recent death-squad victims who had been beheaded no longer had jagged machete cuts across their necks, but neat, almost surgical amputations at the top of the shoulders. Then it dawned on them that the death-squads had "refined" their sadistic techniques: now they were processing their victims through machinery intended for slaughtering animals. So they blew it up.' That particular anecdote – one of a number grimly related by the press corps – exemplifies for me the horror of El Salvador. To see the results of such depravity I had only to visit the local rubbish-tip. There could be seen, at almost any time, the bodies of such victims. Invariably they had been mutilated: ears, noses, fingertips and, in the case of men, genitals hacked off. The women had usually been raped. Of course, within hours the vultures would have picked the bodies bare, eradicating many of the grisly details, but not the reality of what had happened. To have such sights is to have nightmares of the suffering that must have occurred before death. I still avoid rubbish-tips.

During this time of violent instability in the early 1980s, Washington was providing training, advisors and billions of dollars to shore up the Salvadorean government. In 1983 I wrote an article for the *Daily Telegraph* chronicling the real role of the US advisors, who were not officially allowed in combat but who were, I had learnt, directing and running Salvadorean Intelligence, specifically locating and targeting guerrilla concentrations for the Salvadorean army, and thus playing a pivotal role in the combat. (A death-squad defector later described how US advisors handed them money to finance their activities and keep them going, human wickedness I still have trouble believing, although, like so much else going on in El Salvador, I know it to be true.)

I can still recall my concern when publication of my article coincided with the assassination by Salvadorean rebels of a US advisor, Naval Attaché Lieutenant-Colonel Albert Shauffelberger (described chauvinistically in *Newsweek* magazine as 'the first casualty'). He was shot when driving to pick up his Salvadorean girlfriend at the Jesuit University. The window of his bulletproof car was wound down, the air-conditioning being broken, and despite his training in security he made this trip at the same time every day. In response to my article, a BBC reporter telephoned me from England the same day, asking me what I knew and underlining the, to him, extraordinary coincidence of my information and the US advisor's death. I knew all our phone-calls were being carefully monitored, and a colleague of mine had even seen, on the desk of the Salvadorean Foreign Minister, a list of all the phone-calls he had made from his Camino Real hotel room, so I was alarmed when my telephone link to England, normally good, was repeatedly broken. My BBC interviewer patiently redialled at least six times until his deadline finally expired. I thought it sinister then, but it wasn't until later that same day, when I returned to my rented house just behind the hotel, that I realised just how sinister. My front door was closed but no longer locked. When I cautiously entered I found a scene of utter chaos – papers scattered everywhere, the bed overturned, drawers opened and emptied, everything upside down. I was even more frightened when I saw dollar bills I had carelessly left around lying untouched: these were no ordinary thieves. But what alarmed me most were my two telephones lying on the floor, their wires cut.

I knew what could happen – and had – to journalists in El Salvador. My colleagues all agreed that this bore the hallmarks of an inside job: 'Those responsible must be from Salvadorean Security.' Local Salvadoreans, who knew about these things, also warned me to take the break-in seriously: 'This is a warning, pay attention, Susana,' begged my worried landlord. 'Next time they might kill you.' I was reminded of the previous year, when four Dutch reporters were 'accidentally' killed in cross-fire by the Salvadorean Army as they were making a clandestine rendezvous with left-wing guerrilla forces. Even I (no expert) could see the powder-marks on their bloody clothing that showed they had been shot at point-blank range. The press corps interpreted their murder as a none too subtle warning to the rest of us not to meddle with the Left.

I left the country for a few weeks, and even after my return I was terrified of sleeping in that house. Fortunately, nothing further came of it.

Despite such incidents, and whatever one's state of mind, one continued, almost mechanically, to take risks. This was particularly true of freelancers like myself. We constantly drove ourselves, taking chances others avoided, feeling we had to prove ourselves that much better because of our lack of official status. This was reflected in the casualty figures, most of whom were freelancers.

In March 1983 I nearly became one of them when I left Tegucigalpa, the capital of Honduras, with a friend, Richard Cross, to investigate a road on the Nicaraguan border that served as a supply route to thousands of Contras from the Honduran camps dotted along the border.

The official line was that there were no Contras in Honduras, but Richard and I had seen with our own eyes whole villages abandoned and in ruins, coffee plantations untended, farm animals killed by mortars and stray bullets lying decomposing in the road. The only inhabitants of this desolate area were Contras – thousands of them – with their blue-green uniforms (from Georgia, USA) and Che Guevara-style black berets, heavily armed with American-made weapons. We ourselves had been flagged down and warned by Honduran soldiers not to enter the area, because Nicaraguan rockets were falling along our route and vehicles travelling the border road were coming under constant attack. We listened politely, and continued on our way.

Rounding a bend and cresting a hill, we suddenly saw the wide plains of Nicaragua stretched out below us, defended only by a barbed-wire fence that ran beside our track. At the same time, silhouetted against the skyline, like a target in a shooting gallery, we came under intense machine-gun fire. By a miracle we were not hit, but we were badly shaken.

There followed one of the most frightening, eerie nights of my life. Our car broke down while we were still on the border, in the direct line of mortar fire from Nicaragua. We had to stay put until morning. The darkness was periodically lit by the red glow from Nicaraguan flares, and we heard the constant roar of machine-gun fire and rockets. Contra and Honduran soldiers, some limping and covered in blood, kept walking past our car, most of them stopping to warn us for God's sake to move. We explained our broken-down car. They left, shaking their heads.

Despite this narrow escape we decided to return the next day with another friend, Diall Torgersson, in order to gain more on the spot information. It seems extraordinary to me now that I was eager to take such risks.

In the event *The Economist* was so interested in the story that they insisted I file immediately, forcing me, under sheer pressure of time, to cry off the planned return trip. Our reports provided the first eye-witness accounts of the impact of US policy in its so-called 'secret' war against Nicaragua, a conflict that had its front-line in this no-man's land between Nicaragua and Honduras, appropriated by the Contras as a rear base and resulting in cross-border raids by the Contras and retaliatory incursions across the Honduran frontier by the Sandinistas.

On the afternoon of Richard and Diall's trip I received an urgent phone-call from the US Embassy. 'Have Diall and Richard returned?' enquired a tense voice. 'Why? What's wrong?' 'There's been a terrible accident on that road. The bodies of two gringos have been seen. Their car's blown up. We think from their descriptions they're Richard and Diall. But we aren't sure yet. There's such heavy fighting no one can get near. Let me know the second they get back. Don't tell anyone. We don't want to alarm anyone unnecessarily yet. And if it's true we must contact their families first.'

It was many hours before we had positive confirmation. That wait was one of the worst times of my life. I went to a bar – a favourite Contra haunt – to change money and to pass the time. As I waited a Honduran approached me and asked if I knew the two journalists. The news was out on the Honduran radio. 'I hope they're dead,' he said, 'because you foreign journalists bring a bad image to our country.' I screamed at him, tears streaming down my face. Much later that night I heard confirmation of what I had been dreading.

Apparently, on their way back the journalists' white Toyota had hit an anti-personnel mine, buried in the dirt track. The car was hurled yards into the air, and both men were killed instantly. Even after seeing their dreadfully disfigured bodies, Diall's reduced to an amorphous lump in his body-bag, which was about two feet long, I couldn't believe they were dead. I kept thinking of things to tell them. I had been a witness at Diall's wedding only the previous year. I could remember Richard saying to me, on our dreadful night on the border, 'I never thought I'd get to spend the night with you.' I can still remember seeing, poking out of the blanket covering his corpse, his bandaged left fist – injured some time ago when he banged the table at an airline office where he was told he couldn't fly to Honduras.

*

Together with other journalists I had described the reality of America's secret war in Honduras; now I discovered a new development. With the Honduran part of the US plan to destroy Nicaragua in place, a similar development was stealthily taking place in Costa Rica, Nicaragua's neighbour to the south: the ostensibly neutral country was being turned into a springboard for the US-backed Contras to launch their attacks. Until now, America's covert new plans in Costa Rica had gone almost unnoticed.

Despite the difficulties, including scepticism from my editors and, worse, prevarications and disinformation from my Costa Rican contacts, I felt this was a story that had to be exposed. My interest led me, in May 1984, to attend a press conference I would not otherwise have bothered with, having so often been disappointed in the past.

The military leader of the Contra's Southern Front, based in Costa Rica, was Edén Pastora, a controversial and charismatic figure, part Zorro, part Crazy Horse, always capable of the unexpected. He was really a throw-back to the historic *caudillo* – the 'strong man' so beloved of Latin Americans. Nicaraguans of all political opinions still speak of Pastora's extraordinary courage and daring with bated breath. And this is the key to the passionate hatreds, bitterness and loyalty the man inspires. For Pastora – the most charismatic leader of the Contras, whose avowed aim was to overthrow the left-wing Sandinistas – used to be the Sandinistas' most courageous military leader, until he defected in a form as flamboyant and unexpected as the rest of his life. Not surprisingly, the Sandinistas had a particular and virulent hatred for this man, regarding him as the most foul of traitors, and fearing the support he still had among the Nicaraguan people.

In his earlier incarnation as Sandinista hero Pastora was the most famous of all the Frente's military leaders. It was he who dreamed up the idea of seizing the National Palace, where all government business was conducted, and holding the inmates hostage in return for money, publicity and the release from jail of scores of top Frente Sandinista prisoners. On 22 August 1978 he succeeded in carrying it out, with only twenty-six guerrilla fighters disguised as an élite unit of Anastasio Somoza's National Guard. It was this action, above all others, that tipped the political scales in favour of the Sandinistas, by demonstrating to doubters that they could take on the state and win, paving the way for the overthrow of Somoza a year later.

Congress was in session, and there were about 1500 people in the building. When challenged by a genuine guard, Pastora whispered fiercely, 'Shush – the Chief's coming,' and swept up the Palace stairs, flanked by his fake guards. They burst into the Chamber. Pastora said he initially felt fear, rapidly replaced by exhilaration, as he realised he had in his grasp 'the bird with the nest and everything'. Forty-eight hours later fifty-eight freed Sandinista prisoners and their liberators, led by Pastora, were airlifted to exile in Panama and Venezuela. Thousands lined their route to the airport, shouting, 'Down with Somoza'. On the aircraft steps, despite their agreement to remain anonymous, Pastora, who had been given the title Comandante Zero for the operation, could not resist pulling off the black and red bandana that masked his face and revealing himself to the cheering crowd and assembled press photographers. It was this image of Pastora – his G3 rifle in one hand, a grenade hanging from his shirt – and a gold Rolex taken from a hostage on his wrist – that launched him as the hero of the revolution.

But when the Sandinistas swept to power the following July, Pastora was made first Deputy Interior Minister, then Deputy Defence Minister, but not one of the nine Comandantes, a post he felt entitled to. Two years later he defected, whether because he had genuine political disagreements with the Sandinistas or because of pique was never very clear. Now, as military leader of the Democratic Revolutionary Alliance (ARDE), his petty jealousies, egotism and arrogance, and his bewildering political and personal shifts, had succeeded in alienating virtually everyone, friends and foes alike. On the one hand he was probably the Sandinistas' public enemy number one. But on the other, the Americans, who sponsored the Contras, referred to him despairingly as an 'unguided missile' whom they couldn't control and whom they privately held responsible for the failure of the Southern Front.

The Southern Front was supposed to operate in conjunction with the main Contra force in the North, squeezing Nicaragua in a pincer movement in the middle. But Pastora stubbornly refused, on principle, to go along with the US master-plan. He repeatedly told us, in his idiosyncratic, high-flown rhetoric, that the Northern-based Contras were 'genocidal criminals', henchmen of the former despot Anastasio Somoza, and responsible for the murder of his own father.

The Americans – used to dealing with subservient Third World figures – seethed with frustration at their inability to control Pastora. There were serious problems with the image of the Northern Contra force – still perceived by most Nicaraguans as linked to the loathed former dictator, and thus a worse alternative than the Sandinistas. The image was not helped by persistent, appalling human-rights violations. Despite all the money lavished on them by the US, they were manifestly unable to win the hearts and minds of the people. Pastora was the one man, in the American view, who could rally mass support on behalf of the Contras. But far from being able to capitalise on his charisma, the Americans were finding that Pastora's independence and legendary stubbornness extended to them too. Their patience was wearing thin, and they were now putting extremely heavy pressure on Pastora to bring him into line, mostly by cutting off his supplies. There was even a rumour that the US was giving him an ultimatum – that he come through or else – but I could never find out exactly what was involved.

I had met Pastora twice in the spring of 1984. On the first occasion he had been in his 'secret' base of operations – an elegant but heavily armed villa in one of the most exclusive suburbs of San José, the capital of Costa Rica. I had received information from reliable sources of direct CIA involvement on behalf of the rebels. After resorting to a time-honoured journalistic ploy (a marathon drinking session with my best Western Intelligence contact) I had finally confirmed that it was the CIA and not the Contras who had recently mined the ports of Nicaragua. It was a scoop, but I wanted Pastora's reaction.

I was to be disappointed. Not only did Pastora deny all of this, but he stonewalled, bouncing erratically and extremely volubly from topic to topic, leaping from 'control' room to 'communications' room, one moment stabbing his finger at a huge military map of Nicaragua, lit up by blinking lights and marked by flags that purported to show (somewhat improbably, I thought) rebel forces controlling much of the south and centre of the country, the next shouting into a crackling walkie-talkie to various field-commanders (all with nicknames like 'Tuto', 'Ganso', 'Tito' and so on). Then he would pick up a telephone and bark commands into it, and then again he would launch excitedly into a rambling monologue about his prowess, ideology, military strategy, difficulties involving his lack of outside support, all interspersed with his homespun philosophy of life. At one point, late into the night, he even led me upstairs to a room where his poor wife was trying to sleep, to show me piles of new uniforms, boots and guns and to complain that the CIA was cutting off his supplies to put pressure on him. I was later told by a (male) colleague that Pastora had a habit of performing this charade in front of Western reporters, especially women.

I felt thoroughly irritated by Pastora's lies and evasions. The quality of our interview may have been reflected in the fact that although we talked (or, rather, Pastora did) for over four hours, *Newsweek* extracted precisely two questions and answers from it. Even my tape-recorder broke down as I was playing back Pastora's interminable monologue. I sympathised with its attitude.

The second occasion was when I, together with six or seven other reporters, visited the little Nicaraguan town of San Juan del Norte. This had been seized by Pastora – the sole such victory in four years of war. After an exhausting journey walking along a riverbed all night and dragging boats up tributaries of the San Juan river, which had been made impassable by lack of rain, we finally reached the town the day after Pastora had captured it.

There were the shelled buildings lying in ruins, the burnt earth, the stench of rotting corpses, the groups of miserable prisoners – and there was Pastora, every inch the military hero, with his beard and neatly pressed fatigues, giving impressed foreign reporters a blow-by-blow account of his victory. What I didn't know at the time was that Pastora hadn't been present for it. Living up, or down, to his nickname, 'Comandante Kodak' had in fact been flown in afterwards by helicopter, just before the journalists arrived.

Now, on 30 May 1984, a large group of journalists based in Costa Rica was to travel north to a Nicaraguan guerrilla base-camp just across the Costa Rican border in the southern Nicaraguan jungle for a press conference with the maverick rebel leader. I was, rather unenthusiastically, one of them.

My own first notice of the press conference was being woken, at seven-thirty in the morning, by a phone-call from my American colleagues Tony Avirgan and his wife Martha Honey, who had heard there was a meeting organised by the rebels. Tony explained they wouldn't even talk to him after he had made a film about their 'secret' headquarters in San José. (The Costa Rican authorities were forced to close the base, but they gave Pastora's men sufficient warning to enable them to remove all sensitive material to other safe-houses in the city – crackdown Costa Rican style.) 'I've been blacklisted, Susie,' Tony explained, asking me to phone the rebels to see what I could find out.

Tony and Martha were left-wing reporters whose primary aim was to expose US involvement in Central America – and, by extension, Contra operations. Both worked for distinguished US publications, but no one in the US Embassy would even speak to them on the phone, let alone grant an interview. Despite these difficulties, they managed to get a great deal of inside information from disgruntled rebel sources keen to air their views. At the time few other journalists (and none of the local reporters) had the courage to put themselves on the line and carry out genuinely investigative work, so I had no hesitation in carrying out Tony's request. I called Orion Pastora, a cousin of Edén Pastora and the man in charge of the press, who said he hadn't realised I was still in town but immediately agreed that I could attend the press conference, and gave me the place and time of the rendezvous. I promptly relayed this information to Tony.

Our rendezvous was for seven-thirty the following morning, at the Hotel Irazu in San José. There we found two dozen or so reporters, television cameramen and photographers, most of whom, unusually, had only received phone-calls that same morning, telling them Pastora had important news, that the conference would be held inside Nicaragua itself, and that they should be prepared to stay the night because of the distance and difficulties involved. Orion Pastora, bespectacled and perspiring, was fussing in the corridor, checking off names and making urgent phone-calls.

On one level I found it hard to take all this clandestine activity seriously. So many of these earnest Contras seemed like caricatures of themselves – and few more so than Orion, a closet homosexual who was always creating huge embarrassment when dispatched as a spokesman by his cousin, because he would always proposition and try to seduce guerrilla fighters, something not really in line with the Contras' rugged image. But even by the chaotic standards then operating within the rebel forces, these press arrangements were abrupt, smacking of panic or pressure. We were all at least momentarily excited and curious. Why the urgency? Why the meeting inside Nicaragua? I knew Pastora was in trouble with his own troops and that he was hiding from them in the Nicaraguan jungle, but on the other hand he was still constantly, if discreetly, visiting Costa Rica, his rear base. Was he about to reveal US interference? Give us the inside track on the real state of his rebel forces, now so factionalised that they appeared to be tottering on the brink of total disintegration? Would he, in frustration, announce his resignation, as he had done in the past?

Only the day before I had filed a story to *Newsweek* about the rebel power struggles, after extraordinary full-page advertisements taken out by rival rebel factions had appeared in the local press. One, signed by six rebel leaders, demanded that Pastora must go. I had speculated that the US master-plan was to oust Pastora and subordinate the Southern rebels to the US-controlled Northern Command. But Pastora, it seemed, was fiercely resisting this move.

Soldiers and reporters are afflicted by the same curse: 'Hurry up and wait!' Having scrambled to get to the Hotel Irazu we now found ourselves forced to kill time, drinking endless cups of coffee while Orion tried ineffectually to organise our transport to the conference. He couldn't find enough roadworthy jeeps. After two or three hours had passed and still no vehicles had arrived, despite his assurances, our interest had turned to a mixture of irritation and boredom. We knew the trip would take many hours, and we were already worried at the prospect of spending the night in hostile territory inside Nicaragua.

Finally our jeeps arrived. Tony invited Roberto Cruz, Gilberto Lopes and me to ride with him in his own jeep, pointing out that on his two previous trips the Contras' jeeps had broken down. But now Orion Pastora saw Tony and screamed that he could not come, that he was a traitor, a left-winger who was trying to harm the rebel cause. I said the rebels needed US coverage, and that it would look like discrimination if they banned Tony; Roberto and Gilberto backed me up. Orion gave in.

Gilberto Lopes had been brought up in Chile, where his father worked for the United Nations; his elder brother, Sergio, worked for the militant Sandinista newspaper *Barricada*. Gilberto had lived in Central America for a decade, reporting on the tumultuous and tragic events in the area. Slim, bearded and deceptively gentle, he was a tough reporter and deeply committed to his work. He was married to a Nicaraguan psychologist who worked with some of the thousands of Salvadorean and Guatemalan refugees who had fled from the violence at home to Costa Rica, host to an ever-growing number of exiles. One such political refugee was the fourth member of our group, Roberto Cruz, who made no secret of his left-wing views. Grey-haired and intense, he had originally fled into exile in Costa Rica from his native Guatemala after scores of his close friends and colleagues had been murdered by right-wing death-squads and after he himself had received death threats. 'If I had stayed, sooner or later I would have been killed,' he explained matter-of-factly. He had made a new life for himself in Costa Rica, together with his East German wife, and now worked for the Chinese News Agency Xinhua. Surprisingly, for a man with such deep knowledge about political events and such passionately held views, this was Roberto's first journalistic assignment outside the capital.

We wound north by jeep through green, undulating countryside, the paved roads soon degenerating to rutted, muddy tracks bordered by citrus groves. Cattle grazed in scrubby pasture. Sharp hills gradually gave way to gentler valleys of rich, red earth – huge ranches owned almost entirely by US farmers, among them John Hull, the biggest land-owner in these parts. After nearly four hours of driving we eventually arrived at the little outpost of Boca Tapada, on the river San Juan, close to the border with Nicaragua, where the Costa Ricans maintained a constant military presence. Here the track petered out entirely. The only way to reach our final destination, Pastora's riverside base camp at La Penca, just across the Nicaraguan border, involved illegally entering Nicaragua by river. The canoes for the last leg of our journey hadn't arrived, so we spent the time lazing in the humid sunshine, drinking warm Coca-cola and swatting away flies.

At times like this, it was easy to be lulled into feeling that the killing fields of Central America were far away. The tranquil scenery could have formed the setting for an impressionist landscape. Animals grazed among the trees shading the river-banks, from time to time invading the rough football pitch used by the Civil Guard soldiers, whose olive-green tents were pitched conveniently next to it. Chickens and small, hairy, spotted pigs snoozed in the sun or rootled the earth, even entering the gloomy bar that doubled as a dance-hall and general store and formed the hub of what passed for village life. Apart from the soldiers, most of the inhabitants of this remote area were traders or had smallholdings either side of the river. As our group sat watching out for the arrival of our own boats, a steady procession of rivercraft of all kinds chugged up and down, loading and unloading produce, animals and children at the little dock. Colombian Salsa music blared from the bar. Soldiers smoked and chatted. Small boys played football. Men sat drinking beer.

At least Costa Rica, I mused, although a little dull, was safe.

I idly noticed Linda Frazier, the only other woman reporter on the trip, chattering to members of our extended group. I was accustomed to being outnumbered by men, but for Linda such a major news assignment was rare. Despite her interest in 'the story' and her great affection for the Contras, whom she described as 'freedom-fighters', she had heavy domestic commitments that usually restricted her to keeping house in San José for her husband, Joe, the regional Associated Press correspondent, and their nine-year-old son Chris. On this occasion Joe was away reporting in Nicaragua, and Linda had managed to find a baby-sitter.

She now seemed restored to her usual bubbly self. Earlier, at the Hotel Irazu, I'd overheard her phoning her editor at the *Tico Times*, complaining about the delays and announcing in exasperation that we would certainly be late back. I myself, equally frustrated, had been phoning Martha Honey to ask whether she thought it would be all right if I sneaked away and went home. I had spent too many such occasions, waiting and waiting, with little result. I knew my lack of enthusiasm was mirrored by that of my editors (my editor at *Newsweek* told me later he wouldn't even have bothered to run my story on the meeting), and I was having to grapple with my conscience, while another part of my mind was working out my chances of leaving unobserved. 'It could all be a waste of time,' I remember saying to Martha. 'I doubt whether Pastora will say anything worthwhile, and I loathe waiting around like this.' 'I don't think you've got any option, Susie. You've got to go. Pastora must have something really important to say or he wouldn't be holding the press conference,' she replied firmly. Reluctantly, I'd decided she was probably right.

Finally the canoes with outboard motors arrived. We all scrambled in. I was sitting right at the back, next to our bearded navigator. I noticed the care with which a tall, auburn-haired

Danish photographer called Per Anker Hansen carried his camera-case into the boat, even wrapping it in layers of plastic to keep it dry – precautions no one else bothered with. I remember thinking he must be new to journalism to go to such trouble. I also noticed, with amusement, that he spent most of the boat trip assiduously bailing out the water we had shipped early on, when Roberto Cruz, insisting on moving to another, less crowded boat, as he feared ours would sink, had nervously got to his feet, causing the narrow, thoroughly unstable canoe to rock wildly and almost capsize. The photographer was sitting just in front of me, tucked in behind Peter Torbiornsson, a Swedish film director whom he'd befriended, and next to Linda Frazier.

The river journey was magical, with brilliantly plumaged parrots swooping from the river-banks and monkeys shrieking from the thick jungle. I remember trailing my hands in the water, feeling happy and relaxed, although some of my colleagues were starting to become edgy. After all, we were travelling through an area which had recently been the scene of fierce fighting between Sandinista troops and Pastora's rebels. There had been clashes both inside Costa Rica and along the river. Only a few weeks earlier, journalists had come under Sandinista machine-gun fire from helicopter gunships as they had inspected camps further up-river, which the rebels had assured them were safely under their control. Now we were even further from Costa Rica, and the sun was starting to set.

In that part of the tropics there is scarcely any twilight, and it was already dusk by the time we finally reached Pastora's base-camp at La Penca. Our boatman tied the canoe up at a makeshift jetty below a two-storey hut on stilts, and we struggled unaided up steep mud steps cut out of the riverbank. I followed Linda Frazier, commenting sarcastically that there was still some gallantry left among our male colleagues as they let us struggle up first, alone.

The hut was dark inside, although open on one side to the river, and it took time for my eyes to pick out where Pastora was. '*Hola, Susana*,' boomed a familiar voice to my right. '*Cómo estás?*' '*Muy bien, Comandante*,' I replied, realising with a jolt that this was a new, trimmer Pastora. He'd shaved off the grey beard that made him resemble a pocket Fidel Castro (at that time his favourite role model). There was the usual pandemonium as the rest of the journalist pack piled into the hut, lugging their equipment, everyone shouting, pushing and setting up their cameras close to the rebel leader, already firing off-the-cuff questions at him – even though Contra officials kept vainly insisting the conference would be organised later.

This press conference, I told myself hopefully, would be different. This time, surely, Pastora would have something worthwhile to say. I edged right next to him, new tape-recorder, pen and notebook in hand, and tried to get a word into the babble of questions shouted in Spanish. 'What are your links with the US?' 'Do you receive help from the CIA?' 'Why won't you join the Northern Contras?' Pastora, basking in the limelight, all thoughts of postponing the meeting forgotten, launched into his by now predictable tirade. 'I will never unite with those Contras, those genocidal criminals, who have never, in four years of fighting, taken a single prisoner . . .' Concentrating hard, and trying at the same time to take notes, make sure my tape-recorder was working and ask my questions, I didn't notice the tall Danish photographer casually placing his camera-case at my feet, or, remarking loudly that his camera was not working, backing out of the room. Nor, just moments later, did I see the young rebel radio operator, Rosita, a cup of coffee for Pastora carefully balanced in her hands, stumble over the big metal camera-case and knock it over, a clumsy, inadvertent gesture that cost her her life and probably saved mine.

I later learnt that Pastora, the target of the bomb, had miraculously survived, escaping with burns and shrapnel wounds. I had been standing between him and the bomb and had shielded him with my body. Linda Frazier had been standing the other side of me. Both her legs had been blown off, and her abdomen torn apart by the explosion. She died on the way to the hospital. Embedded in her stomach were the cameras that had been in the top part of the metal case – part of the elaborate subterfuge to pass off the camera-case as genuine. Hidden underneath the cameras were packed pounds of C-4 explosive. The bomb was powerful enough to kill us all, had the camera-case not been knocked over at the moment of explosion.

The other journalist to die that night was Jorge Quiros, the young Costa Rican television cameraman, who actually filmed the press conference. His filmed record survived him. The picture disintegrates at the moment of the explosion, but not the sound-track. There is a brief silence, and then you can hear inhuman sounds like dogs or parrots howling. It is the screams and moans of the survivors. A photograph that I saw later of the cameraman lying dead, taken by a colleague still mechanically recording events, shows a young man with a gash severing his thigh, curled up, his arm still shielding his face, even in death. He was just twenty-five. The soundman working with him for Costa Rica's flagship station, Channel Six, a gentle, middle-aged man named Evelio Sequeira, was also mortally wounded by the blast, and died a week later. I saw a film of him arriving at the hospital: he was slowly moving his bloody head from side to side as though trying to escape from the pain.

My own recollections of what happened just after the bombing are hazy. I must have been gradually weakening from shock and loss of blood. The journey, by river, to the hospital, which to me seemed endless, actually took around five hours. Gilberto later told me that the Contra navigator lost his way in the swirling mist and the darkness, and we drifted helplessly in circles for hours. I was one of the first to be evacuated, and the only one with serious injuries. Those like Roberto Cruz and Carlos Vargas, who were critically hurt, were actually left until last, because they couldn't walk to the boats unaided, and because many of those who could have helped them were intent on their own evacuation. I still find this upsetting, an awful comment on human nature. I was shocked, too, to learn later that Pastora, whose injuries were slight, had left for safety immediately in the only fast motor-launch, together with his top military commanders and the sole doctor, despite urgent pleas from reporters to take the most seriously wounded with him.

When our canoe reached Costa Rica and the little hamlet of Boca Tapada, I was laid out on the ground and later transferred to a Costa Rican ambulance. A local journalist told me he saw me lying on my stretcher. He said I was covered in blood and my face was quite black from shrapnel, and unrecognisable. He told me he thought I was dead until he heard me screaming, and that I clung on to him and wouldn't let go. The second stage of the journey by ambulance was dreadful. Heavy rain during the night had washed away a bridge, and my stretcher had to be carried through the river to another ambulance. I was in terrible pain as the ambulance jolted along the bumpy track, hurting my limbs and a seemingly dislocated right elbow. I kept screaming and pleading with the driver to go slower, but the ambulanceman feared further delay could be dangerous as I was losing so much blood. I was vomiting from the pain and shock.

In Ciudad Quesada, doctors were working heroically trying to cope with this sudden influx of wounded, shocked bomb victims, who kept arriving throughout that night, all but overwhelming the staff. Clusters of panic-stricken relatives had already travelled to the hospital after hearing of the disaster on the radio, and stood waiting anxiously for their loved ones to arrive, not knowing if they would still be alive.

In my case, doctors were not optimistic. Reports put out said I had died. And that was, I am told, the prognosis.

# 2

# Between Life and Death

As I lay in the hospital, more dead than alive, swathed in bandages like an Egyptian mummy, blinded, unable to move any part of my body and not knowing how bad my injuries were, I didn't know that news of the terrorist attack had been broadcast worldwide, and that my family and relatives the other side of the world were rallying to help me.

Not for nothing were my father, his brother Hanuš and Hanuš's wife, Rose, Jewish Holocaust survivors, who had escaped by a near miracle from Brno in Czechoslovakia in the last train allowed out, just two weeks before the declaration of the Second World War. They had survived where millions, including most of their own families, had perished. They lived by a combination of dogged persistence, farsightedness, fortitude – and luck. Despite decades in cosy England, they had never forgotten. Now, with that heightened sense of family responsibility, the heritage of having lost so many loved ones, they turned their honed survival skills on me, something to which I probably owe my life.

The genesis of my rescue came about light-years away from the horror of the bombing, in the thoroughly unlikely setting of Guildford, hub of an archetypal Surrey stockbroker belt. There, at lunchtime on Thursday, the day after the La Penca explosion, my uncle Hanuš Morgan was sitting with his mouth open in the dentist's chair. The radio was switched on to distract him from the discomfort of his new bridgework. He was paying no particular attention to the One-o'-clock News until suddenly he caught my name and learnt to his horror that I had been hurt in a bomb explosion in Nicaragua; my condition, a day after the attack, was described by the dispassionate newscaster as 'critical'. My uncle, who has a bad heart, immediately drove home, shaking, and, ashen-faced, recounted the news to my Aunt Rose. What should they do? Rose suggested they call their daughter Annie, a researcher for a television medical programme, and ask her to find out what state I was in and what help I needed. Annie promptly relayed news of the family crisis to her boss who, with great generosity, immediately said: 'Drop everything and concentrate on your cousin. Take as long as you need.' Annie started telephoning all the newspapers I worked for, to see what they knew about me. Information was sketchy and conflicting. The *Daily Telegraph*, one of the better informed, believed I was still just alive, but that both my legs had to be amputated. One Costa Rican TV station said I was already dead. Other reports said I was still alive but was expected to die. Annie confided her fears to a doctor friend. 'If your cousin is that bad,' he said, 'and especially if her legs have to be amputated, you must try and get her immediately to a really top-class hospital, probably in the US.' Annie had sat down, trying to keep calm, she later told me, working out what to do. After a short period of intense thought, she called her elder brother, Ian, a doctor in Vancouver, Canada, at about 3 a.m. his time, to explain what had happened and to see if he had any practical ideas of how I could be moved – if I was still alive.

Curiously, my own parents didn't learn until later that I was hurt. My mother had been out, attending her weekly painting class in Bristol, at the time when the rest of the family had been urgently trying to contact her, while my father had been at his surgery. Eventually they managed to contact my brother-in-law, asking him to inform my parents as soon as possible. But he didn't, unable to face being the one to break the bad news to my mother.

My mother eventually heard about it through a journalist friend on the Foreign Desk of the *Sunday Times*, who telephoned asking if she had any idea that I had been critically injured in Central America, in a bomb explosion. My friend was able to offer little information, and less reassurance. My mother immediately called my father at his afternoon surgery. There was a stunned pause before he answered, 'We must go out immediately to see her. Can you start making the arrangements?' Then, as he later told me, he went back to his interrupted task of treating his patient, the consummate professional to the last.

As my parents were busy packing, buying air-tickets to Central America, obtaining US visas, my cousins were continuing their efforts to evacuate me. By a stroke of the purest good fortune, Ian was at that time working as a medical consultant to a Canada-based, international air-ambulance company. After talking to Annie back in England he immediately called the air-ambulance director, Jerome Edwards, a man he much respected, and told him of my situation, asking for a plane to take me to the States. Jerome unhesitatingly gave the go-ahead, immediately calling up his medical team, and within less than two hours a fully surgically-equipped Learjet was flying out to Costa Rica.

At about the same time, in El Salvador, Rod Nordland, an American reporter friend who had travelled with me on a number of recent assignments, was also monitoring the news and working out what he could do to help. He first heard about the bombing atrocity in the company of Laura, the bereaved fiancée of John Hoagland, a war photographer for *Newsweek* and also a close mutual friend. John, who always told us he would one day be killed in El Salvador, had died eight weeks earlier, caught in a hail of gunfire between the Salvadorean guerrillas and the army. 'Susie's legs are going to be amputated, she's going to die,' Laura had sobbed hysterically, still overwrought by John's death. Deeply concerned by these confused early reports, Rod decided to jump on a plane and leave at once for Costa Rica. He ended up spending nearly all his time rescuing me, instead of writing the story for his newspaper, the *Philadelphia Enquirer*. As he later explained to my father, 'If we journalists don't look after each other, no one else will.'

After speeding down 100 miles of twisting roads from the capital, Rod reached my hospital in Costa Rica well after midnight, to find a tall, fair-haired couple who said they were doctors arguing with suspicious medical staff in the lobby and being refused entry. 'You have to let us in, we've got to see Susan Morgan, take her with us. We've got a plane waiting,' they kept repeating, their raised voices reflecting their increasing frustration. This was the crew from the Learjet vainly attempting to obtain my release from hospital. Their aircraft had been standing on the runway at San José's international airport for some five hours, but the staff guarding the entrance had received strict instructions to keep all unauthorised people out of the hospital. They had been told there was a murder investigation involving the La Penca affair and were adamant that this mysterious gringo couple should not remove one of their critically ill patients. The Costa Rican doctors also deeply resented the efforts to evacuate me to the moneyed US, considering evacuation a slur on their own competence and technology.

I later learnt that the Learjet crew had taken off in such a hurry that they had not obtained prior authorisation to land in Costa Rica; they weren't even sure they had enough fuel on board for the return flight – particularly as they had, at that time, no idea where they would end up, or which hospital would agree to take me in.

Rod flashed his journalist's pass and was allowed in at once, promising to give me the message. He spent some time looking for me, and eventually had to ask a passing nurse to identify me. He then woke me gently, told me who he was – I still couldn't see – and said he had met a medical team outside the hospital. He explained that they had come in a Learjet and wanted to take me to the US. He insisted I leave with them immediately.

I listened groggily, trying to focus my mind on what he was saying, but instinctively resisting the persuasive logic. I just couldn't face any more pain or being operated on again. I couldn't really grasp anything beyond the present. Nor did I understand how bad I was. When friends like Martha had come to my bedside and I begged them to stay with me, not to leave me, they had naturally tried to reassure me by telling me I would be all right, that I was in good hands. I was so tired, in so much pain, so confused and disoriented, that I needed someone to think for me, to make the right decisions. Luckily, Rod was just that man. He sensed and understood my reluctance, but realised he had to convince me, not just override my fears. He was extraordinarily patient, calmly explaining how much better my treatment would be in an American hospital, where there were vast resources and the latest equipment. He promised to accompany me, and I remember he recounted in detail how his own brother had suffered a very nasty car accident, landing up in a tiny rural hospital, just like this one, and how he had arrived just in time to stop surgeons from amputating his brother's leg. He had then engineered his brother's transfer to a major hospital, and his brother, he ended triumphantly, was now so much better he could even play football again.

I was, despite such strong initial doubts, eventually quite won over, and after quite a while, and much pleading and arguments from both Rod and myself, we obtained reluctant authorisation from the doctor on night duty for me to leave. After even longer I found myself being wheeled, still on my stretcher, complete with intravenous drips, catheter, enveloping bandages and my medical notes, down a corridor to an ambulance, which drove back up those same winding roads that Rod had travelled only hours earlier, to San José and the waiting Learjet.

The timing of my rescue was fortuitous. Just after my departure the Costa Rican security authorities belatedly ordered that no one who had attended the press conference should leave the country – even for medical treatment – in case one of them turned out to have been involved in the bombing. I suspect this delayed decision, an effort to show the authorities were in control, was actually sparked off by intense speculation in the Costa Rican press about my own 'mysterious' departure in the dead of night.

Banner headlines reported that what they dubbed my '*fuga muy sospechosa de medianoche*' – 'very suspicious midnight flit' – was due to my own involvement in the attack; other reports had me hiding the bomber on my plane in order to help him escape. As it turned out, the sole effect of the ban was to stop other injured victims leaving the country. For instance, the Learjet sent by the US television network ABC News to evacuate Tony Avirgan, the day after my own rescue, was grounded in Costa Rica for the best part of a week, pleas for Tony's departure on medical grounds being curtly refused. The belated travel ban might have been more useful for the investigation had the Costa Rican authorities not already allowed the man who turned out to be the bomber to slip out of the country. Since then, I have thought a great deal about why the Costa Ricans neither sealed the international borders, nor questioned any of the victims at our little hospital, nor even prevented any of them from leaving that night.

It may be unfair to blame the Costa Ricans for not doing more. I think it is hard for foreigners, inured to a regular diet of horror provided by newspapers and television sets, the routine recording of violence from Beirut to Belfast, and with a police and investigative force practised at preventing and solving crimes, to grasp the searing emotional blow of the La Penca bombing on the Costa Rican nation. For Costa Ricans the bombing, a minor event on the world scale, was simply the worst atrocity ever to hit the country. They had never before been exposed to this kind of organised, international terrorism, nor had they any professional or technical training in dealing with it. It had the effect of wiping out at a stroke most of the nation's leading media figures, since of those who survived, none was in a physical or mental state to work for a long time to come; also, there was simply no money available to replace valuable television and radio equipment that had, like its owners, been blown to bits. I find myself in an anomalous position in this affair. On the one hand, I am a member of that sophisticated international community (and one, moreover, whose living has been earned precisely by the reporting of violence, rather than peace). On the other hand, I cannot condone the extraordinarily malicious campaign launched by the local Costa Rican press and directed against fellow journalists, the very people who had suffered most. In the guise of 'investigative' reporting, they indulged in a sensationalist witch-hunt, focusing on the foreigners and those of the group attending the press conference it deemed 'left-wingers', spinning an exotic web of half-truths, innuendo and downright lies.

I slept nearly all the way to the States. I am told my pilot and the doctor kept radioing SOS calls to hospitals *en route*, telling them there was a critically ill patient aboard suffering from severe burns, shock and multiple fractures: did they have a bed? 'No,' came back the answer from the major Miami hospitals with the best-known burn units (at this stage, from looking at my misshapen face, swollen from the burns and blackened from the powder and shrapnel from the bomb, the Canadians believed my burns were my most serious injuries). So we flew on, the medical team now starting to get seriously concerned. Finally, as they flew over the flat, muggy plains of central Florida, a major teaching hospital, Shands, in Gainesville, responded to their urgent pleas and agreed to take me in. It was now seven-thirty in the morning. The admissions surgeon on duty, David Orbach, later told me he was deeply moved by my plight because he had earlier served as a surgeon in Vietnam, and had treated hundreds of victims suffering from a similar array of injuries to mine. The tough but kindhearted head of the hospital public relations department, who was on hand when I arrived because of all the attendant publicity my arrival had caused, said, 'My heart went out to you: you looked like a little wounded animal.'

The next events are blurred in my mind. I remember being X-rayed again and again, and screaming from the pain as the technicians moved my injured limbs, even though they were as gentle as they could be. They explained how vital it was to note all the fractures. One of them said, 'Each time we took pictures, we found more fractures.' Then I had to undergo more emergency surgery. I know this because I can still remember a voice saying to me as I was wheeled on my stretcher through endless corridors, 'You do realise that if you have this operation you may die.' I was later told this advice was necessary (and indeed is now common practice in the US), in case I should later decide to sue. The US is a very litigious society. Later, to my amusement, I saw in my thick pile of hospital notes the laconic comment, 'Patient seems to understand.' I still couldn't see or move at all, and I couldn't stop my teeth chattering from the shock. It was hard to keep track of time or place, since I couldn't distinguish between day and night. I seemed to be constantly drifting in and out of consciousness, coming round from yet another general anaesthetic, or else being wheeled down once more to the operating theatre. Thankfully, my memories of this time were further blurred by hefty doses of morphine.

I do remember my parents arriving. By now I could open one eye a tiny bit and could see, very blurred, my mother's wonderfully familiar form wearing one of her home-made floral print dresses. She looked terribly apprehensive. I wanted to hug her and my father, but since I was lying naked under a blanket, flat on my back, punctured by three separate intravenous drips, and attached to different pieces of apparatus that constantly monitored my heart and other vital functions, movement of any kind was impossible. My mother later told me I didn't look quite as bad as she had expected: my face was so 'fat, pink and swollen' that I looked like a chubby child, rather than a woman near death. She also expressed relief that my voice as I greeted her sounded quite strong and normal.

Before she reached my bedside my mother had begun to panic that I might die before she could see me. As soon as they arrived in Miami, after a gruelling flight from London, she insisted that instead of waiting for their connecting flight to Gainesville the following morning, they hire a car and drive through the night. My father had demurred, concerned that he was so tired he would be liable to have an accident. 'If she's survived the trip to the Costa Rican hospital from the jungle, she'll live,' he argued. He was right. After two weeks on the critical list I was moved from the intensive care ward to a room of my own. My life was no longer considered to be in danger.

Most of my days from then on were taken up with the cleaning and dressing of my many burns, cuts, bruises, fractures and other injuries, many still infected and oozing pus. My hands had swollen up like a giant's paws, as a result of severe bruising and broken finger-joints, shattered from the sheer force of the bomb. They were also burnt, blistered and infected, and it was weeks before I could use them at all. Their treatment – like that of my other wounds – was unbelievably painful. My arm was the worst injury, shattered, infected, the elbow dislocated and the nerve in shreds. I would scream in agony when its dressing was changed (three times a day at first, because of chronic infection), while its throbbing used to keep me awake night after night.

According to the doctors, including my father, the lingering infections were a legacy of the initial treatment in the Costa Rican hospital. Surgeons there had incorrectly sewn up our wounds, even though they were infected, instead of leaving them open to the fresh air. Oxygen deprivation, I was told, is a classic cause of gangrene and other infections. Two major operations I underwent in the Florida hospital shortly after my arrival involved not only hours of complicated surgery, but also opening up all my infected wounds. Had this not been done, I would almost certainly have lost my arm. I dearly wish my companions could have benefited from the treatment I had. I still feel guilty and sad that while I was evacuated and given the very best treatment – the reason I am so fully recovered today – they had to make do with what medicine was on hand. My cousin Ian, who played such a key role in my rescue, remains convinced that my transfer saved my life.

The hospital evolved a novel way of cleansing the wounds in my arm and leg. They would slowly lower me on a pulley suspended from the ceiling, still securely strapped on to my stretcher, into a great tank of warm salt-water; this would gently whirl to and fro like a giant jacuzzi, painlessly cleaning my wounds as it went. Several times a day literally yards of bandages impregnated with brown, strong-smelling disinfectant were carefully wound, figure-of-eight style, into the gaping holes in my arm and leg where the blast had torn away great hunks of flesh and had pulverised the bone. This bone damage raised a further problem: the potential danger of blood-clots caused by fragments of shattered bone and marrow circulating in my bloodstream. To prevent this happening, a blood-thinning agent was injected into my stomach twice a day during my entire stay in hospital.

My parents – exhausted by the worry, the Florida heat, concern about paying my enormous (and ever-mounting) hospital bill, my constant need for reassurance and love, my refusal to eat and my nasty outbursts of temper when everything got too much to bear – were wonderfully supportive. My father spent a lot of time talking to the specialists who cared for me, comparing notes on my treatment, and even writing them all thank-you letters on my behalf – a gesture that surprised and touched them. He wrote up copious pages of descriptive and highly technical notes on my medical progress and appearance – 'Hair burnt off; what little there is seems to have all the soil of Nicaragua in it' etc. – and sent them off to relatives and friends (and even, for good measure, to my medical insurance company). In between this flurry of activity, he accompanied me twice daily to have my wounds washed, marvelling at the resources in American hospitals compared with the underfunded National Health Service back in Britain. And apart from all this, my mother said reprovingly, he still found time to flirt with the nurses.

I was in that hospital for two and a half months. It seemed much longer. I was starting to make progress, albeit excruciatingly slowly (and after a false 'high' caused by the trauma of the explosion I was now so physically exhausted I slept nearly all the time), but my mental state was less good. My underlying anxiety was revealed when I developed a stress ulcer, in reaction, so my doctors told me, to the trauma. It was diagnosed after I complained of shooting pains in my stomach, which felt as though it was being burnt by acid. I found it ironic that, after years of being forever on one crash diet or another to get fashionably thin, I was now being threatened with forced feeding unless I ate more. They explained it was vital to eat so that my body could create new bone, skin and tissue and to combat the terrible stress. They explained, too, that the effect of severe burns was drastically to speed up the body's metabolic rate. In less than two weeks I had already lost two stone, but I was simply unable to eat, gagging when I tried to force the food down. I ended up by cheating, offering my food to any hungry visitors, as the formidable chief nutritionist would personally monitor my food intake twice a day.

Apart from the acute discomfort caused by the ulcer, I found the whole process of eating both demeaning and unpleasant. I had to lie flat on my back, my broken hands and arms suspended in splints and heavily bandaged, so I had to be fed by a nurse by spoon, like an infant. Not only could I not eat, I could do hardly anything else either. I couldn't hold up a book to read, and my eyes, after surgery involving cuts in the cornea to establish how deeply embedded the shrapnel was, were anyway still inflamed and sore; I couldn't pick up a telephone, couldn't even turn on the remote control of my television set. People have commented on the extraordinary patience I must have needed to have endured all of this. In fact I was so ill, and receiving so many painkillers, that I was more docile and groggy than any normal person. And while much of my treatment was indeed frustrating, boring and painful, it was, after all, designed to help me. I had a choice: drive myself crazy from frustration, or resign myself to the inevitable. Curiously, too, although this period was intensely difficult and painful, certainly one of the hardest of my life, it offered a unique experience that was not all negative. It gave me an opportunity for reflection.

Now more or less recovered, I am struck by how frequently I am asked what special insight I have gained into life as the result of my accident. People seem to feel that, because of my close brush with death, I must have gained some unique understanding, akin to the secret of the philosophers' stone. But while I'm sure the bombing has changed me, it's very hard to know just how. As Gilberto Lopes later put it, 'La Penca has changed us all in ways we may not understand. Life can never again be the same for us.' I think the main difference is that my sense of values and priorities became clearer as a result of this suffering. Giving and receiving love seemed to me back then, and still today, to be the only really worthwhile thing. And, feeling as I often do that I am living on borrowed time, life seems infinitely more precious. I also feel somehow protected. Nothing, I believe, as bad as the bombing can ever happen to me again. I remember saying to the Public Relations head, Ginny Hunt, who would find time every day to come by my bedside and chat, that if I let this bombing ruin my life, it would be my fault. It was then, I now realise, that I made a conscious decision not to let this happen.

Although much of my day involved things that hurt – the dressings of all my wounds, the continual injections and blood samples, painful efforts by the physiotherapist to try and restore movement to my stiff, broken fingers and even stiffer arm – there was a comforting bustle and routine about the day-time. My father had had to return after two weeks to his medical practice and the family dachshund, but my mother remained with me for the whole time, and accompanied me home on the plane. She was with me constantly – a rock of support. I had, with the accident, become totally vulnerable, like a child; utterly dependent on love and support. The veneer of sophistication, toughness and aloofness that I had prided myself on completely disappeared. Even at weekends, when the hospital virtually shut down and my rehabilitation classes stopped, my mother would always visit me, making the long trek in to my bedside from her temporary home way out in the Florida countryside, where she was staying with the godparents of a close friend of mine. My mother was not just a source of moral support; she also busied herself in practical ways. She would help me eat, help me with exercises for my fingers and arm, write thank-you letters to all the dozens of people who had written to me (complaining gently that I used long words she couldn't spell), and read to me. It seemed appropriate that an old family friend sent my battered teddy-bear to the hospital. He was given a surgical gown and the same bandages that I had.

So my days would pass peacefully enough. Nights were a different matter. I still remember them with a shudder. Lying alone in the gloom, with no distraction save a constant, sometimes excruciating, pain that prevented me from drifting off to sleep, or woke me in agony, my thoughts would turn gloomy and depressed. I would go over aspects of my life in my mind, endlessly blaming myself, punishing myself for what had happened, irrationally convinced that the bombing was my fault. I would reflect time and again on the choices I had made, somehow convinced that the key to my current predicament lay here. If only I had done this and not that, I would reflect, everything might have turned out differently: why couldn't I have realised then that it would all turn out so badly? I became obsessive; I thought in irrational circles, always returning to the same theme. Myself. The bomb. My fault. It was all my fault. I should have known the bomb would go off. If only I hadn't gone that day, hadn't listened to Martha, had been further away, maybe a little further to the left, maybe further back. I would torture and goad myself to the point where I went nearly mad.

My career as a journalist, which had earlier seemed so important and worthwhile, and in which I had taken so much pride, now seemed to be an aberration. After all, I reasoned (and my thoughts all had this mad logic), if I hadn't chosen to be a foreign correspondent, I wouldn't have got blown up. I thought enviously of my friends with the kinds of humdrum lives I had previously despised as 'boring' and 'cop-outs'. Now, I thought, these 'humdrum' lives didn't seem so dull. These women had children growing up around them, husbands, homes, solid existences, solid futures, love, emotional support, security. And I – what did I now have? Nothing. Everything had just gone up in a puff of smoke. I had, I knew with a terrible certainty, blown it: irrevocably blown my life. It was all over. I felt stuck in some dark, limbo-like tunnel, with no way out. I used to catch myself saying, 'When I was killed . . .' and realise what an extraordinary Freudian slip I was making. It was as though my spirit had died, and my body, by some aberration, some animal vitality, had failed to die along with it.

I also remember wondering how on earth I had spent so much time and energy on doomed love affairs (although I suppose, in my defence, I hadn't considered them doomed at the time) with men who had never cared for me. I could remember my chagrin when one or another of them took off for Beirut or somewhere, or for someone more exotic or more radically chic, but feeling I could never admit to it, since many of my male editors had a jaundiced view of 'unreliable' female reporters, and any hint that one was prey to emotions would serve to reinforce their prejudices. All of us woman reporters were very anxious not to let the side down, to show we were at least as good as our male colleagues, even if, as I sometimes suspected, many of us found the job more of a strain. Our male counterparts, after all, often had the emotional support of a wife and family tucked away. We also felt obliged to be discreet about our love affairs, and tended to want lasting, serious relationships. My male colleagues were happy to frequent the local brothel as a way of getting rid of their tension and frustration, and would then boast about their prowess. A charming male journalist once put it to me that he could burst into tears, throw a tantrum with an editor – 'but a woman like you could never afford to, Susie'. Even now, when my invariably male foreign editors from the *Telegraph* or the *Observer* called me in hospital, their reaction if I broke down and cried was one of acute embarrassment.

I dreaded lying awake all night, watching the hours on the clock by my bed tick slowly by, but in some ways I was even more afraid of falling asleep. This was the time for flashbacks and nightmares – dreadful, vivid nightmares in which bombers, terrorists, fiends, were out to stalk and kill me. I would wake sweating, panicking, hallucinating, screaming aloud in fear. Often I would have wet my bed, something that embarrassed me greatly. But I was quite alone, with no one to comfort me, no one to tell me not to worry, to go back to sleep, that I wouldn't die, that I wasn't dead. It was simply not possible, in that busy hospital, for anyone to stay with me. The next night the nightmares would start up all over again, and the next. There was no escape.

My state of mind was made worse by the unnerving presence of a mildly deranged Vietnam veteran who apparently worked in the hospital. He had taken to visiting me, stealthily creeping up to my bed at night and stroking my hair and face as he murmured to me. He began this practice when I still couldn't see, and frightened me out of my wits. To protect me, the hospital arranged for a guard to be stationed at my door twenty-four hours a day, with a list of family and friends who alone were allowed to enter my room. Much later I received a letter from this strange acquaintance, explaining that he had meant no harm, but had suffered great trauma during the Vietnam war and was seeking expiation through me, with whom he identified as a fellow victim.

In retrospect it seems extraordinary that I didn't feel anger towards the bomber who had reduced me to a scarred, bed-ridden invalid. Instead, I felt anger only against myself. Only once did I feel a flash of anger at someone else. It was about three in the morning, and I had been trying, unsuccessfully as usual, to get to sleep; my infected arm was throbbing unmercifully and the nurses refused to give me any more painkillers because of the danger of addiction. I was watching television to distract my thoughts when a familiar figure strode across the screen. It was Edén Pastora. I listened intently as the reporter blandly announced that the maverick rebel leader was in Washington trying to drum up further support for the remnants of his rag-tag army.* In disbelief, I watched Pastora closely: apart from a slight limp, he looked unhurt. Why, I asked myself bitterly, was he able to walk around freely? While I, who had inadvertently taken the blast intended for him, was now lying in hospital, my life destroyed.

Watching investigative reporters on television or seeing the by-line of a colleague writing about 'my' journalistic turf as I lay helplessly

* I was later told that Pastora had come to Washington to lobby Bill Casey, head of the CIA, for more aid, even though he told a reporter at the time that he knew the CIA had tried to remove him, even suspected they were behind the La Penca bombing. Realist – or cynical opportunist – to the core, he was still hoping he could wangle more US support, backing which he would deny receiving, as that would be harmful to his 'independent' image.

on my back, I would feel a curious pang of jealousy. My moods veered from despair to flashes of unrealistic hope, when I longed to return to Central America as a reporter. Seldom did the example of my appalling accident curb my desire to return to cover 'the story' when, or if, I recovered sufficiently to walk again, something I frequently doubted. I remember talking, in one of my rare upbeat moods, about badly missing 'being out there' to a woman journalist friend who had phoned from El Salvador to see how I was. 'Central America will still be there when you're better,' she advised with gentle irony. But would I ever be better? Would I ever be able to walk again?

During this time I was able to glean little about the fate of the other reporters who had accompanied me to that press conference. Once Gilberto Lopes called from Costa Rica to see how I was. He was glad to hear I was making progress, and described his own near-miraculous escape, with only slight burns to his hands and face, the result of his having fallen through the huge hole in the wooden floor made by the bomb as it went off. 'La Penca was a lottery, Susana,' he said, philosophising about the blast that had left some dead, some critically hurt, and others with minor injuries. He recalled the superhuman effort he had made to clamber out from his crater because it was 'infernally hot' and he was being burnt. He also told me that most of the other victims were still in hospital, while those only slightly injured, or not hurt at all, had suffered severe trauma. Some members of a Costa Rican film-crew who were in another room, trying to fix their faulty equipment, harboured dreadful feelings of guilt that they had been spared and yet were unable to save the wounded and dying.

When I asked whether there were any clues about who carried out the bombing, he replied, 'Of all our group, the only person not accounted for is the man who said he was a Danish photographer. He just disappeared. And then all his papers turned out to be false, stolen. So, for the moment, suspicion is centred on him – but of course no one knows where he is – or what his real identity is.'

In mid-June, Martha and Tony paid an unexpected visit to me in hospital *en route* to Costa Rica from Chicago, where Tony had been receiving treatment for his mangled hand and shrapnel wounds. I was impressed by the surgery on Tony's damaged fingers, and envious that he could walk around while I still couldn't move, but I was distinctly unamused by his oft-repeated 'joke' that my injuries were due to my being a 'rebel groupie' and standing right next to the bomb's target, Pastora. Tony himself had been lounging against a far wall, having been promised an exclusive interview the next day, and his injuries were correspondingly less serious. He told me I kept screaming his name after the explosion but he couldn't reach me because I was the other side of the gaping hole in the floor.

With her characteristic energy, Martha was trying to find out who was responsible for La Penca. On the day of the bombing an important article by her on the crisis in Pastora's movement and the ultimatum delivered to him by the CIA was published by the *New York Times*. Now, lying flat on my back, I listened with growing fascination to her account of what was known so far: the identification of the bomber as the Danish photographer by the Costa Rican authorities; the disinformation by the Costa Rican press, featuring Tony and me as prime suspects; all sorts of phony-sounding culprits being 'named'; her suspicions of other Contras; her still unproven theories of CIA involvement.

It provided a welcome distraction. The doctors had decided that my right arm was so shattered, with a big gap where the bone had been pulverised, that they needed to insert bone-shavings from my hip, which would knit together to form a new, stronger arm. I was impressed by the capabilities of the human body, but less enthusiastic about going under the knife yet again, particularly as I was warned that any further surgery would exacerbate the arm's infection. At this stage it never occurred to me that I would one day be well enough to return to Central America to investigate the bombing for myself.

Finally, my doctors, worried about my becoming institutionalised, started to prepare me for going home to England. Above all, I had to be as mobile as possible, so that my elderly parents would be able to manage. I was far too emotionally and physically weak to live by myself. I had, in effect, to learn how to walk again. At first I would regularly faint when slowly tilted upright strapped on to a curious Heath Robinson-like machine, designed to prepare me once more for vertical living. But then, with a plaster cast from foot to hip, I took my first tentative steps. How could walking be so hard, I wondered, clinging exhaustedly to a rail after about three steps. How did I keep my balance?

I finally left the hospital that had become my home in a wheelchair, wearing thick pancake make-up to disguise facial scars that looked to me like the mountains of the moon, and with a raging ear-infection, my bandaged arm in a sling and my leg in a plaster cast. Many of the staff, like me, were in tears. They warned me that I was far too cheerful and 'stiff-upper-lippish', that I should allow myself to grieve or else I risked sinking into depression. I was surprised I gave this impression, feeling far from cheerful, even if I didn't show it, but at home in Bristol the combination of enforced idleness, the lack of a sense of identity (far more bound up with my work than I had ever realised) and feelings of guilt and embarrassment at being dependent on my parents again combined to make living in the 'real' world again far harder than being in hospital.

For one thing, I could no longer put off thinking about my future, although in my heart of hearts I didn't believe I had one. I couldn't walk more than about five steps, couldn't get in and out of the bath, couldn't wash my hair or get dressed by myself, couldn't leave the house, was quite unable to lead a normal life or to imagine I ever would. Once I fell over when both my parents had gone out. I couldn't get to my feet, but had to lie on the ground until they came home, hours later, and helped me up. I felt utterly despondent about my scars and believed I would now never have a boyfriend; no man would ever be interested in me. To my hypercritical self I appeared hideously disfigured; several times, after explaining to a stranger that I had been in a bomb explosion, I would be asked, 'Were you hurt?' – a question I at first took as some cruel joke. Only after about the ninth time this happened did I come to realise my scars were on the inside; they didn't really show.

It was a strange, disturbing time. I still had friends in Bristol, people I had known in my teens, but I had nothing in common with them, couldn't relate to their concerns – their children's schools, the price of houses. I had been involved with what were to me titanic struggles between good and evil, left and right. I had watched people fighting and dying for their beliefs. That life was 'real' and intense in a way that life in an English suburb could never be. I didn't believe I would be able to adapt. I felt like an outsider, a character from a Kafka novel, watching the world go by, my face metaphorically pressed to the window-pane. Only rarely did I rouse myself to self-assertion, as when the physiotherapist I saw twice a week told me to weave raffia mats and I drew myself up to my full height of five foot two to explain that former foreign correspondents don't make mats. More often, I succumbed to despair.

In the autumn of 1984 I moved to London, staying first at my sister's flat in Battersea and then with a friend in Hampstead, as I still couldn't cope by myself. Gradually, almost imperceptibly, and despite terrifying panic attacks when my heart would pound madly and I would wake sweating from recurring nightmares, I turned the corner.

My friends rallied round with suggestions of activities that would take me out of myself. But I was still weaker than I cared to admit and tired easily. The wound in my arm was still infected, my hearing impaired; I still couldn't walk properly. I had to face further operations on my elbow and shattered eardrum. Although I would love to have bounded back to my pre-bomb life, I was simply no longer able to push myself as I once had. But at the same time I found it hard to be patient. Desperate to fill my days, I started trying to write a book about the bombing, but I was too close to the events, too raw emotionally: brooding on those painful experiences was just too destructive and hard. And anyway, all I could write about was what it felt like to be the victim of a bomb attack – nothing about who had done it.

Eventually, months later, with the encouragement of my friends,

I timorously applied for a job at the BBC. My main reason for doing so was hearing that some former 'friends' had been saying I had been reduced to a human vegetable. I was upset, all the more so because I feared there was a grain of truth in the report. I decided the best way to rebut the rumours, and prove I could still 'hack it', was to hold down a 'proper' job. To my astonishment I got it.

The warm, stimulating atmosphere of the BBC's World Service helped me to feel happy for the first time I could remember. Going in to an office every day and writing talks about Latin America also provided a badly needed structure to my life and helped restore my professional confidence. I was working, coping, even though for the first six months I had to go to bed, exhausted, the moment I arrived home.

As I got better and the depression finally started to lift, I began to brood obsessively about the man who had planted the bomb and ruined my companions' lives. I would sometimes dream of vengeance; ponder for hours on who the bomber really was, and where; how he could be brought to justice. I read everything I could find about what others were doing to try and uncover the crime. In fact, apart from Martha Honey's investigations, scarcely anything had been done, but she had been working solidly on the case and now claimed to have solved it.

I was enormously excited when she sent me a copy of the preliminary report she and Tony had written on the bombing. To my surprise, though, I found I had misgivings about their conclusions. Here was an astounding tale of involvement by Miami Cubans, by the Northern-based Contras of the Nicaraguan Democratic Front (FDN) – and by the CIA. John Hull, the American whose ranch we had passed on our way to La Penca, was a key figure; there was collusion by high Costa Rican officials. It read like a thriller, but there was no proof, no mention of sources. And somehow the material just didn't ring true; it all seemed too pat. One of the first maxims I had ever been taught as a journalist was, 'Never believe anything you haven't seen with your own eyes.' If only I was there, I found myself thinking, I could try to do just that.

It was then, in June 1985, that by one of the chances that have occurred since my 'accident' I met at the home of a mutual friend a documentary film director named Judy Jackson. Judy had made several highly regarded documentaries about Latin America. Her concern was with injustice, poverty, government brutality and corruption. She had a reputation, in a field where taking risks was not exactly unheard of, for going to considerable lengths in the pursuit of the truth. She listened to my account of the bombing and said she thought a wonderful investigative documentary could be made if I returned to Central America to try and track down the bomber.

It seemed the perfect opportunity – but did I really have the nerve to take it? Could I really face reliving all that horror? Gently, little by little, Judy persuaded me. She put together a proposal and sent it to Central TV, who responded enthusiastically. They asked to meet me – 'I think they wanted to check you were really all right now, could do the film, weren't some grisly, mauled over sort of person,' explained Judy later, a shade less than tactfully. Then they said yes.

# 3

# 'No Stranger to Terrorism'

In the event it was not until February 1987 – eight months after Central TV had formally commissioned *In Search of the Assassin* – that Judy left England for a preliminary 'recce' of Costa Rica, Honduras and Nicaragua. I was still working for the BBC, and would meet her in Miami for the American leg of the trip, as I couldn't take more time off. The delay was due to a ghastly and quite unforeseen problem. Judy's Chinese-Canadian fiancé, Ed, a TV cameraman, died quite unexpectedly and very suddenly in July 1986. Judy, very understandably, felt so devastated she didn't feel up to embarking immediately on what we both knew would be a gruelling enterprise. Without her energetic support I began to worry all over again about the feasibility of our undertaking this film at all. I seriously contemplated calling the whole thing off, even going back to Central's bosses and telling them that, having so recently dragged myself back from the trauma, I couldn't risk descending that awful path again: my sanity meant more to me than the film. But then I decided I had to go ahead. The project meant so much to me. I had been given just this one chance. I couldn't throw it away: somehow I – we – would cope.

We had read up as much about La Penca as we could lay our hands on. We became instant experts on terrorist groups, ranging from neo-fascist to left-wing, learning how, on occasion, far-left and far-right groups linked up and made common cause, and how truly international their links were. We read up on the background of intelligence networks – from the KGB to Mossad to the CIA – studying dozens of individual cases and 'ops' from South East Asia to Iran, Latin America, the Middle East, Europe. We honed up on guerrilla wars, including those in Central America, noting how they attract gun-runners, drug-smugglers, kidnappers, mercenaries, spies and terrorists of all kinds, all anxious to make capital out of the chaos. Even at this early stage I could glimpse what a murky, vicious, amoral world I was entering.

I went to endless lengths to talk to anyone I believed might help, even tracking down in London men like Stewart Christie, ex-Angry Brigade, to see if he had any left-wing or anarchist contacts who might help us. He didn't. I started making phone-calls to check up on the veracity of early leads. I called Belgium, I remember, to check with a police chief if a Libyan (allegedly the bomber) had been killed there in 1985, a version put out by Pastora's former associate Alfonso Robelo; he denied it. I called Spain to see if a Basque suspect had been under house arrest at the time; he had. I talked to spies, former spies, SAS men, ex-SAS men, self-styled 'experts' and fellow journalists specialising in terrorism. To all of them I brought the by now slightly battered photographs of the Danish photographer whom the Costa Rican authorities had identified as the bomber fifteen days after the event. This photograph, accompanied by packets of information and explanation, all translated into the relevant languages, were sent to contacts as far away as Uruguay, Argentina, Chile, South Africa, France, Israel and Spain, in the hope that someone might remember something or would try and find out for us. That photograph – our one piece of evidence – became a kind of leitmotif. I even had it on the wall of my BBC office, despite the horrified comments of my colleagues, who marvelled at my constant, obsessive pursuit. Despite these efforts, scarcely anyone replied, and no one recognised our man.

On La Penca itself there was little. After the first flurry of news reports expressing outrage and shock, succeeded in the following days by analyses dredging up flimsy and ill-informed scenarios as to who might be responsible, the topic was virtually dropped by the media. A number of short reports, mostly quoting unnamed Pentagon and State Department sources, hinted that the Left was responsible, but the allegations looked curiously insubstantial. Bucking the prevalent 'Left was responsible' scenario were Martha and Tony, who right from the start were certain the Right and the CIA had done it. I have a note from Martha dated 1 September 1985, dashed off in her usual hurried manner, in which she offers sympathy for the operations on my eardrum and elbow, and then goes on to say:

> I also wanted to let you know we have now solved the La Penca case . . . basically we were right all along – it was a CIA plot involving John Hull, Cubans and the Northern FDN Contras and some Americans in Honduras. The bomber is supposed to be a right-wing Libyan named Amac Galil. I don't know much about him yet. The group continues to function under the control of Hull – and no one has yet been arrested, even though we have told the Costa Ricans everything. There were – and continue to be – high Costa Rican officials, mainly in the Ministry of Security, involved. We have been dealing directly with [President Alberto] Monge's office in trying to get something done to stop and arrest this group but nothing has happened.

I would have been less sceptical about Martha and Tony's information if it hadn't gone directly against the prevailing theories, and if, as a former colleague of mine in Central America said, 'I can't get rid of the gut feeling that Martha wants it to be the CIA'. But although their second report still provided no proof, the evidence being mainly circumstantial, it was nonetheless an invaluable working document for anyone following the case, even if I could still not bring myself to believe the Americans would do anything as awful, or indeed as stupid, as the bombing. Even the IRA – no stranger to violence – never harms journalists.

It was only when I racked my brains that I realised there were precedents: the Salvadorean Right had, after all, murdered four of my Dutch colleagues; and the Contras had killed my friends Diall Torgersson and Richard Cross. And then I was given a new theory for La Penca, which provided a role model for the bombing in the form of the assassination in July 1979 of the American TV presenter Bill Stewart in Managua, Nicaragua.

Stewart was killed during a desperate rearguard action by President Anastasio Somoza's National Guard to halt the onslaught of the Sandinistas, who were only days away from victory. The whole gruesome episode is on film. You see Stewart walking ahead of his crew down a hot, deserted street, looking for action. Locals shout to him to stop, as the National Guard are shooting everyone. Stewart, who spoke no Spanish, nods and continues on his way. Next, you see him being made to kneel by a Guardsman. Stewart smiles, clearly not understanding what is happening; kneels obediently; then his body goes limp. The picture, flashed across the world, did more than any other factor to turn the tide of US public opinion against the Somoza regime. I was told those who planned La Penca had intended to kill dozens of journalists (and if the bomb hadn't been inadvertently kicked over, many more of us would have died) and blame the episode on the Sandinistas, in order to inflame US opinion against them when a crucial vote on aid to the Contras was due in Congress.

Judy was less doubtful than I about Martha and Tony's report, but once she reached Costa Rica she too came to see we had problems. When she arrived in February, mercifully just after the long rainy season (no one ever tells tourists there is torrential rain for half the year in this 'paradise'), she went straight to Tony and Martha's elegant house in Rohrmoser suburb. They were busy racing about working for different media, and Judy found it hard to compete for their attention, but slowly she came to realise that, for all the persuasiveness of the report, they simply didn't have the proof to back up their allegations. There was no solid evidence on which to base a serious documentary film that we hoped would reach damning conclusions.

'I thought I'd go to Costa Rica, talk to Martha and Tony, look at their files, interview their witnesses – and we'd have a film. Only it wasn't like that,' Judy later explained. The American couple reacted badly to her misgivings, even though she kept explaining that she didn't doubt their information. 'I understood their reaction,' she told me. 'After all, they'd done all this work, and they were sure they were right. But there wasn't enough to make a film. That was when I realised the only way was to start totally from scratch and examine all the evidence from an unbiased viewpoint. Carry out a totally fresh investigation.'

Our preliminary investigation was vitally important to work out a provisional timetable for the shoot, develop the script, see how much information (and interviewees) were available, and what areas were uncovered. We had to try and save time for the actual shoot, which was scheduled for July and for which a mere three and a half weeks were allotted. It was vital to have an idea in advance of who knew what, who would go on camera and where everyone was.

Judy's problems didn't end in Costa Rica. She went on to Nicaragua, where she spent a frustrating ten days holed up in a very hot house in Managua waiting for Nicaraguan Security to contact her and give her any information they had. When they finally turned up, they wanted to find out what she knew, but offered no information in return. She also met up with the Swedish film director whom the bomber had befriended, Peter Torbiornsson, who was making a documentary film in Nicaragua, persuading him, though with considerable difficulty, to revisit La Penca and talk about it on film. He kept saying he couldn't face it: returning would awaken too many bad memories. Eventually, reluctantly, he accepted.

Judy then passed briefly through Honduras, where she found traces of the bomber in the shape of a hand-written form in the name 'Per Anker Hansen' from a car-hire firm dated two months before the bombing. The firm's manager recalled him, describing him as a 'tall, cold man', and immediately recognised the photograph Judy showed him. What had he been doing in Honduras, and where was he now?

In March 1987 I flew out to meet Judy in Miami. I had forgotten quite how infernally, exhaustingly hot Miami was, and how getting anywhere took at least forty-five minutes and often longer. We started out by trying to get in touch with all the relevant suspects, telephoning contacts we'd already been given, leaders of the Cuban community, a Watergate plumber (also Cuban), Contras and ex-Contras, Sandinista defectors, detectives, ex-spies, local journalists (particularly those working on drugs and terrorism), lawyers involved in our concerns, academics – and then following up all the leads and contacts they provided. We spent a lot of time driving around – and almost as much waiting in our hotel rooms for promised phone-calls that never materialised. When we did see people we often felt we were getting the run-around.

It was in Miami that I had my first glimpse of just how hard we would have to push ourselves. Judy was relentless, always feeling there was more work to be done, one more contact to be seen, always believing our breakthrough lay around the next corner. In theory I was all for this. But in practice I found the 'all work and no play' approach made me short-tempered and irritable. I found myself longing to escape, just to sit by the beach, go to a film, do nothing for half an hour. Instead I ended up so exhausted I would unwind by watching dire soaps on late-night television – and I still couldn't sleep.

After about two weeks of non-stop racing about we flew on to Washington. One of our aims here was to talk to Brian Barger, considered to be a brilliant investigative reporter, with a deep knowledge of US involvement in Central America. We were very anxious to recruit him on to our team, and after considerable persuasion he agreed. Then, in another whirlwind of activity, we contacted and picked the brains of everyone we hoped might know something, from the CIA to authors of books on, respectively, the killing of the left-wing Chilean politician Orlando Letelier (Miami Cubans were involved) and ex-CIA renegades Wilson and Terpil. We questioned more investigative reporters, Central American lobby groups and think-tanks (a growth industry); we talked to more diplomats, ex-spies and terrorist experts.

We visited the Christic Institute, a left-wing public interest law firm which had taken out a $24 million criminal suit on behalf of Martha and Tony for the La Penca affair, naming twenty-nine defendants. The experience was intriguing. Entering their agreeably rundown premises, consisting of two low clapboard houses in a 'no-go' area of north-west Washington, I met a bright-eyed young woman wearing a smock who exclaimed, on discovering who I was, 'You're a La Penca victim! I feel so moved, I'll have to sit down and think about it, to take in the experience.' They were all friendly and doing good, but I couldn't help remembering friends telling me that 'Christies' resembled members of a religious cult. We had a copy of the suit, which incorporated Tony and Martha's information and which for 300 pages dealt with a massive round-the-world conspiracy. But we were not privy to the Christic's sources and, once again, were reluctant to take highly controversial information on trust.

Our search continued to be gruelling. I have never, in my life, put in so many hours, so much work, for so little reward. We ate, breathed and slept La Penca. People have often said to me, 'Your film and book must have been so cathartic,' and to an extent I think they were. But beyond that it just kept me in a kind of time- and subject-warp, going over and over the same material. I'm not sure if other people doing documentaries go to similar lengths, but our subject proved extraordinarily hard to crack, and many 'normal' channels (police help etc.) were denied us. Also, Judy is the most painstaking perfectionist I have ever met, while I, being rather slapdash and happy-go-lucky by nature, wanted to do my best for the sake of the other victims. And on top of that, as if it weren't enough, I have to say, quite simply, that I became obsessed.

We returned to London towards the end of March. In May I returned to Washington to see Ed Wilson, a renegade ex-CIA man now serving a fifty-year jail sentence in a high-security prison in Marion, Illinois, for providing arms and explosives to terrorists. (In one shipment alone, according to Peter Maas, author of *Manhunt*, a best-selling book about Wilson, 43,000 pounds of plastic explosive left Houston for Libya.) I went to see him principally because a reporter in Miami had confided enigmatically that the key to La Penca was 'the fish-farm' and that Ed Wilson knew all about it. I must say I took this information less seriously than Judy, who was quite desperate for new leads. I spent seven hours with Wilson, who claimed to know nothing about any fish-farm, but as he was a consummate liar I had slender hopes anyway that he would give anything away. I later learnt that 'fish-farms' is a euphemism for assassination training camps – 'fish' probably distorted Mafia slang for dead. We discovered they existed in the US but were never sure quite how they fitted in to La Penca, although our bomber could well have been trained in one.

We had been following the Iran-Contra affair closely to see if the La Penca bombing would come up. It didn't – except for a single reference when Oliver North's deputy, Rob Owen, was questioned about it. Its exclusion was almost certainly a result of 'damage control', the drawing of a veil over CIA involvement, aimed essentially, I understand, at preventing the collapse of the Reagan government in a rerun of the Watergate scandal which had brought down Nixon. In the event, Reagan hung on by a whisker. Even if La Penca itself was a black hole in the hearings, we reasoned it was worth investigating whether North's gang – who were up to their ears in almost everything else in Central America – knew something about the bombing. Then we discovered that one of Oliver North's Security operatives, Glenn Robinette, had been sent down to Costa Rica to bribe officials and see what Tony and Martha had found out, and to smear them. I began to reconsider my original, unfavourable assessment of their work.

Then it was another wait until July, when we were all to leave for the shoot. I resigned from the BBC that June and rushed around obtaining visas, foreign currency, inoculations, malaria tablets, suitable clothes (we decided I should wear the sort of practical clothes I wore when I was a reporter, no shoulder-pads or lip-gloss; 'I think they didn't want you to look too attractive,' said my mother loyally when she saw the film).

Our expanding team now consisted of Judy, myself, our American investigator Brian Barger, who was to catch up with us in Miami from his Washington base, Brian Moser, who was brought in because he was a very experienced film-maker with impressive investigative, Latin American credentials. We hoped his enthusiasm and background in sleuthing would make a big contribution. (It did.) The other members of the team – Noël Smart the cameraman and Mel Marr his sound-man – had worked together for fifteen years; they were to catch up with the rest of us in Costa Rica. They were, quite simply, the best. I can't think how we could have got by without them. They were unflappably professional, always good-tempered and had a terrific line in repartee. They coped with tracks that were technically impassable because of the rains, with tantrums, with interviewees who suddenly refused to go on camera, dug me and my Landrover out of ditches – and still cracked jokes in execrable taste. When the relentless shooting schedule, the sheer difficulty of the investigation, differences of opinion as to how to proceed and utter exhaustion led to severe strains among our little team, Mel and Noël kept us going.

On 16 July, via Miami and Houston, I arrived in Tegucigalpa, Honduras, in order to pursue one more lead before filming began. The Honduran connection was very important because of our information that the bomber had been there in March 1984, two months before La Penca. Also, we thought the Contra set-up could provide vital clues. A CIA operative I had met in 1983, down from his base in Panama and wearing the regulation dark-glasses and crew-cut, described the Honduras operation as a 'secret Vietnam' and boasted about the amount of money and arms going to the rebels based there. In Houston I had interviewed General Walter López, a Honduran army commander at the time of La Penca, but it had been a waste of time. All he could tell me was that since Honduran Intelligence could find nothing out, 'the operation must have been very professional'. There was another conclusion to be drawn, I thought, which might have something to do with Honduran Intelligence, but this I kept to myself. Similarly with the car-hire firm lead. Looking at 'Per Anker Hansen's' writing – almost unnaturally neat and regular – gave me a strange feeling: here was one of the few traces of this elusive man, whom Martha had established to be one Amac Galil and whom she considered to be Libyan. He had changed hotels in Honduras several times, and cars three times, something that struck the car-hire man as very odd. 'It seemed he had something to hide,' he commented. Hansen had said he was going down to Honduras's second city, San Pedro Sula, but there was not enough mileage on the clock for him to have reached it. I wanted to know where he had gone, what he had been doing, but the trail was cold, the cover-up had been clamped firmly in place.

The lead that had brought me here promised, I hoped, some real answers to these questions. It came through a British journalist friend of mind, David Adams, who was based in Honduras. He said he had a remarkable contact who might be able to help. He couldn't give me his name, but his pseudonym was 'Morris' (after Adams's car). David had sent me long, carefully written letters about this new contact and called me late at night with new tips. I was very grateful, but perplexed about his contact, and the information, which kept changing. The names altered; the information shifted; as in a dream, facts, dates, personalities, countries seamlessly metamorphosed – but David was sure his informant had the goods. And we were desperate for leads.

Brian Barger, Brian Moser, Judy and I finally met up, severely jet-lagged, in a pleasant down-town hotel in Tegucigalpa. David met us and took Brian Barger and me to meet our contact in a dingy café called the San Francisco, just up the street from our hotel. 'Morris' was actually called Ferrari, and was the Honduran equivalent of a Kray twin. He was a self-styled Intelligence officer, but after some time with him I came to suspect his 'Intelligence training' had been acquired in the death-squads.

As we talked I became more and more uneasy, suspecting, as he asked casual but leading questions about our own, still embryonic, investigation and tried to get us to show him our files 'to save time', that I was being checked out by him, rather than the other way round.

There followed three of the most exhausting and frustrating days I have known, often requiring six-hour sessions sitting in that grotty café drinking undrinkable coffee or Coca-cola (Ferrari refused all alcohol, saying he had once killed someone in a drunken brawl) while our 'lead' talked on and on in Spanish spoken at a machine-gun speed that made my head ache. It took all my concentration to keep track of what he was saying, with its shifting details and changes of subject, but when I complained that he was contradicting himself he told me angrily I hadn't been listening. Brian Moser was convinced he was a con-man, but it was hard to be sure; some of his information was correct; some of it utter rubbish; but there was always just enough gold among the dross to keep us going. And some of his theories sounded vaguely plausible. He told us, for instance, that the attempt on Pastora was carried out by drug traffickers from the Colombian Medellín cartel after Pastora had reneged on a deal, pretending the cocaine shipment had been lost. Ferrari also talked about the involvement of an Iranian 'Savak' mafia which had moved to Central America after the fall of the Shah and was based mainly in Costa Rica. (The mafia did exist; we checked.)

Finally, he came up with some straight, important information. The bomber had left Costa Rica for Honduras the day after La Penca and had been given a Honduran diplomatic passport. Ferrari said he could obtain this passport – for $20,000.

We beat him down on the price, with Brian Moser arguing fiercely that we should give him nothing. We agreed to hand over the money, though, only if we were satisfied that it was the bomber's photograph on the passport.

Ferrari became even touchier than he already was, sulked – and then disappeared for two days. The whole thing was not just a nightmare; it was becoming a black farce. Finally, through an intermediary, he let us have an appalling photostat.

'It could be the bomber, couldn't it, look at his ears – and his nose is nearly the same,' Judy kept saying wistfully. But it absolutely couldn't.

It was on this note of, I have to say, some demoralisation, with lots of 'told you so's' from the two Brians, and hopes (by myself at least) that the rest of the trip couldn't, simply couldn't, be so embarrassingly awful, that we took the plane to Costa Rica. There was a horrible thunderstorm *en route* and we all had several stiff drinks.

# 4

# THE WITNESSES SPEAK

Costa Rica is an anomaly of a country. Famous for its neutrality, its genuine democracy, its tradition of peace (it is frequently compared to Switzerland because it has no army, a comparison that Graham Greene has observed is unfair to Switzerland), it was in fact, in the early 1980s, being turned by the Americans into a staging-post for their war against Nicaragua. The urbane social-democrat image concealed a staggering level of corruption. A telling joke doing the rounds was, 'You can't buy a Costa Rican official, but you can rent one.'

Scarcely anyone had ever been extradited from Costa Rica, and so the country was full of criminal fugitives from all over the world, especially the US. The most famous was Robert Vesco, the US financier, who lived in Cuba (socialist countries have good security and need hard currency) but kept a huge villa in Costa Rica, guarded by Costa Rican Rural Guards. The bland explanation given by Costa Rican officials for their refusal to allow extradition was both neat and devious. The crimes for which these fugitives were wanted – drug- and arms-smuggling, financial skulduggery etc. – did not exist when Costa Rica's extradition laws were first enacted in 1923.

Costa Rica derived considerable benefit from maintaining the status quo. But while some unextraditable villains lived peacefully (protected by dogs, local guards and electric fences) on their ill-gotten gains, more enterprising – or poorer – criminals turned their expertise to an array of ingenious schemes, such as the marketing of 'Young Weimar Republic Bonds'. (I confess to an uncharitable feeling that anyone buying these deserved to be taken for a ride.) Other dubious schemes involved gold and silver mines, oil-wells and forests of valuable hardwoods, few of which existed outside their creators' fertile imaginations. A number were given credibility by the many Christian-backed financial newsletters that serve Costa Rica's large population of retired Americans. There is also a flourishing market in compliant child brides (or playmates) for elderly American men, who regularly advertise for them in the *Tico Times*, the local English-language paper.

During the Contra war drug-trafficking increased with the active connivance of the CIA. The aim was to fund the Contras after Congress banned aid, and the man behind this scandal was Oliver North, who in 1985 did a deal with Panama's then leader, Manuel Noriega, paving the way for Costa Rica to be involved in the smuggling of guns and drugs, the profits from which were to be funnelled back to the Contras. The key player in Costa Rica was John Hull.

Returning to Costa Rica in 1987 was like entering a time-warp. For the first time in three long years I was seeing again the reporters with whom I had attended the press conference. They were my starting point, in more ways than one. For the film, I wanted whatever clues and information they had, because it seemed to me that those most directly affected would be the most motivated. On a more personal note, I wanted to ask them how they had managed to cope with the bombing and its traumatic aftermath. I had frequently been asked why I was still obsessed with the bombing – why I had not 'got over it'. Others would tell me I was not emotional enough about it, that I seemed indifferent and remote. Now I wanted to share my former companions' insights and offer my own, and to talk about these feelings.

Soon after we arrived I saw Roberto Cruz. He was horribly hurt still, unable to walk more than a few steps on his heavy, crudely made wooden leg, unable to work, unable to support his family. I went with him to the slums of San José to visit the elderly mother of Jorge Quiros, the young cameraman killed in the explosion. Her son had been her sole support, but she told us she had never received any money to help her after his death, and that not one government official had bothered to visit her. The shock and grief had affected her mind and she had become a religious fanatic.

To get there we had to walk down a narrow, badly surfaced alleyway and Roberto tripped and fell, despite my supporting arm. As I bent to help him up I felt him trembling with the shock. I could still recall, as I looked at his kindly, damaged face, hearing him, after the blast, scream over and over again, 'My eye, my leg,' and, since I was blinded, not being able to see him. He told me he had heard me cry, 'Help me, please help me,' but that when he had reached out an arm to try and console me I had screamed in panic, 'Don't touch me.' He told me, 'I saw a hellish yellow-blue light. Then I think I heard a couple of shots. I fell down. I had a great pain over my body, but especially in my back. I reached down with my hand and I touched something like a *palo de escoba* [broom handle]. It was wet. I shook it to see what it was. Then I realised it was my leg. They had got my leg. Then I felt my forehead and I felt it was very destroyed and I thought, well, they have got my eye.' He added, 'I thought I was bad, but not one of the worst, and I thought the most wounded should go first. I didn't think then I would die, but I thought I needed medical treatment pretty badly.'

The reverberation of the bomb still echoed, the wounds still festered. Carlos Vargas, after thirty-eight operations, was also dreadfully hurt, his leg amputated, his elbow mangled, grotesque lumps of flesh sewn into his fist to replace the missing fingers of his left hand. He wanted to bring to the interview the pair of spectacles – completely melted – that he had worn at La Penca, but he had mislaid them. A devout Christian, he told me he accepted the bombing and its terrible effects on him. Gilberto Lopes, who helped save me after the bombing, had been sacked from his job at Agence France Presse. He believed his boss engineered his removal because he was jealous of Gilberto, who was seen as something of a local hero. Gilberto's marriage had collapsed as a result of the strain. Now, stolidly but without bitterness, he was trying to rebuild his shattered life.

Reid Miller, an American reporter who had suffered shrapnel wounds, told me he still had to make a conscious effort every day to blot out of his mind the image of Linda Frazier dying beside him and of the hideous carnage surrounding him. He was still racked by guilt at having been unable to help her, or even pass on the last messages to her loved ones that he believed she was whispering as her life ebbed away, because he was temporarily deafened by the blast. He still has severe hearing problems, as do many victims of the bombing. He, too, has had a long-standing relationship break up, and friends who had known his girlfriend, Pauline, said she had changed beyond recognition and that in some ways she had suffered more than did Reid. His was the archetypal Anglo-Saxon reaction to the horror: to ignore it. This distanced Pauline unbearably from the man she had left her long-term staff job in Washington to follow. For six months she had been a recluse, spending her days weeping and shaking, trapped in the luxurious home they rented in San José.

I learnt that my treatment had been far better than theirs. Nearly all of those left behind in Costa Rica developed chronic infections. Roberto told me that he had first turned a yellowish-green colour and swelled right up. It was then that the doctors, to save his life, had been forced to amputate his leg no fewer than five times, starting just below the knee and ending at the top of his thigh, as each time the stump became infected. At the end, he told me, they had used a wire brush to clean his wound, without recourse to any painkiller. He used regularly to faint from the pain. Reid Miller told me his German-born 'Nazi' doctor also cleaned his wounds without any painkillers, by the brutal method of scraping and digging out the infection with a scalpel every day for a period of several months. He said he had never been in so much pain in his life and that Pauline, who would come along to lend moral support, used to have to rush out to vomit from the horror of it all.

He admitted, though, that this 'sadistic' treatment was none the less very effective. The infection cleared up and did not recur.

As well as my fellow victims, I talked to Dr Pacheco, who had treated me on arrival at the hospital. He said he had been reluctant to have me removed from there: 'You were about the worst to come in that night. Of course, there were others badly hurt too, but you were suffering from acute shock. You were very nearly dead. You had no pulse at all, you had terrible injuries – your arm was very nearly completely severed, your leg was torn apart, your eyes were badly cut and burnt, full of shrapnel pieces and dust, your face, hands and neck were badly burnt – and you had lost so much blood. With that and the shock, we thought it very likely you wouldn't survive that first night.'

I believe I probably owed my life to his and the nurses' dedication and care, and I was impressed by his evident kindness and conscientiousness. But I also found out that he was a close friend of John Hull, whose vast ranch was just a few miles down the road from the hospital, and that he was alleged to have treated wounded rebels in the hospital and to have provided other help to the Contras. He certainly misled investigators about the injuries of some of the victims, notably the time they arrived at the hospital, and implied that Tony Avirgan and Peter Torbiornsson, the Swedish film-maker, were both involved in the bombing. I didn't know what to make of any of this.

About the bombing itself, to my surprise, many of my fellow victims spoke freely and easily, some with almost perfect recall. 'A fireball', 'a brilliant flash', 'a sudden, terrible explosion' were some of the descriptions. And Roberto Cruz, despite his dreadful condition, could remember every word of Pastora's futile diatribe before the bomb went off.

There were common threads to the folk memory of that night. All the victims spoke of the pain; the terror; the lack of help; the endless waiting on that dark, muddy river-bank. Of the feeling that this was the end of the world. Some had a weird 'out of life' experience of travelling down an infernally bright tunnel just after the explosion. Peter Torbiornsson remembered thinking he was going to die: 'I was going somewhere at very great speed; it was very bright; kind of nice, comforting. But then you came back to all this . . . mess, blood, screams, everyone around me dying or wounded. I saw Jorge Quiros who had a terrible gash up the whole of his leg and beyond; you knew he couldn't last very long with a wound like that.' Carlos Vargas described 'a very curious experience; for two or three seconds I felt myself in a very bright tunnel being sucked towards a brilliant light at the far end . . . I thought if I reach the light I will die . . . but I'm not going to die, so I made an effort and came back . . . then I realised what had happened. I heard Linda and the other people screaming and asking for help.' Some victims, including Roberto and Carlos, thought they heard shots. Several recalled watching Linda Frazier die from her terrible wounds. Roberto could even remember two Contras discussing whether or not she was still alive when they were both dumped in the bottom of a dug-out canoe with filthy water lapping around them. 'One rebel said he thought she had stopped breathing. Then the other one tried to move part of her body and confirmed that she was indeed dead.' Her body was actually touching his. Carlos observed, with a truly saintly lack of rancour, 'I think the rebels were so horrified by our condition that they couldn't cope. Just left us; trying to ignore the reality. And other journalists rushed out to file the story: that is normal for our profession.'

Few, however, noticed the tall Dane, 'Per Anker Hansen', with mud on his face and in a state of apparent shock. He had been outside the hut when the blast went off, so was unhurt. Gilberto, one of the lesser wounded, remembered seeing him in hospital in the next wheelchair. 'I felt very sorry for him,' he told me. 'He was quite silent. I assumed he was very badly shocked.' In the immediate aftermath many victims were in no state to wonder who had done this to us. 'We were just fighting for our lives,' explained Carlos.

By a strange coincidence, at about the same time that Carlos and Roberto reached hospital, the Danish photographer was already leaving, having pressurised a reluctant Peter Torbiornsson to take a taxi back to the hotel they shared in San José. They were the first to go. Nurses commented that the curiously unwounded Dane, who chain-smoked Marlboros throughout the night as he sat in his wheelchair, seemed on edge and appeared to be waiting for someone. He was constantly asking if a woman had called for him, if there were any phone-calls; he also kept asking about Pastora. In the chaos, his anxiety to leave aroused no suspicion.

I was surprised to find that, though the bombing itself was etched indelibly on the victims' minds, few had made any real effort to investigate the crime. Even Reid Miller, who had covered news stories over five continents for four decades, had done nothing. 'I don't mind someone else looking into it,' he told me, 'but I want no part of it.' He was unhappy about offering support to Martha Honey and Tony Avirgan when they wanted to take a legal suit to the US on behalf of the victims, claiming they had found out who the perpetrators were. 'I told them,' Reid explained, 'that I didn't believe they had the evidence to back up their case and that therefore, in all conscience, I couldn't offer them my support. But I wished them luck.' He even refused to be interviewed by an American producer making a film about La Penca, unhappy, as he explained curtly, about exploiting the bombing and its victims.

His reticence contrasted with the extraordinarily malicious campaign launched by the Costa Rican press just after we were blown up, directed against fellow journalists, the very people who had suffered most. They had already accused me and then Tony Avirgan of being involved; next newspapers pointed the finger at the four of us reporters who had travelled in Tony's jeep to Pastora's base-camp. We were doubly suspicious: we were foreign, and also 'ultra-leftists'. This line of argument was bolstered by the information that we had 'refused' Contra transport. (Quite why that made us potential murderers was not explained.) Orion Pastora told the local press that I had actually turned up with the bomber, with whom I was very close, and insisted he join us. He added, for good measure, that he had not invited me to the press conference. Even Edén Pastora, the intended victim of the bungled plot, interviewed at his hospital bed, said that, from his recollection, I had been closest to the bomb at the time of the explosion. (This was given to imply my involvement.) Not content with blaming those badly hurt in the attack, several newspapers ran a story asserting the real culprit was Linda Frazier, whose mutilated body was still lying in the morgue. It was Martha who pointed out the sinister nature of this deeply unpleasant aspect to the affair, explaining how the press had been used at every level: 'The bomber was posing as a journalist. The journalists were his vehicle for getting to the press conference. They were its victims. Afterwards the press was used to put out false stories, as part of the cover-up. Journalists were its prime suspects. I think one of the most insidious things is that the backers of this plan, basically the CIA, despite US laws forbidding their use of the press, has used both the Costa Rican and the US press in a myriad ways.'

Supporting Martha's assessment of the operation as both cynical and calculated was a report in the *Tico Times* shortly after the bombing: 'Only a professional could have patiently plotted and pulled off such a complex mission. Experts agree: this killer was no hastily-hired thug, no lower-echelon hit man. Cold-blooded enough to chat and joke with the people he would soon be mutilating, cool headed enough to give a radio interview and gaze brazenly into the camera a few hours later, "Hansen" is clearly no newcomer to terrorism . . .'

Martha also said the US Embassy had done nothing to correct the early press reports that Linda Frazier, Tony Avirgan and myself were prime suspects. After the bombing they told Dery Dyer, the editor of the *Tico Times*, that there were no Americans among the dead. Neither the Embassy nor the Costa Ricans made any serious attempt to organise an evacuation by helicopter, although one US official said, 'We're on top of it. We're doing everything we can.' In fact, they did nothing; they didn't even keep track of events so as to provide information to relatives. It was the same story during the investigation. According to Dery, 'Never has the US Embassy been so incompetent and unhelpful.' This was certainly my experience. We were refused a film interview with US officials on the grounds that, 'We had nothing to do with it.'

On the motives for the bombing, Carlos told me vaguely, 'Maybe it was the Sandinistas who wanted to get rid of Pastora; maybe it was the Contras from the north; maybe it was the CIA who couldn't deal with him. There are so many people who are interested in killing him – it could have been anyone.' He added, 'Of course I have my ideas, but it is too big a step to accuse anyone. If I named somebody I would have to be sure . . . and I'm not sure. If I had a proof I would say the name, but I don't have it.' With terrible earnestness he went on, 'We must tell the world how stupid, how criminal, attempts like this are . . . none of us had anything to do with politics . . . we were just doing our job . . . this terrorism, the worst kind of murder of innocent people has to be stopped somehow . . . but we don't have the force or the power to stop it or do the investigation.' Carlos had talked to the Dane on the way to the press conference. 'He was a very cruel man,' he recalled. 'He didn't smile; he spoke as little as possible; he didn't try to make friends; he was what we call a lonely wolf.'

For the few who had tried, obtaining proof – or indeed making any headway at all in the investigation – proved immensely hard. One who made a valiant effort was the identical twin brother of Carlos Vargas, Joaquín, publisher of the conservative *La Republica* newspaper. He told me that he and Dick Dyer, the publisher of the *Tico Times*, attempted a joint investigation. Joaquín told me, 'We contacted Interpol, the FBI, tried to get our own authorities to investigate. Interpol and the FBI never replied. We contacted people in Venezuela allegedly linked to the bomber. They promised to help. But nothing happened. I even hired a Mexican detective at my own expense. He said the bomber was in Mexico and how I could reach him. But I was never able to. And then the detective disappeared. I got absolutely no help from any single authority. They never even answered my letters. From Venezuela, nearly a year later, I got a message which simply said, "Beware of the boys with the blue eyes."' Shaking his head, he went on, 'Our own authorities abandoned the case.'

Joaquín believed there was a lack of political will to find out the truth: 'As a paper we have neither the means nor the capacity to solve this horrible crime. But there are governments who, if they were honest and defended human rights, should be involved.'

'Why,' I asked, 'since we suffered so much, has this not been done?'

'Because there is the possibility, I repeat the possibility, that friends and not enemies were responsible. Yes, I mean the CIA.' He explained this could have been very tricky for Costa Rica, a poor nation economically dependent on the US.

Dick Dyer found he too was blocked. He devoted a year to contacting authorities everywhere, telephoning and writing endless letters, but got no response. No official body was interested in taking up the case. He even published a Wanted poster of the bomber in the *Tico Times*, with all the relevant physical and personal details as well as the offer of a $10,000 reward to be paid out of his own pocket. But no one came forward. Finally an FBI official told him brusquely, 'Call the US Embassy in Costa Rica and ask for the CIA Station Chief. He knows about this.' When Dyer did so he was turned away. 'They told me there was no CIA Station Chief,' said Dyer. 'After a year,' Joaquín ended, 'we both gave up, our money and energy exhausted. And we had got absolutely nowhere.'

This all sounded extremely discouraging. Now, in retrospect, it sounds extremely familiar.

The staff at the hotel where the bomber had stayed, the Gran Via, on a busy street in the middle of San José, remembered Hansen for his quietness: '*No hablaba*' – 'he didn't talk' – said Mauricio, a waiter, shaking his head at such an un-Latin trait. I remembered all those times I had been on flights at ghastly hours with everyone chatting like mad. What I would have given for someone like the bomber who didn't, I thought. 'The man in 606,' he went on, 'was not friendly like the others, but polite. He seldom went out, and then only for short periods.' He spent much of his spare time alone in his room, which was so tidy the others often used it to work in. Mauricio never saw him with a girlfriend (although Rosa the cook disputed this). He had a short temper which flared when he thought he had been overcharged or 'done down'. The overriding impression was of ordinariness, a man who did not stand out. 'We never, ever imagined this man would turn out to be an assassin,' said Mauricio's colleague at the reception desk with a laugh, shaking his head. Behind him the lobby was lined with mirrors. I couldn't help thinking what a metaphor they were for the search I had undertaken: every time anyone found anything, it was a chimera; each clue hid another, and so on . . . It was an Alice-in-Wonderland world where nothing was as it seemed.

The hotel records – unsorted – were dumped in the basement. To get in you had to pull up a trapdoor in the lobby and then gingerly swing your legs round and climb down pitch-black steps until you could reach the light switch. I spent several cramped days in this dungeon, leafing painstakingly through ten years' worth of curling records looking for clues about the bomber's stay. Here at least there were traces of the man: on 12 May he had fruit-juice, toast, two eggs and coffee for breakfast. The bill was signed 'Per Hansen' in a careful, rather flowery hand. Unlike Torbiornsson and the others, he had made no phone-calls from his hotel, claiming it was cheaper to make them from public phone-boxes. I tried to obtain these records but was told they had been thrown away. Back inside the hotel I found little: the bomber's Paris address, rue St Bauve (I checked this later; it didn't exist); and one fascinating detail – on the day after he arrived, 8 May, he asked for a wake-up call at five in the afternoon. He must have come from far away to be so tired he needed waking then. But where?

It was strange looking through the records, at the name 'Per Anker Hansen' in the hotel registry, and even stranger going to the room he once used. I sat on the bed he had slept in, with the roar of San José's traffic just outside, and wondered again what must have gone through his mind as he calmly planned to blow us all up, including the men he had befriended.

Inevitably, there had been all sorts of theories, rumours, 'sightings' of the bomber, none of which, equally inevitably, tallied: according to one version, he left for Honduras; according to another he slipped into El Salvador; a third had him 'without a doubt' entering Nicaragua. A more imaginative version had him leaving the subcontinent entirely, flying first to Madrid and then Morocco. The most favoured exit route (at least four versions, although they may have originated from only two sources) was to Panama; each time I was told John Hull helped the bomber to get out on a light plane. This seemed the most likely explanation for where the bomber really went as he strolled casually out of the Hotel Gran Via, the day after the attack, saying he was going to Miami.

I suspected Hansen's bland, chameleon-like personality and appearance were probably part of his professional armoury, to be worn or discarded at will. Leafing through photographs and videos of him – and seldom can there have been a more photographed terrorist – seeing him taking pictures in a boat, standing around at a Contra camp, wearing a little white sun-hat, with or without a beard, smiling, concentrating, I was struck by his uncanny ability to look different in different poses. But from all this speculation and mystery, one thing was clear: the man was a professional. As Jesús García, a Cuban prisoner I interviewed in jail in Miami, put it: 'He's a mercenary who works for anyone if the price is right.'

My problem was simple, and so far insoluble. I had no legal powers, could force no one to tell me the truth, could not get hold of vital evidence and above all could not get anyone with real authority to help me. I remembered an American friend, Saul Landau, whose colleague Ronni Moffitt was killed along with the former left-wing Chilean minister Orlando Letelier in a car-bomb attack in Washington on 21 September 1976, telling me, 'We couldn't have solved the case by ourselves, Susie. It was only because the FBI worked on it, could force witnesses to talk, offer them deals, bring real weight and resources to bear, that they – not we – were able to prove it was the Chilean Secret Police with help from the Miami Cubans. In your case, none of these people are going to help – they're simply going to block any investigation because of their own involvement.'

I was sure he was right. But what else could I do?

# 5

# Assessing The Evidence

In some ways I was surprised that the President of Costa Rica, Oscar Arias, winner of the Nobel Peace prize in 1987 for his impressive efforts to end the conflicts in Central America, had not done more to help solve La Penca. But I recalled that Arias had not been in power at the time of the bombing, and had had to fight a rearguard action against the Costa Rican Right, with their close links to the US, who fiercely resisted Arias's attempts to restore Costa Rica to genuine neutrality after it had been turned into a virtual US base under his predecessor, Alberto Monge. For President Arias to have taken on the case would have exacerbated problems that had already nearly brought down his government.

Two extreme right-wing organisations were allegedly created with CIA funds, some of which were also employed to influence the local media. Also busy expanding at the time was a secret (and outlawed) far right-wing paramilitary group that wanted to fight alongside the Contras – and to form an internal front to do away with 'communism'. It was closely linked with John Hull, and Dr Pacheco was a prominent member. Many of the supposedly neutral Rural and Civil Guard not only sympathised with the Contras, but provided intelligence, tip-offs about raids and even, on occasion, military back-up.

Because of the unwillingness of officials to investigate or even discuss La Penca I found myself going round in endless circles. I spent days tramping round the city, waiting in dusty anterooms to see officials who never turned up, waiting patiently for promised phone-calls that never materialised. I badly needed to see people who had been involved in the investigation. A number had since left government employ, and they were extremely hard to track down, as often I had no home address or telephone number; I soon found out that they were trying hard to avoid me. '*Qué pena, acaba de salir*' – 'What a shame, he's just left' – is a phrase that still rings in my ears after hearing it at office after office where I had been reliably informed a man by the name of Campos, or Monge, or Tacsán worked.

One man bucked this trend and at once agreed to see me. It was wet and windy on the day I turned up to see Fernando Cruz, Attorney General at the time of the bombing and now a Supreme Court judge, and I clutched my full skirt firmly as I climbed the steps of the Justice Ministry, anxious not to do a Marilyn Monroe in full view of the camera-crew. His office was on the ninth floor and commanded a magnificent view of the city's red-tiled roofs and the volcanoes beyond. Huge law books lined the walls from floor to ceiling. Fernando Cruz sat behind a mahogany desk, which was adorned with one of those fussy pen and ink sets usually given to officials on retirement. Although very short-sighted, he none the less took his spectacles off for the filmed interview, and squinted – albeit charmingly – at me.

I asked him why so little had been done to solve La Penca. He explained that Costa Rica lacked expertise in dealing with organised crime of this kind. He also admitted there was a lack of political will to carry out a thorough investigation because of fear on everyone's part at what it might turn up. Haltingly, and after fairly relentless questioning, he told me about the infiltration of the security and investigative forces supposed to be working on La Penca; the distortion of information; the slippery slope of 'a conspiracy of silence, not just by the authorities, but no one wants to talk; everyone is afraid'. He admitted there was a cover-up, 'an organised attempt to prevent the truth coming out'. He too was afraid. 'I believe there is a big network behind La Penca, but I am afraid for my position to say more, to name names. And I have no proof, only suspicions.' He explained how hard it was to get anywhere because 'those in the north, near where La Penca happened, gave us no facilities or help'. And this, I thought, was the only man genuinely concerned to help; who said he believed passionately that La Penca ought to be solved and who had even, very honestly, admitted his part in the error that still haunted him, of not immediately sealing all Costa Rica's borders after the bombing.

His attitude was a thousand times more positive than that of Angel Solano, Interior Minister at the time of La Penca. I wanted to see him because not only was he supposed to have information about the bombing and the lack of progress in investigating it, but he had been sacked from the government shortly afterwards for his independent views. I hoped he might be angry enough to want to talk.

Solano was nearly three hours late for our interview. I spent my time playing with his enchanting tiny children (six of them) and studying my surroundings with awe. The nouveau-riche décor of his home was ostentatious in the extreme: enormous gilt chandeliers hung from the ceiling; gilt and china gew-jaws – china bambis, gilt madonnas, bleeding Christ figures and three-tone vases of staggering vulgarity – fought for every available inch. The heavy pseudo-baroque furniture would have suited a mausoleum. There were back-lit grottoes in the bathroom and pictures on the walls depicting Dickens-type waifs, all blond curls and tear-stained faces. One of the curious aspects of Central America is the use in so many pictures and in nearly all the advertisements for clothes, cigarettes and so on of craggy blond men and leggy blonde women who bear all the resemblance of Martians to the small, dark, indigenous inhabitants of the area. It's sad, because it reflects a widely held belief that the white (and particularly American) race is inherently superior, and that its habits and values should be emulated.

Finally Solano arrived, apologising profusely. He started by explaining that since he left office before the La Penca investigation got under way he knew nothing directly; he could tell me very little, could certainly not name names, didn't want to speculate, but after forty minutes of prevarication grudgingly conceded (and even this was like pulling teeth) that in his view the Left was not involved. But he didn't know who was, and he was not going to venture an opinion. 'You can draw your own conclusions,' he kept repeating. Not for nothing was the man a lawyer. I left wondering why on earth he had granted me an interview at all.

Despite the intense pressure to 'get the story' I was finding it increasingly hard to keep psyching myself up. Was it really worth making yet another phone-call or waiting for hours outside yet another office or insalubrious meeting spot at midnight, driving miles out of town for yet another rendezvous to be told by yet another frightened ex-minister, 'I know nothing; I don't dare say anything'? I was becoming conditioned to expect rejection.

I had contacted one of the two main Costa Rican investigative organisations, the OIJ (Judicial Investigation Unit), which a few weeks after the bombing assumed major responsibility for the case. Unlike its rival organisation, DIS (Directorate of Intelligence and Security), OIJ had a criminal laboratory in which it analysed the evidence Pastora's group had brought from La Penca. Now, hoping that at last I might find something more than veiled accusations and innuendo, I visited the warehouse where the La Penca remains were stored. The sight that greeted me when I arrived was enough to dash this hope.

All the material from all the crimes that had ever been committed in Costa Rica were dumped on the second floor of a huge warehouse belonging to the Security forces. In one corner, lying higgledy-piggledy on the floor, covered in dust and rat-poison, was the mouldering evidence collected from La Penca. There was something unbearably poignant about these relics – the tattered remains of T-shirts, torn and brown from encrusted blood; the shattered bits of tape-recorders and cameras; the sheets of rusting corrugated-iron from the hut, ripped apart by the explosion. But none of it looked remotely useful in providing clues – if indeed anyone had tried.

The OIJ director had told Martha Honey that a year after the bombing the extensive files and the investigation of a hundred and twenty people believed to have been involved in La Penca had produced no concrete leads. He had added that the bomber 'undoubtedly had local contacts helping him before the incident'. Martha believed some of these local contacts included members of Costa Rica's Security forces. She was convinced that while much of the bungling of the La Penca investigation could be explained by interagency rivalry and a lack of professional competence, there was also evidence of a cover-up. She also believed some Costa Rican security officials had prior knowledge of the assassination plot and that they and others helped to circulate false leads afterwards.

Now, after some persuasion, the OIJ finally allowed me to meet the head of their crime laboratory, Fernando Castillo. A decent-seeming man with the erect bearing of a former military officer, silver hair and beetling black eyebrows, Castillo had one piece of remarkably interesting information: he said vital pieces of evidence – including the bomb's detonator – had been taken away by American experts just after the bombing. The Costa Ricans had asked them for help 'because we do not have any experience in these matters'. The Americans were supposed to return both the evidence and their analysis to the Costa Ricans when they had evaluated them, but, said Castillo, 'we never saw them again'. Nor were the results of the analysis ever made available to the Costa Ricans. Castillo admitted that these pieces of physical evidence from the bomb were crucial in ascertaining its provenance – and, by extension, its perpetrators, since each batch of plastic C-4 explosive has separate 'fingerprints' from which its place of origin can be determined. The detonator could provide further corroborating evidence. One of the main difficulties in solving the bombing, he said, was precisely the lack of physical evidence. It seemed highly suspicious that all these vital clues went missing just after the bombing. Did he think the Americans had been trying to cover the bomber's tracks?

Castillo was clearly embarrassed and reluctant to tell me what had happened, and he could never bring himself to accuse the Americans of a cover-up. But he was a lot more forthcoming than the rest of his department. Allan Solano, a short, stocky man who looked like a Costa Rican Lenin, with his huge head and thick, black, spade-like beard, was now in charge of the investigation. It was a long time before he would agree to see me; even when he did, he was evasive, suspicious and unhelpful. I hoped that by turning up at his office every day I might wear down his defences, get him on my side. I would walk from my hotel, through the relentless rain, to the tall Ministry of Security building, take the lift to the fourth floor, turn right, past signs for the public morgue, and come to the unmarked door of the investigative unit, which opened only from the inside. Gradually Solano's team started to give me more information – but only after I had had to go to humiliating lengths, losing my temper or bursting into tears to show them I really cared. Even then I was rewarded only with fragments of information, whose accuracy I was never able to double-check.

On one occasion, about two weeks into my visit, Solano produced the unit's 'pièce de résistance': a huge cardboard cut-out flow chart about seven feet long and two wide, criss-crossed with lines and arrows with place names and dates drawn in different coloured crayons that required two men to carry and hold up. It purported to show the movements of the bomber (whom they had codenamed 'Aguila': eagle) and a mysterious woman companion (codenamed 'Halcón': falcon) for two years before the bombing. I was invited to photograph this important piece of 'evidence', but as I studied it I was disconcerted to overhear a heated squabble breaking out among the members of the La Penca crime squad as to which codename referred to whom. Had I not been so desperate, I might have found some black humour in this Inspector-Clouseau-like incompetence.

For two years before the bombing the chart showed the bomber moving regularly around Central America. He was apparently based in Panama for a while, and travelled constantly to Costa Rica, Honduras, El Salvador and back to Panama. He had visited Costa Rica in November 1983 – presumably to plan the bombing. I had learnt independently that a man named Per Anker Hansen had been arrested during that month near the Gran Hotel for illegally carrying firearms, together with a notorious Miami Cuban named Felipe Vidal, known to be a hitman and to have links with Hull. Official records of the arrest and charges had mysteriously disappeared, released after a phone-call from a 'senior official'; I was unable to find out who. When I asked about the incident Solano blusteringly insisted it had never taken place, and blamed inaccurate and meddling journalists. My difficulties in checking the veracity of Solano's information were increased by his refusal to allow me access to any of the sources of his information about the bomber's movements – which he said came from authorities in Honduras, Panama and elsewhere – because 'they are between official investigators; not for journalists or the public as the investigation is still under way'.

According to the chart, the bomber left for Miami the day after the bombing, and disappeared into thin air. Solano had no idea where he was. But he would be grateful if I could find out.

The woman who featured on the chart was supposed to be the bomber's beautiful raven-haired companion, travelling on a stolen passport under the name Patricia Anne Mariscot de Boone. The passport was French, a language the bomber was apparently familiar with. But Solano's office said she had not accompanied 'Hansen' to Costa Rica, and although a chambermaid at the hotel where he stayed before the bombing said a woman regularly visited him, others working there didn't remember this. Martha Honey, on the other hand, was convinced the woman was with him at the Hotel Irazu, where our trip started.

One witness she spoke to even claimed there was a black wig left at La Penca. Martha became convinced that the woman was María Lourdes de Palacios, an extremely glamorous niece of Somoza, one of whose brothers had died fighting for the Sandinistas.*

To complicate the issue, Solano had a second woman suspect, a blonde for whom an odd, inhuman-looking photofit was issued. But a nice young deputy of his confided to me that he didn't believe the blonde was an accomplice at all, just a casual girlfriend 'Hansen' had picked up in Honduras, possibly as a cover. I later heard rumours that the physical descriptions of the women had been deliberately altered.

Why was Solano apparently at odds with his own investigators? He constantly complained of being underfunded; described how he had virtually had to abandon the La Penca investigation 'although the files aren't closed' precisely because of lack of support and had had to fund a Wanted poster out of his own pocket. He was vitriolic about other attempts to investigate and told me that Martha and Tony were 'making capital out of the blood of their dead colleagues' – an extraordinarily vicious remark. Certainly he disliked the press in general and smarted under criticism that his department was idle and ineffective. (One cartoon in the *Tico Times* depicted a half-open filing cabinet covered with cobwebs and marked 'OIJ La Penca investigation'.) Was this because of what they had discovered? Because their findings had shown him up? Or because of their aggressive personalities and left-wing political views that were out of step with his and the majority of conservative Costa Ricans'?

* In 1989 I questioned the British correspondent whom María had married. He said she had indeed been suspected of working for the CIA but that in 1988 Tomás Borge, the Nicaraguan Interior Minister, had boasted that she had been a Sandinista double-agent all along. This was the first her husband had heard of this. He also told me that she had been in Costa Rica at the time of the bombing, although Immigration have no record of her entering or leaving the country.

Finally, we got on to the subject of John Hull. Solano was vehement that he had 'no evidence' that Hull was involved in La Penca. Once again, though, other members of his investigating team gave me a different story, notably one young woman who wore extremely high-heeled thigh-length boots in which she was constantly to be seen miraculously racing up and down stairs, who told me 'everybody' believed John Hull and his people were responsible for the bombing.

Some of Martha's most important leads on La Penca came about by extraordinary coincidence. It was hard not to be suspicious about some of them, and even to suspect that some were actually an attempt to provide not information, but disinformation. Ernesto Guevara, a petrol-pump attendant, was just such a badly needed 'break'.

One evening, a year after the bombing, Martha had stopped her blue station-wagon (the same one that had taken us on the La Penca trip) at a San José garage to fill up with petrol, then realised to her embarrassment she had forgotten her purse and couldn't pay. At this point the petrol-pump attendant, a small, intense, dark-haired man, suggested he accompany her home as security. The moment they set off he said, 'You're Martha Honey; you're doing an investigation into La Penca, aren't you?' Martha, astonished, said she was. He then revealed an extraordinary story. He said that at one point he had been designated as a driver to DIS. In May 1984 he had been ordered by the head of DIS, Carlos Monge – whose name had already come up during Martha Honey's investigations – to drive a tall, well-built man with a beaked nose, hooded eyes and Middle Eastern appearance – a man he was told 'was working with the government' – down to the river on the Nicaraguan border, and to wait for him. He assumed the man, who did not speak during their trip, was carrying out a reconnaissance. 'This was the same man who appeared in the photographs in the newspapers after La Penca as the Danish photographer, the bomber,' he insisted. He told Martha his name was Ernesto Guevara, and that he had on two occasions driven the young man and John Hull on a reconnaissance up the San Juan river, to the area where the bombing took place only weeks later.

The information was extraordinary – vitally important if true – but, like so many parts of the La Penca investigation, hard to prove. Guevara stuck to his story even after being thrown into jail on apparently trumped-up charges after his information was made public. He was released, but the intimidation seemed to have worked. When I tried to find Guevara I was unable to track him down, even though I spent first days and then nights driving round with Roberto Cruz in his old car, stopping at every garage to see if they had an Ernesto Guevara working for them. No one had heard of him.

I did, however, manage to get a single interview with Carlos Monge. I didn't expect this to be easy. I had already been told by an aide to Edén Pastora that Monge had received death threats and had backed off from the investigation. I also heard several versions of a debate about whether Guevara really had worked for the Security organisation. One version had his name being erased from the files; another, that the relevant page had gone missing. The *Tico Times*, whose reporting was usually accurate, said it had information that Guevara had indeed worked for the organisation, initially as a general 'gofer' and later as a driver, as well as being involved in Intelligence work. Subsequent attempts to deny this – and in addition to smear the man as an unreliable crook – were part of 'damage control'.

After a dozen or so phone-calls from me, Carlos Monge eventually turned up at my hotel, armed and accompanied by a burly minder with a tape-recorder who not only listened in to our conversation, but conferred in a whisper with Monge about key bits. I was less than happy about this arrangement. Carlos Monge, however, looked genuinely affected to see me and kissed me with emotion as we met. He told me he could never forget the horror of La Penca, of seeing the shocked and wounded victims. As soon as he had heard the news about the bombing on the radio, he had immediately jumped into his car and sped down from the capital to Boca Tapada. There he watched us arrive in canoes in swirling mist in the early hours of the morning; we were laid out by the jetty and then transferred to ambulances. Monge said he remembered seeing us, seeing how horribly hurt we were, hearing our screams and moans; seeing Linda, dead. He was on the verge of tears at the memory. Then, he said, he followed us to the hospital and started to interview the survivors until an overwrought photographer yelled at him, 'How can you interrogate us at a time like this? Don't you have any sense of human decency?' Carlos said he was shocked, and immediately stopped. 'I couldn't bear anyone to think badly of me,' he explained. 'I felt terribly upset, ashamed.'

It seemed almost inconceivable to me that the head of the Security force could be stopped dead in his tracks like that. But given the gentle, courteous Costa Rican tradition, I can believe it. I asked Monge whether he had received threats during his investigation, but he emphatically denied this. I wanted to get all this information out of the way and to soften him up before I started asking him about Guevara.

Monge at once became agitated and denied that he had ever heard of a man named Guevara, let alone that the man had worked for him in any capacity. He denied Guevara's story about being sent as driver with the mysterious man whom Guevara identified as the bomber. 'It's a total fabrication, a lie,' he shouted, pounding the table with his fist. I then asked him about the most incriminating part of Guevara's story. Guevara had claimed to have seen a large silver camera-case, with a yellow sticker marked 'Made in the US', which, Guevara said, he later learnt had contained the bomb, inside Monge's office where it had been stored for some weeks. 'That story is a wicked calumny, a lie,' shouted Monge, rising to his feet and going red in the face. 'There is no truth at all in the accusation. How can you possibly think I had anything to do with that bombing – helping to kill and maim innocent people like you? I swear I had nothing to do with it.'

I found myself moved by Monge's distress. If he wasn't sincere, the man had to be a fantastic actor. On the other hand, Guevara's story seemed credible. Why would he have made it up? And if it wasn't true, why had he been jailed for no good reason? Unable to track Guevara down or to see Monge again, since he didn't return my phone-calls and was never there when I went to the down-town bank where he worked part-time as a security officer, I was left with no way of being able to prove or disprove this tantalising piece of 'evidence'.

If my interviews with the Security forces were frustrating, those with the strange mixture of characters who seemed to gravitate towards anyone trying to find out about the bombing were even more so. They would surface, with no warning, from the anonymous underground of Central America. Some had stories incriminating the Left; others, the Right.

One such was a tall, well-built, sexy black Nicaraguan Contra from the Atlantic coast, that languorous, tropical area once under British rule and now for the most part bitterly opposed to the left-wing Sandinistas. Rudy Sinclair was the friend of one of Martha's contacts, and he told me he harboured 'deep human feelings for me' (after hitting me for large expenses for himself and his friends). He had a charming slow Caribbean lilt, expressed himself in an archaic, almost Elizabethan English and sometimes worked as an assassin. He was now in charge of an Atlantic coast rebel force which was languishing from lack of funding. He told me he had been asked to infiltrate a hit team formed in order to assassinate Edén Pastora. The leader of the team was none other than Enrique Bermúdez, military leader and *jefe maximo* of the Honduran-based Contras.

Bermúdez, an authoritarian figure who had been an officer in Somoza's feared National Guard and then Military Attaché in Washington, had a reputation for cruelty and ruthlessness. Rudy said he had been driven twice at night to meet him in the spring of 1984, both times in the Honduran capital, Tegucigalpa, in the Contra safe-house, which lay, more than coincidentally, just one

Carefree and relaxed, journalists – and the bomber (in peaked cap) – travel to the press conference at La Penca. *(La Republica)*

Pastora – otherwise known as 'Comandante Zero' – as Sandinista hero in 1979, after 'El Triunfo'. *(Joe Frazier)*

Pastora – to my eye practically indistinguishable from his previous incarnation – as Contra leader of the Southern Front. *(Joe Frazier)*

These three journalists died later from wounds suffered during the explosion, Linda Frazier and Jorge Quiros within hours, Evelio Siqueira a week later.

At Pastora's jungle HQ moments before the explosion. I am standing to the right of Pastora. *(Costa Rican police)*

One year later: the first reunion of La Penca survivors. Front left in wheelchair is Roberto Cruz, who lost his leg and an eye; behind him just to the right is Carlos Vargas, also critically injured. In the back row, right to left, are Tony Avirgan and Gilberto Lopes. *(M.E. Esquivel, Tico Times)*

Cartoon by Arcadio Esquivel in the *Tico Times* on the lamentable state of the police investigation into the bombing.

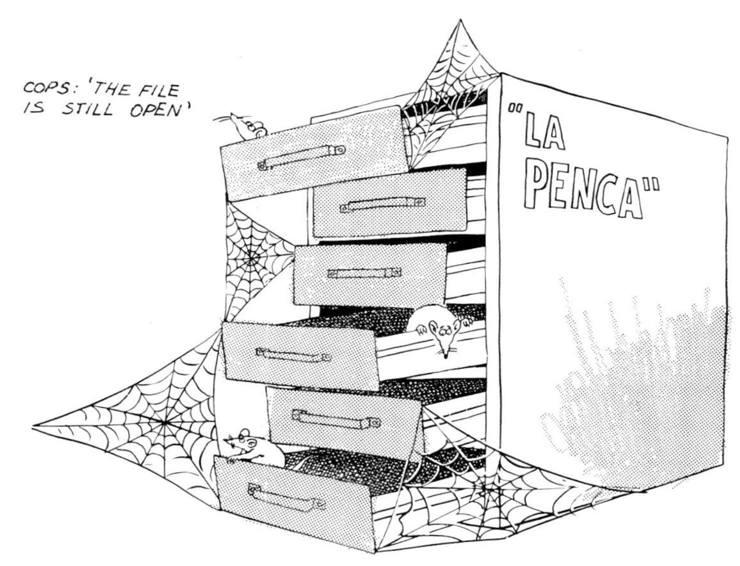

La Penca one year after the bombing: the remains of the hut. By the time we arrived to film in 1987 it had totally disappeared, cannibalised by the Sandinistas for their military base. *(Tico Times)*

Some of the 'evidence' collected from La Penca by the Costa Rican police: most lay mouldering in a huge warehouse, despite claims that 'the files on La Penca are still open'. *(Tico Times)*

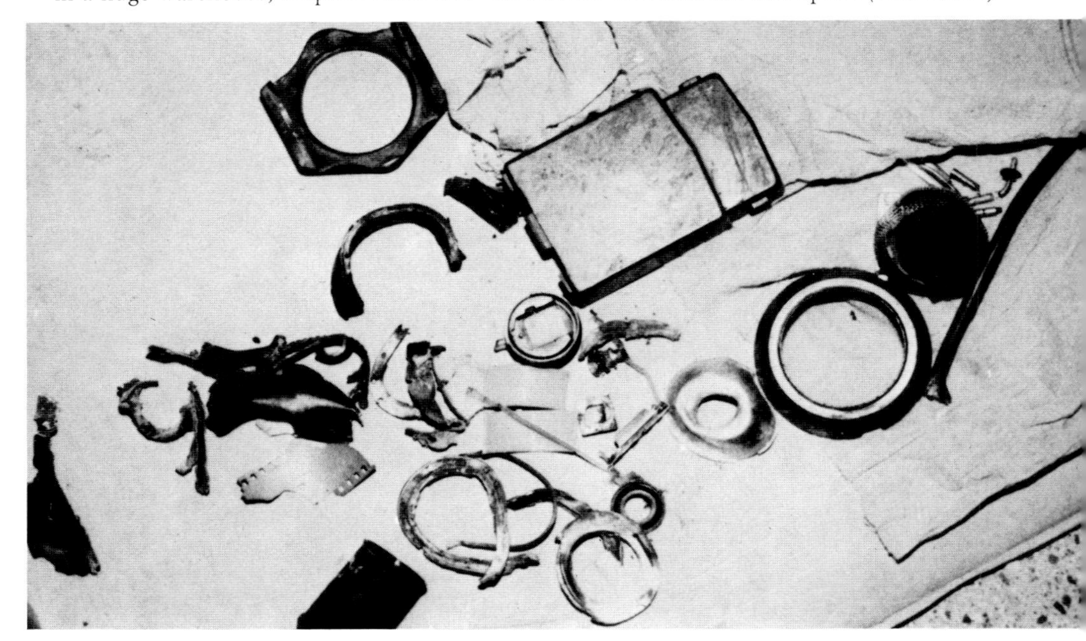

block from the US Embassy, whose main function at that time was to liaise with and direct the US-sponsored Contra operation. At the meeting Bermúdez told Rudy that he would support his commando group, but on one condition. In return, Rudy had to complete a mission that involved 'eliminating Edén Pastora and Brooklyn Rivera'. (Brooklyn was the Misquito Indian leader whose forces were fighting in conjunction with Pastora.) He was to infiltrate Pastora's bodyguards in readiness for an assassination attempt in May.

Rudy said he was appalled by the idea: he had nothing against Pastora, and baulked at the thought of killing him and his colleague. But he understood instantly he had to appear to go along with the plan or his own life would be in danger. 'Because I was apprised about the plot, if they thought I would back out they would have to kill me, to keep me quiet.' Pretending to acquiesce, he managed with some difficulty to slip back into Costa Rica. But there CIA agents were waiting to meet him and discuss the plans in greater detail. Rudy said he had lengthy meetings with two men he knew to be CIA agents in various hotels in the capital as they worked out the details. 'Then,' said Rudy, 'I decided things were getting too hot and soon I would have to be involved – and I didn't want to – so I disappeared.' He wouldn't tell me where. 'I was truly shocked when La Penca happened,' he went on, explaining that he believed the bombing was the plot Bermúdez had been talking about. 'I never realised they intended a bomb or for innocent people to die. I assumed they would just assassinate Pastora – that's how it's usually done.'

I made Rudy retell his story at least three times, and kept going over all the details to try and trip him up. But he faithfully repeated exactly the same version, each time listing the complicated series of meetings and events, of place, character and motivation, until I became convinced he was telling the truth. But how would I ever know for sure this was the plot that led to La Penca, or whether, in those feverish months in the spring of 1984, as the crisis on the Southern Front was reaching a climax, this was one of a number of different assassination plots being hatched in smoke-filled rooms throughout Central America and Miami? As one witness put it to me: 'Every time we had a meeting with those people' – and here he meant the CIA – 'at the beginning of the meeting and at the end, every time, the discussion always turned to the same theme: how to get rid of Edén Pastora.'

# 6

# The Spider in the Web

In all my investigations one figure – the spider at the centre of the intrigue – always seemed to come up: John Hull, the rich, powerful American rancher who ran the north of Costa Rica as though it was his personal fiefdom. I had first visited him with Martha Honey in March 1984 – two months before the bombing – because even then I had been warned that John Hull could be much more than the simple, 'good ole boy' farmer he purported to be; that in reality he used his status and his enormous, strategically sited ranch and sympathetic neighbours (many of whose farms he managed) to help in America's secret war. A young researcher from *Newsweek*, whose correspondent I was, had called me from New York to tell me of a sudden surge of interest in him. She read out newspaper clips that suggested Hull provided weapons, money and training to the Contras, and hinted at conspiracy and plots. We both decided I should take a closer look at the man.

My interest heightened after I had pored over a large-scale map of Costa Rica to look for Hull's land. I found, to my surprise, dotted about close to the border with Nicaragua, half a dozen airstrips all marked 'John Hull'. Clearly, the man was important.

A few days later, Martha and I left the noisy, smelly bustle of the capital and entered volcano country, our route taking us high over tortuous hill roads, with glorious tranquil vistas of cloud-capped cones, corn taller than a human being waving beside the road, chocolate-box villages of low, white-washed adobe buildings, colonial churches and streetside vendors selling flowers and sticky sweets. The air was thin, cold and clean. I remember passing a graveyard in the village of Zarcero with yew-bushes lovingly clipped into surreal birds and beasts – peacocks, lions and giraffes; then the road began to wind down the far side of the volcanic spine into the red-earthed San Juan valley. On our descent, as we negotiated alarming hairpin bends, chasms and waterfalls, the air already felt warmer and wetter; giant ferns bordered the road, and there were flowering shrubs and trees, festooned with moss and creepers, and cascading with orchids. An hour later we arrived at the hill-billy town of Ciudad Quesada, the gateway to this fertile agricultural region that shades off into impenetrable tropical rainforest near the Nicaraguan border. This was the town to which I was to return, critically injured from the explosion, eight weeks later.

The bustling main square had the feel of the Wild West. Muddy four-wheel-drive vehicles, farmers wearing stetson hats and cowboy boots loading up with provisions from general stores that bore Lebanese names and provided everything from cowfeed to kerosene and candles. We got out to stretch our legs, drink a quick cup of coffee and take directions for the ranch of 'Don John', as Hull was called, a mark of respect for his status. His office was in a side street, we were told – but he wasn't there. A dark-haired young secretary directed us to Bruce Jones, a red-haired American in his mid-forties. Yes, he was a friend of John's. He was at the ranch. We should go there. After making a rendezvous later in the day with this forthcoming man, who freely admitted he supported the rebels – 'They're everywhere,' he told us, 'and everyone here supports them' – we set off on the last, twenty-minute, leg of our trip.

We drove slowly down the road to Hull's ranch, accompanied by the sound of frogs and cicadas in the grass where humped white cattle grazed. Following our instructions, we turned left across an unmarked stony drive flanked by huge palm-trees and parked next to a small hangar containing a one-engine plane. It was used, Hull later told us, to check out sick animals. The man we had come to see was in his sixties, tall, with a permanent tan, a laugh that never reached his curiously wary blue eyes and a jovial manner that struck a false note; even without the information I'd been given about him, there was something that made me think he was giving a performance. He seemed friendly, inviting us into his house for a chat, even though we had no appointment, and his tiny common-law wife Margarita, a Costa Rican, offered us lemonade. We sat on the verandah of the airy ranch-house with its arched porticoes, looking down on a tributary of the San Juan river – containing both alligators and fresh-water sharks – and beyond it to 8000 rolling acres of cleared jungle mostly devoted to cattle, timber and citrus groves. Palm-fronds swayed in the breeze; parrots squawked. A distant volcano was wreathed in cloud. It seemed incongruous, in this bucolic, apparently tranquil setting, with the misty hills of Nicaragua in the background, to catch sight of Hull's ten or so armed minders discreetly patrolling the estate, and to be questioning the 'boss' about training terrorists and trafficking in weapons.

Confident and relaxed, 'Don John' sat back in his rocking-chair and laughingly dismissed my and Martha's accusations of his running guns, drugs and a private army as 'communist misinformation', insisting the extent of his help to the Nicaraguan 'freedom fighters' was humanitarian and that he helped Nicaraguan refugees only for 'humanitarian reasons'. He was just a farmer, he kept insisting, trying to make an honest living in this charming country.

We got nowhere, but as we drove away I wondered again what John Hull – with his stories of living the frontiersman's life, literally hacking down the virgin jungle with his bare hands when he arrived, complete with soil-testing kit, with his father over twenty years earlier – was really like. I became even more suspicious after we stopped the car and talked to Hull's young American neighbours, whose ranch-house was down the road. The wiry blond American and his heavily pregnant wife, who had bought their ranch only two years earlier, said they were nervous about speaking out, afraid of the powerful 'Don John' and his armed guards, but admitted that covered trucks rumbled mysteriously through Hull's estate twenty-four hours a day, and that light planes would land on his private airstrips and take off again at odd hours.

Back in Ciudad Quesada, Bruce Jones, Hull's friend and business partner, also claimed to be 'just a farmer', but he was much more open about helping the Contras. Later, to an American journalist working for *Life* magazine, he couldn't resist boasting about his exploits with the 'freedom fighters', and had himself photographed, wading across the San Juan river with a bunch of rebels. The article, entitled 'A CIA man in Costa Rica', caused a furore and forced the Costa Ricans to expel him, even though Hull kept telling everyone the photo had been faked. Much later I heard rumours that Jones might have been involved with Hull in the La Penca bombing, but I have been unable to prove this.

Two weeks after this visit, I climbed up a steeply wooded hill not far from Hull's ranch with a frightened, elderly peasant guide to find the wreckage of a DC-3 that had crashed into dense tree-tops during a night mission to resupply the Contras nearby. Not only was the broken-up fuselage still smouldering, but I could feel the heat from the freshly turned earth of a crude grave, marked by a cross fashioned from two branches. Stirring the ground nervously, I uncovered charred bones that looked human. The most mysterious and macabre aspect of this incident was that I knew the plane had in fact crashed a full two weeks earlier. Why, then, was it still smouldering?

According to my guide, both the wreckage of the aircraft and much of its contents – including uniforms, boots and the corpses of the pilots and crew – had repeatedly been doused with petrol and set alight. He said the Contras in the area had originally been ordered to remove the jawbones from the charred corpses to prevent identification, but they found the operation too ghoulish, even for them. Finally, I was told, John Hull flew one of his light planes to the area to take the bodies away and bury them secretly on his ranch. The peasant said he had heard there were gringos aboard as well as Salvadoreans, and that it was crucial to remove this evidence.*

It was in 1985, a year after the bombing, that the operation at John Hull's ranch was exposed. Even then, few took the information seriously, or realised that what they were hearing fitted into a larger, more sinister scheme.

The unravelling of this part of the operation started at dawn on 25 April when a group of Costa Rican Guardsmen led by one Colonel Badilla, who was acting, he later said, on direct orders from the government, entered a remote Contra training camp in dense jungle close to Hull's ranch and arrested five gringo trainers. To their horror, the foreigners were driven straight to San José and charged with violating Costa Rican neutrality and possessing explosives. The military trainers – two Americans, two Englishmen and one Frenchman – were initially shocked at their treatment: they considered themselves an officially sanctioned part of the US operation in Central America, and were used to friendly relations with the Costa Ricans. After being transferred to the La Reforma jail the five were divided on tactics: to keep quiet, or to spill the beans. Peter Glibbery, an ex-British soldier, originally from Birmingham, and Steven Carr, an American, decided to talk. The decision was to cost Carr his life.

The stories Glibbery and Carr told to the press, the FBI, the US Justice Department and finally the US Senate were extraordinarily detailed and completely consistent; they also tallied with earlier testimonies. The US Embassy in San José, in particular, went to great lengths to denigrate them, describing Glibbery and Carr as 'unreliable jailbirds' telling 'fairytales'. Their tactics were

* This was nearly three and a half years before the Southern Air Transport C-123K carrying an American mercenary, Eugene Hasenfus, on a Contra resupply mission crashed, shot down inside Nicaragua by Sandinista troops, and made world headlines. This accident revealed the extent of clandestine US involvement because Hasenfus – unlike those aboard the DC-3 – survived. I was to find out more about this on my Miami trip. See p. 147.

partially successful, but there was just too much information available for the story to go away; too much of it could be independently corroborated – and was. The two mercenaries said they had been working for John Hull, who had described himself to them as the 'CIA-Contra liaison' in Costa Rica, for which he received $10,000 a month from the National Security Council in Washington. They described him as the 'boss' of the whole area. His work included supplying, arming and training the Contras; overseeing the war on the Southern Front after Edén Pastora had been pushed aside as a result of the La Penca bombing; paying the commanders; operating two Contra training camps, including the one on his ranch where the mercenaries had just been arrested; and liaising with Rob Owen, Oliver North's deputy, as well as with the hard-line Contra leaders from Honduras, the FDN, run by Adolfo Calero.

Glibbery described how a man named Robert Owen had gone with him and Hull to redirect a Contra arms-supply plane that had landed at the wrong airstrip, and said he had been told that the pilots were Salvadorean. He had been impressed by the size of the operation, and by the importance of its participants. Meanwhile, Steven Carr described how he had come to Costa Rica from Fort Lauderdale, boarding a chartered aircraft loaded with six tonnes of weapons. It had flown to the Salvadorean air-force base of Ilopango, where US military had watched as the cargo was unloaded by Salvadorean military personnel for transshipment to the Southern Contra Front.

Needless to say, Hull was extremely worried by 'his' mercenaries talking, and paid visits to the prison to pressurise them to say they had been paid to spin this story by local journalists, agents of the Nicaraguan and Cuban governments and of the KGB; if they agreed, he said, he would get them food parcels and legal help. Meanwhile, to reinforce the message, a friend of Hull's told them if they continued to talk their lives would be in danger. Despite the threats and bribes, the two men continued to talk for some time.

Eventually, the five were bailed out, Hull putting up the money. Three – the Frenchman and two Americans – decided to keep quiet, but Carr and Glibbery continued to talk. On his release from jail in April 1986 Glibbery, after wavering slightly, even chose to enter the waiting vehicle of Tony and Martha Honey in preference to that of John Hull, and the two put him up at their house. At this time the American journalists were being sued by Hull, who claimed the information in their La Penca book was libellous. Glibbery and Carr agreed to be witnesses against him. Carr was released from La Reforma jail shortly after Glibbery, but although he turned up for a reunion with Glibbery at Martha's house, he then decided to move in with an old girlfriend in the Costa Rican capital. He kept telling everyone how afraid he was, particularly of 'Hull's pet bulldog', Felipe Vidal, who had earlier confided he 'did Hull's dirty work for him'.

When the day of the trial came, in May, Carr had disappeared. Martha and Tony frantically tried to find out what had become of him, and were told by a clerk of the court that he had been picked up outside their home by a US diplomatic car. It later turned out the US Embassy had forced Carr immediately and illegally to leave the country via Panama, contravening the bail agreement which required him to remain in Costa Rica. On his return to the US, Carr was imprisoned on old charges of stealing his mother's cheque-book to pay for drugs. Interviewed in jail by American television reporters, he once again expressed his fears about being killed by Vidal.

About a year later I received an urgent phone-call from a journalist friend. He told me that Carr had been found dead – and in distressing and mysterious circumstances. I was shocked, but not that surprised. A police report dated 13 December 1986 said Carr's body had been found in the driveway of a house in Van Nuys, California. The two women who lived there said Carr had seemed chatty and normal earlier that evening but then, at around three in the morning, appeared looking very distressed, saying he'd drunk too much and could someone stay with him. He then collapsed, foaming at the mouth, saying, 'I paranoided out; I ate the whole thing.' The police report said he may have overdosed on cocaine. But three separate autopsies failed to agree on the cause of death.

The first, by the police pathologist, found no alcohol in the body and only small traces of cocaine; the cause of death was 'deferred'. The second, carried out at the insistence of Danny Sheehan, head of the Washington-based Christic Institute, gave the cause of death as 'acute cocaine intoxication'. The third, carried out at the request of Carr's family, decided that marks behind the mercenary's left elbow, earlier ignored, were the marks of injections.

We visited Glibbery in the La Reforma prison, where he had returned after Hull, angry at losing his libel suit and at Glibbery's starring role as prosecution witness, persuaded officials to revoke bail. Peter Glibbery had agreed to go on camera and describe his role – and, more crucial for us, Hull's – in the Contra operation, including meetings between Hull and Rob Owen, and phone-calls made by Hull to Oliver North. We anticipated no trouble, although we had noticed that our distinctive white TV van was followed all the way to the prison, about an hour's drive outside San José, by a beige Landrover with tinted windows, which stopped when we did and waited a discreet distance from the prison gates. To our surprise, when we got inside to interview Glibbery, he refused to talk to us 'on the record'.

Unusually for him, Glibbery seemed extremely nervous and agitated. He told us he had been visited by John Hull, who 'told me the CIA had killed Steven Carr and they could kill me too. I can't talk to you. I'd like to, but I'm too afraid. I just want to get out alive from here.' Much though we wanted Glibbery's information, we sympathised with his predicament. As our cameraman said, 'If I were him, after all he's gone through, all I'd be interested in is getting out.' Reluctantly, we left the ramshackle prison, with its rusty barbed-wire fence that looked as though it couldn't keep in anything fiercer than a sheep, its inmates playing football or dozing in a dusty courtyard, and returned to San José. Our tracking vehicle had disappeared. We later traced its owner from its numberplates: it belonged to an American 'evangelist', a much-used CIA cover.

The Carr and Glibbery evidence was one thing I needed to talk to Hull about. The other involved what was among the most tantalising and frustrating of all the leads in the La Penca investigation, the tale of the Contra defector named David. His story was told to Judy by Martha and Tony, and my major difficulty in confirming it is that I never met him, because by the time I started my investigation he had disappeared. He was thought to have been murdered because he knew too much, but his death is hard to prove. As Tony said, 'There's no body and his killers didn't leave paper trails.' Despite such problems, the David story is more substantial than it appears, because apart from Martha's detailed notes and tape-recordings of David's voice, Judy also had contact with a man named Carlos Rojas, the dead Contra's go-between. Carlos, too, paid heavily for his role in bringing the truth to light. He is now living in exile because his life was threatened by John Hull and his men.

As with Guevara, the circumstances that brought David to Martha's notice are very strange. Martha first learnt of him when Carlos called his neighbour, because she was American and he needed help. The neighbour, Julia, happened to be Martha's secretary.

Carlos, desperate to unburden himself, relayed to Julia a strange tale. He had recently met, in a working-class bar situated one block from the US Embassy, an extremely nervous young man with a Nicaraguan accent. The young Nicaraguan had told Carlos that he was a Contra whose group was planning an attack on the life of the US Ambassador to Costa Rica, Lewis Tambs. He opposed this proposed assassination plot, he said, just as he had opposed another murder plot, involving Edén Pastora at a press conference, but his life was in danger if he backed out.

David, near tears and speaking very rapidly in a low voice, said he was an anti-Sandinista, 'but these people are much more evil than the Sandinistas'. He said his group was made up of Nicaraguans, Costa Ricans and Miami Cubans who ran a 'dirty tricks' commando group within the Contras. The Cubans, the main part of the group, had close links with anti-Castro terrorist groups in Miami, such as Alpha 66, Omega 7 and the 2506 Brigade, as well as to the CIA. He added that his group operated from safe-houses and Contra camps in Honduras, Panama, Costa Rica, Nicaragua and Miami. In Costa Rica they were based on the farm of John Hull, a key Contra supporter.

The group had important connections and 'moved in and out of Costa Rica like a dog from its own home'. It had three main functions: to eliminate Edén Pastora so that Contra forces could merge, something Pastora opposed; to provoke conflict between Nicaragua and its neighbours Honduras and Costa Rica and thereby help provoke direct US military intervention in the area; and drug- and arms-smuggling – 'they are making money off the blood of the brothers and using our cause to get rich'.

At a second and a third meeting, David (he still would not give his full name) said his commando force, then based on Hull's ranch, had been involved in the La Penca bombing and was planning new attacks. He'd met the bomber several times with John Hull; the bomber had been using an alias and was passing himself off as a journalist. David also kept warning Carlos about the planned assassination of Tambs, who, in his former post as envoy to Colombia, had antagonised drug-smugglers by demanding their extradition to the US.

Carlos, a carpenter, who had never been involved in any political activity, let alone murder plots, was appalled by David's information and moved by the young Nicaraguan's passionate sincerity and fear. He asked David why he didn't go to the Costa Rican authorities with the information, but David said he was too afraid as he had learnt some of them were involved. Carlos was at a total loss as to what to do. His mother told him to keep his mouth shut and to forget what he had heard. But Carlos couldn't. Finally, after hearing about the arrest of five mercenaries on Hull's ranch, he decided to tell his neighbour what he had learnt, thinking that as she was an American, she might know what to do; Julia, who was Martha's secretary, in her turn, passed on the information to Martha. David then met Carlos on a number of other occasions and asked a series of questions to amplify his information, questions that Martha and Tony would devise and give Carlos. Their conversation was recorded.

Martha believed utterly in her informant, even though neither she nor Tony actually met David (Tony once saw David at a distance). 'He wouldn't meet us, he was too scared,' she explained. 'He had already warned Carlos that his group suspected him of passing on information, and said they would kill him and his brother who was fighting with a Contra unit inside Nicaragua, if they could prove any of this.' They never found out David's surname, where he came from or any other personal details that could properly identify him. All they had was a tape-recording of his voice.

The story then takes a violent turn. Carlos failed to turn up for a meeting with Martha. After a week of silence, he turned up again, utterly distraught. He was crying, shaking, covered in blood and mud and his clothes were torn. Between sobs, he described how, during a secret meeting with David in Sabana Park, they were set upon by a group of armed men who forced them at gunpoint into the back of a flat-bed truck where they were made to lie face down.

Carlos was certain they would be killed. He heard one man say, 'We'll take them to John Hull's ranch,' and the truck rumbled off. *En route* they stopped, and, as their captors were trying to contact Hull by radio, David kneed their guard in the groin and they managed to escape. They both ran off as far and as fast as they could. Then Carlos told his companion he would try and get back to the capital and the protection of Martha's house. David insisted he would make his own way, and that was the last Carlos ever saw of him.

Judy had interviewed Carlos in exile, and he had said, breaking down in tears at the memory, that he had been told David had been recaptured, then taken to John Hull's ranch where he was tortured and murdered: 'I wish I could think he was still alive, but I was told he was dead.' He himself had received death threats afterwards and had had a police guard assigned to him, 'but for us, it was impossible to live like that'. A Costa Rican policeman, Harry Barrantes, assigned to guard Martha's house after she and Tony received death threats, became quite friendly with them and confided that he had heard David had been secretly murdered by John Hull's men and buried somewhere on his sprawling ranch.*

I could take the David story no further forward. But I did receive further corroboration of his tale. In Costa Rica, Beth, a pretty young journalist working for the *Tico Times*, told me about another renegade Contra, known as 'Sebastian'. She promised to track him down for me, saying she had lost contact with him because he was so 'tiresome', always suspicious, constantly changing rendezvous, paranoid about being followed and 'not worth the hassle'. She also told me she was very nervous about covering this bombing story, despite the zeal of her editor, Dery Dyer, and feared repercussions. In the event she was as good as her word, and set up a late-night meeting with this new 'deep throat' at his work-place, an underground garage in the red-light district of down-town San José.

Beth and I waited for hours for him to turn up, hanging around on windy and insalubrious street corners with men wolf-whistling and accosting us and Beth telling me nervously that this was where people got mugged. I wondered, for the umpteenth time, why I was doing all this when I could, after all, have stayed comfortably in England. Finally 'Sebastian', a short, powerfully built, ugly man with a pockmarked face and wearing dirty overalls, appeared for his late shift, but only to make another rendezvous. Our next

* I interviewed Barrantes in September 1987 to ask him about this, but he denied it. 'Sure I told them David had been killed,' he said, 'but that was because it was what they wanted to hear; it wasn't true. I made it up to humour them, find out what they knew.' Martha had a story about Barrantes that could explain this volte-face. She said that one day, after spending months as their sympathetic bodyguard, he simply vanished. No one, not even men from his own Civil Guard unit, knew where he had gone. Then it transpired he had been invited to the States on a military scholarship to Fort Benning in Texas. He returned three months later a changed man, having undergone a Pauline conversion – or, rather, having been 'bought' by the US. He even turned up at the libel trial brought by Hull wearing a T-shirt with 'Fort Benning' emblazoned across it.

meeting, three days later, was in the leafy Sabana Park, where Carlos had met David.

Once again, 'Sebastian' turned up late, and seemed extremely nervous, telling me he thought he was being watched. All I could see through the thick grey-green eucalyptus groves and pine trees were high-spirited young men playing football nearby, paying us no attention, and 'Ticos' walking their dogs. 'Sebastian' started by complaining that he and the other Contra fighters, who had given up the war because of political and moral scruples, were destitute. He also said he hadn't eaten for several days and had to sleep on park benches or in his filthy garage.

He didn't look like the sort of man who would have many scruples about anything. But perhaps I was wrong. By now, after months of mixing with the strange assortment of people who knew, or professed to know, something about La Penca, I had little faith in my ability to judge people. I needed to assess why he was prepared to talk; whether he genuinely had information he wanted to impart, or whether he had a grudge, perhaps had been kicked out of the Contra movement. Or whether, like some other 'informants', he was trying to find out what I knew.

I started by chatting to him about his work with the Contras and why he had left. He told me he didn't mind killing Sandinistas but he didn't see why they had to be tortured first. Finally, revolted by this kind of brutality and the callousness and corruption of his comrades-in-arms, he abandoned the fight. Once I thought I had his confidence, I started asking him about the bombing. His story, in its broad outlines, dovetailed with that told by David. 'Everyone', it seemed, knew the CIA was behind the La Penca bombing, that it was carried out by a group of Cuban Americans based on John Hull's ranch. CIA officials working in the US Embassy helped with the planning, including hiring the assassin, and then paving the way for escape to the US. He also said the bombing plot was linked with drugs. The whole conspiracy, involving dozens of names, aliases and sub-plots, was incredibly confusing. I must keep track of it all, I kept thinking, because there are important clues here.

Later, when I came to look at my notebook, I found an unsolvable muddle. Under the heading 'Beth's deep throat' I had scribbled a list of names, some Nicaraguan, some Cuban, all aliases, of a group of men who had apparently been staying on Hull's ranch; there was 'Gato Negro' ('Black Cat'), 'Vilgero', 'Chichi Meco', 'Omega', 'Chama', 'Caminante' – and so on. My notes say: 'After this commando group left John Hull's farm, they went to a ranch in Alajuela, then to a Contra camp called Mojón 9 on the Nicaraguan border. They had an operation to eliminate Pastora: money obtained from Gorman, black gringo working in the US Embassy. Bomber recruited from South America by Contra called César Aviles. Aviles went to El Salvador just before the bombing to meet CIA officials there. From there he flew to either Paraguay or Uruguay in the days immediately before the bombing to recruit the assassin.'

According to 'Sebastian', Aviles was given a US immigration greencard by a man from the US Embassy named Ron Godard and was now living in the US. I found out independently that Aviles had been a fighter on the Southern Front who was now living in Los Angeles. His wife had recently died of cancer. I obtained a phone-number but no address. I could hardly call him and accuse him of the La Penca murder; he would almost certainly deny everything, hang up the phone and change his number. In the event, that is exactly what happened.

Yet more complicated, my notes said the bomb-plot was linked to drug deals and that Costa Rican Security officials – the ones supposedly helping in investigating the plot – were involved. Even when I had made sense of all of this – and it was clear that 'Sebastian', no intellectual, had only half grasped the outlines of some plot, but couldn't really tie it together – I couldn't manage to make it add up to a convincing whole. How, for instance, was I to get to the bottom of a drug-smuggling group called the '*Círculo Verde*', allegedly linked through Aviles to Costa Rican Security? A Costa Rican named Tacsan, a key figure in helping the Contras but also linked to the La Penca plot, came in somewhere, and members of the Venezuelan Embassy in Costa Rica were also allegedly involved, including a Mata Hari figure called Beatríz who was a secretary there and was Tacsan's mistress.

Some details differed from David's story. For instance, while both agreed the plot was carried out by Cuban Americans with Contra support, on CIA orders, they differed significantly on the recruitment of the bomber: David had told Carlos that he had been recruited by two Cuban brothers from Chile, where the assassin had worked for the Intelligence organisation, DINA.

I hoped to be able to firm out a definitive version from names that 'Sebastian' gave me from a battered old notebook, but the problem was they were not real names, only nicknames and *noms de guerre*. The directions for finding them were extremely vague. One read, 'Go to a bar frequented by Cubans in the town centre after 11 p.m.; it's five blocks south-east from the María Auxiliadora church; ask for a man called "Gato Negro".' I turned up at a very seedy clip-joint, following the directions; inside there was red lighting, banquettes in torn red velvet; drunk and leering men; and many obvious tarts. No one had ever heard of the barman. I widened my radius, visiting all the bars I could find nearby with my nervous taxi-driver hovering protectively outside.

On no occasion was I able to track down this man, who 'Sebastian' said had been one of the Cuban gang on Hull's ranch and knew about the bombing. I methodically called the other names he had given me, in Panama, in the US, Costa Rica, Honduras, and checked out addresses of distant farms in Costa Rica, where ex-members of Hull's gang were allegedly hanging out. Not once was I able to track anyone down. No one on the end of the phone knew anything about the person I was trying to contact. In the end, it was no disappointment when Beth told me 'Sebastian' refused to see me again.

Meanwhile, getting to Hull was proving a nerve-racking business. At first he agreed to see us. But then he called back, telling us his lawyer had advised him not to talk to any journalists, and cancelling. Had I been Hull's lawyer, and given his propensity to talk and incriminate himself, I would certainly have advised him to keep his mouth shut. Only I wasn't, and I badly needed the interview, one we all thought crucial to the documentary.

At this point, Judy decided she could no longer go on with this 'impossible film'. She announced she was going home – this time for good. She had threatened to leave before, but this time I felt she meant it. We all rallied round, telling her the film was possible, that it was politically important and could be wonderful – something I think none of us genuinely felt at this point. I remember assuring her with tremendous passion and sincerity that John Hull would 'come round'. I didn't really believe this. I simply refused to contemplate the idea of giving up now, after putting so much time, energy and emotional commitment into the project.

Judy, however, kept telling us that she had never, ever, tried to make a film that was so difficult; now, with Hull's defection, it was literally impossible. She is a beautiful woman, with enormous blue eyes. When tired, she becomes all eyes. Now they looked simply huge, full of pain and suffering. It just can't be done, she kept repeating. We had all busted a gut – but the project was doomed. We were exhausted, strung out with worrying and fretting about reluctant interviewees who frequently would say one thing and then, on camera, deny it all out of fear. Hull's defection was, quite simply, the final straw.

Eventually, we managed to get to Hull through a combination of chutzpah, cunning and luck – and by appealing to his considerable vanity. Our breakthrough came when we learnt he was to host an agricultural fair at his ranch. We decided to exploit the atmosphere of bonhomie, and the guaranteed access, by rolling up in our Landrover along with everyone else, buttonholing our target, who would find it hard to throw us out in front of all his guests, and then pleading with him to do the interview. It was our best – indeed, our only – chance.

There was an atmosphere of carnival outside the low white ranch-house, where local farmers wearing cowboy boots and sporting rather hideous baseball caps milled around chatting, drinking beer and eating delicious-smelling barbecued meat, beans and rice. Trying to blend in, though not, admittedly, looking much like Costa Rican ranchers, we wandered casually through the throng, searching for Hull. He was inside the house, expounding in Spanish, with a pronounced Indiana drawl, to a packed audience on the evils of communism, squatters and falling farm prices. The thought flashed through my mind that he enjoyed the sound of his own voice as much as his arch-enemy Pastora. During a break we managed to talk to him.

'Please, Mr Hull, please. Just give us five minutes of your time – it's so important to us, and we really want to put your side of the story . . . set the record straight . . . after all the terrible things said about you. Please, Mr Hull . . .' I grovelled on, pleading with the fluency and urgency born of desperation, sensing instinctively this was the way to get through to him. I could see Judy and Brian Moser exchanging glances and looking slightly embarrassed at my shameless display: I was going TOO FAR. But it worked. As I all but clutched at his trouser leg, following him from room to room, Hull finally said, 'OK. Five minutes. Come back tomorrow.' We did, and he not only gave us a two-hour interview, but insisted we return the following day to meet 'his' David. He would, he said confidently, explain everything.

Looking back now at the transcript of my interview with Hull, I realise how extraordinarily revealing it is of the man: how paranoid, how extreme, even crazy, are the far-right views he expressed; how totally out of touch he was – but also how out of control. And yet, for all this, he was cunning and highly dangerous. It was crucial not to underestimate him. He may have been 'out of control' in a personal sense, but he was a key part of the war in Central America, with direct ties to the White House. That they could sanction a man like Hull is shocking and very frightening.

Not many men who express such views are actually in a position to do anything about them – even in Central America. Unfortunately for me, and many others, Hull was. On communism, he told me in all seriousness, 'If the Russians capture Central America they can throw fifty to eighty million refugees into the

US. They will break the economy of the States and Russia will never have to fire a shot, and if the States falls, make no mistake, the empire's finished.'

'Do you think Nicaragua is a threat to the stability of the region?'

'It's a threat to the stability of the world.'

He denied working for the CIA, although he had previously admitted this to journalists, and claimed $50,000 he had been given in 1984–5 by the top Contra leader Adolfo Calero was compensation for 'ragged, starving Contras' as they left Nicaragua. But he could not help adding, paradoxically, 'Why should I deny something I'd be proud of? Although I don't work for them, the CIA are all that stands between us and being overrun by the red tide.' According to him, liberals like Senator Kerry – whose investigation for the US Senate in 1987 detailed Hull's involvement in smuggling cocaine and weapons and alleged he 'was a central figure in Contra operations on the Southern Front when they were managed by Oliver North' – had 'the morals of an alley cat and a Marxist–Leninist ideology'.

He ranted on . . . and on . . . Communism was taking over the world; Martha and Tony were a threat to world peace, had been denounced as spies, as KGB agents; their witnesses had been paid by the communists to make up stories; Pastora was a traitor and a communist; Pastora had actually carried out the bombing himself. Not only was what he said banal, predictable, knee-jerk stuff; the man was also astonishingly stupid, incriminating himself while trying to defend himself, his arguments childish in the extreme. For instance, when I asked him about the story that he had travelled on the San Juan river with the bomber before La Penca, to reconnoitre the area, as Martha's informant Guevara had claimed, he tried to disprove it by bringing out a contrasting version 'in which Martha, not me, is on the river – it's the same story, only reversed'. This interesting episode had, he said, been witnessed by 'Oscar', one of Pastora's commanders who was apparently also working for Hull. According to Oscar, Pastora's people had put the bomb there. 'It was a propaganda thing to stain the people on bail . . . the bomb was supposed to be weaker. The hospital said most of your injuries were caused when the case caught fire . . . Oscar did intercept the fellow that put the bomb; he did have him under a gun . . . he was ordered by Pastora's people to release him . . . Believe me, I want to know who did the bombing as much as you.'

So far as he was concerned, Martha and Tony's La Penca report was 'a fantasy'. But while rubbishing the two journalists he made an incriminating slip. 'They claim the bomb was manufactured here . . . it was taken across by a fellow of the name of Morgan.' (Morgan is the codename for Felipe Vidal, Hull's 'pet bulldog'.) But the report said nothing about the bomb having been manufactured in Costa Rica, or about Vidal taking it. No wonder Glibbery said of Hull, 'He's the wrong man for the job. He can't resist boasting about his connections. He only opens his mouth to change feet.'

We moved on to Pastora himself. 'I don't really have an opinion except that he was very incompetent . . . had a bad reputation among his men . . . they wanted Pastora to step down and put in a competent military man.' Hull admitted there had been a meeting with Pastora and 'a number of Contra leaders, including the Indian faction and a couple of black leaders from the Atlantic coast' at his ranch a month before La Penca. 'They all wanted him to go and of course Pastora threw a screaming fit that lasted from four in the afternoon until four the next morning . . . The line of those who wanted to kill Pastora is pretty long, but I wasn't in it.'

He went into great detail about battles Pastora had lost, explaining that 'anyone who wanted to win would not try to fight when he was totally surrounded. He manoeuvred himself deliberately into a position where his troops were massacred. He was not present at these battles.' In his peculiarly slow, emphatic way of speaking, which made each syllable sound like a separate word, he explained, 'All the people in this valley are anti-communist. We all provided help to Pastora – gave him rice, beans, so long as we thought he was trying to win. And when we realised he wasn't we shut off our help.' He spoke simply, matter-of-factly. I wondered exactly what 'cutting off our help' entailed. Did it, for instance, involve trying to eliminate Pastora?

'What do you think about Pastora's future?' I asked.

'Pastora's future lies in his past,' was the cryptic reply.

I now brought out an extraordinary piece of evidence that pointed directly to Hull's involvement. On the night of the bombing three Americans had met in a 'safe-house' in San José; they were Robert Owen, Oliver North's deputy; Dewey Clarridge, the CIA Chief for Latin America; and John Hull. This information first came to light during the Iran-Contra hearings, when Owen was asked where he had been on the night of La Penca. Owen admitted he was in the CIA safe-house in Costa Rica together with John Hull – 'and the CIA Station Chief of that government, I mean, that country'. (This blunder earned him a reproving look from his dark-glassed minder.) Owen claimed that this meeting, which took place at the same time as the bomb went off, was 'sheer coincidence. I was just as shocked as anyone else when a Contra came to the house at eleven-thirty or so that night and told us what had happened. Some say,' he went on gratuitously, 'that John Hull was responsible for the bombing. That's absolutely scurrilous as well.'

Hull hesitated before admitting he was in the safe-house, and then his recollections differed in one significant detail: 'I don't remember the Station Chief.' Then he said the first he had heard of the bombing was at 'three-thirty in the morning when Dr Pacheco had phoned me and asked if I could help evacuate you in my plane, but by that time you were already out and in the hospital'.

This raised more questions than it answered. What was the doctor doing phoning Hull at the CIA safe-house?* Why was there a discrepancy of four hours between Hull's and Owen's version of the same incident? And why did Hull sound so unaccustomedly nervous and hesitant when he answered?

I told Hull, who now had a fixed, empty smile on his face, that

* In fact Dr Pacheco called John Hull's secretary, who passed on a message requesting help in the form of aircraft. Hull refused.

I had heard his ranch was a centre for both gun- and drug-running. My informants, I said, had actually landed on his ranch and had flown back to the US, their planes loaded up with cocaine.

Hull first tried to laugh these accusations off. 'Look at my face. Would you take the word of convicted drug-traffickers and felons over mine?'

'Yes,' I said.

Hull's smile gave way to a malevolent glare as he replied, in his slow drawl, 'I don't like you. You must have had real bad damage in that bomb blast.'

His expression as he said these words is recorded on film. More than anything else it convinced me that this man was capable of planning the bombing at La Penca.

'Were you involved in La Penca at all?' I asked.

'In no way whatsoever; in no way whatsoever.' And for good measure he added, contradicting his earlier insistence that he was as concerned as we were to find out who was behind it, 'I'm not much interested in the bombing. I know it's of great interest to you, but I'm far more concerned if my cows get sick.'

'But surely you have to be concerned if people are saying you did it.'

'Those people don't make my living,' he replied.

I asked him about Glibbery's accusation that Hull had made murder threats against him when he was in jail. As I expected, and right on cue, Hull described at length how he had never turned up at the jail, that Glibbery and Carr were unreliable, untrustworthy individuals prepared to say anything, that he had never threatened Glibbery – in fact he had helped Glibbery, whom he scarcely knew, because he 'felt sorry for him'. I reminded him that his name was in the prison's visitors' book, and he 'remembered' that he had turned up there, but only to bring 'toothpaste and toilet-paper'.

Scrabbling under an untidy pile of papers he managed to unearth letters signed 'Peter Glibbery' in which the Englishman denied all of his allegations against Hull, claiming he'd been paid by Martha and Tony to make them up. 'I am showing you here sworn documents that show Honey and Avirgan offered bribes to try and make the thing look like I did it . . . or the CIA did it . . . or the Costa Rican government had people who were involved in it . . . If it weren't for the fact that people had been hurt – like you – that lives were at stake, it would all be almost laughable, but it's a kind of tragic comedy it seems . . .'

Finally, the interview over, he told us he was going to produce 'the real David', even though he continued to insist that Martha and Tony's David never existed.

The next day, we returned to Hull's ranch to be driven for hours, through pouring rain, up to our axles in mud, in his battered blue pick-up truck to a distant corner of his vast ranch. Hull made small talk, saying his wife had kept him up all night nagging him, insisting that he shouldn't talk to me, that it would bring nothing but trouble. I was probably as bad as that communist Martha Honey. I scarcely knew her, I lied. Throughout that slow, bumpy trip I kept thinking how extraordinary it was that I was sitting next to the man I strongly suspected was deeply involved in the bombing, and having to be nice to him.

Finally we arrived at a distant part of the ranch. By a barbed-wire fence on which washing was hanging stood a small wooden shack. A thin, dark teenage girl stood inside the dripping porch, surrounded by tiny, rather ragged children. David was out, tending the cows, she told us. So Hull strode into the driving rain, returning some twenty minutes later with a young man wearing a hat and carrying a huge machete, presenting him rather as a conjurer produces a rabbit out of a hat. This man, David, was so shy he fixed his eyes to the ground during our whole conversation, and spoke so softly I had to strain to hear him. Scarcely articulate, he muttered that he was a former Nicaraguan Contra now farming here, and couldn't understand why he was in so much trouble. He said he was being persecuted, but seemed to have little idea why. He had never heard of Carlos the carpenter, nor of Martha and Tony, nor of the plot described by their David. Finally, and most damningly, his voice sounded nothing like the voice I had heard on the tape-recordings. Hull told me, 'There's a rumour that David was killed and hidden somewhere on my ranch and

Carlos is supposed to be in exile. They say he's in Canada. Until he is produced,' he said, looking defensive, drawn and every one of his sixty-odd years, 'there's no proof.'

We spent the best part of an hour in this distant part of Hull's ranch, the rain never letting up. It was a long, slow and sobering drive back. We were all wet and tired, and the crew were having to sit in the back of the truck, protected by black plastic bags with holes for their heads, as our Landrover couldn't negotiate the quagmire the road had turned into. The David exercise had totally backfired, producing quite the opposite result to that Hull had intended, something he was apparently not intelligent enough to realise.

It was only when we finally returned to our hotel that I recalled something a lawyer friend of mine who knew Hull had said: 'He's stupid – but surprisingly crafty and quite ruthless.' We knew he had previously stolen the notes and files of an interpreter working for a US journalist interested in his activities, and we had ourselves been followed more than once during our trip. Once we saw men taking photographs of us as we filmed, and heavily armed men with dark-glasses took to turning up at our hotel. We never found out who they were, and we never received overt threats. Nevertheless, we took the precaution of hurriedly shipping our film out of the country the next day, so that it couldn't mysteriously 'disappear'.

# 7

# Commander Zero

The key to La Penca increasingly seemed to lie with John Hull and the network around him – the one that ran all the way from the White House to his ranch. So far, nearly all the credible information had pointed in that direction, and although, taken separately, it often didn't seem that significant, the cumulative effect of the evidence was gradually shaping a picture. Nonetheless, I remained sceptical. There were many more avenues that needed to be explored before we could draw any firm conclusions.

One man who might be able to provide some missing links was the very person Hull had so comprehensively smeared – Edén Pastora. He had struggled unsuccessfully since the bombing to regain his position as military leader, but, despite his efforts to rally and regroup his demoralised and scattered men, had found himself blocked and isolated. His efforts to drum up outside support (such as the visit to Washington I had witnessed from my hospital bed) all came to nothing. Washington and most of the Contras were determined he was to stay out.

By the time of my investigation, Pastora had been replaced by one Fernando 'El Negro' Chamorro (nicknamed 'Comandante Johnny Walker' because of his fondness for the bottle), but the Southern Front was all but extinct. (Ironically, the one place it still operated was in the thick forest around La Penca.) In the spring of

1986 Pastora himself realised the futility of his attempts to remain a rebel leader and asked Costa Rica for political asylum. He then returned to his former work as a shark fisherman on Costa Rica's isolated west coast, commuting there from his home in San José. I had been told these visits tended to coincide with requests from journalists for interviews. And that was where I found him in July 1987.

He had agreed to my request for an interview, and we left at the crack of dawn in order to reach the west coast before nightfall. As we drove, I thought that it would be interesting to know who Pastora thought had tried to kill him. The choice was certainly wide. At the time of the bombing he was under siege from all sides: vilified in Managua because of his defection to the Contras; a thorn in the side of the CIA, whose directives he would not obey; rumoured to have angered a number of his followers, not only because of his conduct in the war but also for being staunchly opposed to their dealings in drugs; and, as if that were not enough, with enemies among his military allies, like Brooklyn Rivera, the Misquito Indian leader whose forces fought alongside him, and Alfonso Robelo, another defector from the Sandinista government, who now directed political activities for the Southern Contras.

The more I found out about Pastora, the more I came to understand how impossible was the position of his allies. By the spring of 1984 his conduct of the war on the Southern Front had even given rise to rumours among the CIA and its supporters that Pastora was a fifth columnist, secretly working for the Sandinistas, fighting as a spoiling manoeuvre to throw the Contras into disarray and to demoralise his troops. I had rejected this idea out of hand, putting it down to disinformation. Now John Hull had said virtually the same thing, and while this was no recommendation to me of the truth of a statement, I could not help recalling what I had learned of Pastora during a visit to some of his own foot soldiers in February 1984.

I had gone to Tilarán refugee camp in Costa Rica after Pastora, failing to obtain military aid from the CIA, declared, not for the first time, that he was leaving the struggle and, in a public-relations gesture that rather backfired, brought several hundred unarmed soldiers into Costa Rica, declaring them refugees. These 'resting' soldiers recounted how they had not been militarily trained or prepared for battle against crack Sandinista troops. Pastora, they said, merely made the occasional visit to their camps in the damp, low-lying jungle area, where it rained for nine months of the year. There they existed with few firearms, less ammunition, hardly any boots or uniforms. They had inadequate food, suffered frequently from illnesses such as malaria, and were bored, hungry and demoralised. On his visits, Pastora used to deliver speeches about glory and victory.

'Did you train?' I asked.

'No, we did nothing. No one showed us how to fire a rifle. We just lay in our hammocks getting wet and waiting. There were no medical supplies and hardly anything to eat. We were always hungry. And for much of the time we didn't get rifles or ammunition.'

I asked them why they had joined Pastora's forces. Their replies did not reflect well on the Sandinistas. About forty Nicaraguan youths I interviewed separately described how they had been suspected of being Contras, even though they said they were apolitical and just wanted to tend their land. They were arrested, interrogated, jailed, then released but rearrested. In some cases this harassment continued for two years. Dozens recounted how their land had been burnt to prevent it from being used by Contra forces. Several said they had been tortured and one or two had even been killed, but I was never able to confirm this. They said they became so fed up with this treatment that they joined the rebels. It seemed that, in this war, there were no good guys.

I had asked Alfonso Robelo what would happen to these soldiers, as their presence was embarrassing for Costa Rica. 'There are many ways to skin a cat,' he had replied in his good English, winking at me. Shortly afterwards, there was a mass 'break-out' and they all returned to fight.

After catching a ferry across an estuary in Guanacaste province and negotiating a stretch of bumpy, unpaved road in one of the more remote parts of Costa Rica, we arrived at the Nicoya peninsula just before yet another downpour. We spent the night before the interview at a small tourist hotel by the sea where we were the only guests, leaving early the next morning to drive to the edge of the beach where Pastora now fished. There we tracked him down to the tiny hamlet of San Juanillo and a ramshackle wooden hut that housed fishing-tackle, boats (including rubber dinghies that I recognised from the San Juan river and Pastora's fighting days), and an ice-making machine, on which we had been told Pastora was working.

I'd never seen Pastora out of uniform. He'd always been totally absorbed by the war, by politics, the ultimate man of action. Now he emerged from the dark hut, blinking in the brilliant sunshine. He greeted me with a smiling, 'Hola, Susana,' just as he had at the press conference, and the years fell away. My last memory of him was of hearing, right by me, his piercing, frightened screams as the bomb went off. I hadn't expected him to scream like that.

As he explained that he had been struggling with the ice-making machine, but had failed to coax it to life, I found myself thinking that, unlike the majority of Contra commanders who had enriched themselves at the expense of their soldiers, and whatever other reservations I might have had about the man, at least Pastora could not be corrupt. He wasn't even making a success of shark-fishing, and according to one of his men hadn't caught anything for weeks.

I had nursed a grudge against Pastora for so long, blaming him and his wretched press conference for my injuries, for those wasted years. Hadn't I inadvertently shielded him from the full force of the blast with my own body? Now I realise – and it has taken me all this time to understand it – that the reason I felt so dreadfully bitter about Pastora was because I couldn't physically get at the bomber, the real, and missing, culprit. I now understand my deep, and unsatisfied, psychological need to get my hands on the person who did it: to extract a terrible vengeance from him; retribution. A recurrent theme in my earlier dreams and nightmares had involved my torturing, killing, physically eliminating the man who had blown me up. I wanted to hurt him as he had hurt me. His face was always there. I hated him, and was obsessed by him.

The television director had always believed the assassin was just a professional terrorist who killed for a living. It was important to track him down because we could then prove the link to those behind him. Far more important, we believed, was the network behind the bomber. That was all very well, intellectually. But it was all too abstract. It didn't satisfy my feelings, only my mind. I needed to find the bomber himself, just as a bereaved person physically needs the body of their dead to mourn. My feelings towards Pastora – and to a much lesser extent Martha, who had told me about the press conference and then urged me to stay when I wanted an excuse to slip away – were the result of displaced anger: the result of my inability to track down the real culprit.

My meeting with Pastora should have been extremely emotional. Instead I felt awkward, my emotions blocked. I was disarmed by his friendliness, by convention, unable to say, as I wanted to, 'You bastard, if it wasn't for you I would have been fine,' because somehow when I saw him, smiling and saying, 'I am pleased to see you here,' I couldn't. I still believed he had behaved appallingly when he had left the scene of devastation behind him, ignoring the pleas for help, but anger takes up so much energy. I've never been able to sustain it for long. And now I had other priorities.

We started slowly, gropingly, to talk about the bombing, describing to each other how it felt, what we remembered of that terrible moment that 'changed all our lives for ever', as Gilberto had put it. For some reason, we felt a compulsion to recall every detail and to talk about it. Then Pastora explained that although he had given specific orders only for the critically wounded to be taken out, and for the *compañeros* to keep a check on those who left, so as not to lose track of the person responsible, 'in that situation, with so much desperation and confusion, with the darkness, so much pain and blood, the *compañeros* lost control'. Afterwards, he said, a man was identified lying outside, who turned out to be the bomber, 'but he took advantage of the panic and was the first to leave. I kept asking for you, Susana, and the *compañeros* kept telling me, "She hasn't recovered, she hasn't recovered."'

I felt more sympathetic towards Pastora than I had expected, and also that we had formed some kind of bond through our shared experience. I leant over backwards to be fair, to understand how he had come to have abandoned the wounded and dying, but I still couldn't finally understand or forgive it, particularly as he evaded my direct questions as to why he left first, in the only fast motorboat, with the only qualified doctor. (Pastora later told journalists he had waited until everyone else was evacuated before leaving.) He told me he had nearly died, and that both his legs had been fractured, but when I told him I didn't see how the injuries to his legs could have been that serious, since I'd seen him walking around Washington only weeks after La Penca, he didn't deny it, but, with a macho flourish, retorted, 'Washington? By then I was back in the mountains, fighting. I healed very quickly.' He was torn between listing his injuries – larynx burnt, nearly died in the hut, in a coma for two days, numerous fractures, burns, shrapnel wounds – and insisting he had struggled to stay on his feet after the bomb went off, thinking it was a mortar attack and preparing to fight whoever was responsible.

My urgent need, however, was to find out what Pastora knew. Had he or his people reached any conclusions about the bombing or its perpetrators since then?

Pastora then told me that about two weeks before the press conference, when he had been deep inside Nicaragua – hiding from his troops because his aides feared for his life – he had been contacted by 'Hansen', the bomber, himself. 'Hansen' had put through a call on Pastora's radio telephone and had offered him money for an interview and photo session, something no professional journalist would do. And then, a month after the explosion, something had kept niggling at his mind. He thought he had seen the 'Dane' somewhere before. Searching his memory, he thought 'Hansen' may have been a member of the hit squad that had assassinated Somoza in Asunción, Paraguay, on 17 September

1980. Somoza's limousine had been blown to pieces in broad daylight in a main street. The official Sandinista line was that the operation was carried out by left-wing Argentine Montonero guerrillas independently of the Sandinistas. The unofficial version was that although the operation had involved Argentine guerrillas, the whole thing had been authorised by Managua. Pastora would be likely to have known some of the members of such a team, through his former role as Sandinista Deputy Defence Minister, but I none the less found this story unlikely.

He went on. 'The perpetrator is a piece within the terrible machinery of those who ordered us to be killed, a professional criminal, without scruples, one of the coldest criminals that I have seen. To travel, to go in a launch, down a river with those he is going to kill, to go back calmly, hearing cries, the pain, the shock of those he destroyed with his bomb – that has never, or hardly ever, been seen in the history of humanity . . . But the most important thing is, who sent this perpetrator? What diabolical mind was it that conceived that terrorism, that terrorist act?'

I asked who he thought it was, but Pastora, constitutionally incapable of answering any question directly, started by asking rhetorically, 'What policies were operating in the spring of 1984, in the weeks leading up to the bombing?' He went on to describe the immense pressure he had been under from the CIA but denied that he had been given an ultimatum to merge with the Northern Contras: 'The CIA wouldn't dare to talk to me like that.'

I could tell, as I stood on the white sand, with the sea and boats behind me, that this new, civilian Pastora hadn't really changed: he was poised to launch into one of his interminable rhetorical explanations. I remembered once exhaustedly asking Pastora's aide, Carol Prado, if Pastora always talked at such length. 'Oh yes,' replied Carol. 'We were once in an important meeting with some Americans, trying to get money, and they asked Pastora a question. I knew his rhetoric irritated them, so I slipped him a note. It said, "Just answer yes or no."' 'And did he?' I asked. 'Oh no,' replied Prado, shaking his head and laughing.

But now I was impatient. I needed concrete evidence, not

rhetoric. I interrupted him, a trifle sharply, demanding details. Who had put pressure on him? What meetings? Who was involved? How could he be sure? What proof was there? Anglo-Saxon pragmatism met Latin bombast.

Pastora hesitated only for a moment before replying. 'The pressure was terrible. It came from Dewey Clarridge [the CIA chief for Latin America, who was in the San José safe-house on the night of La Penca]. He used Alfonso Robelo against me. The CIA wanted to kill us at La Penca. Look, these ultra-right forces in the United States wanted four objectives. One, to end a legitimate opposition to the government which showed up the false pretensions of the other counterrevolutionaries. Two, they needed a flag, and by killing me they could raise my flag in the name of the other Contras. Three, they wanted to blame the Sandinistas. Four, they wanted to turn the international press against the government in Managua by this act.'

'Like Bill Stewart?' I asked.

'Yes.'

I had never heard Pastora so succinct. But I needed more. All this was information we already knew. What about the ultimatum, I insisted. What kind of pressure did the Americans put on him?

Pastora then told me he had been kidnapped early in 1984 and held for nearly a month in Honduras, in a house next to a brothel. He visited the country five times in all, the last time in May, only weeks before the bombing, when he had been pressurised by General López, whom I had interviewed in Honduras to such little effect.

'What else happened that led to the bombing?'

'They did it through Robelo, took advantage of his weakness. Robelo told me they were tired in Washington, tired in Costa Rica, tired in Honduras. They started the idea that if the Sandinista government didn't fall it was my fault, because I wouldn't unite with the henchmen of Somoza, the Somocista guards in the north. The slogan was headlines everywhere: "UNITY WITH OR WITHOUT PASTORA". So it's logical, this is the obstacle to liberation, he has to be taken out with a bomb, or a feather, or whatever. I realised that, and at nine o'clock on the morning of May 30th I got together with 150 *compañeros* on the river at Sarapiquí [upriver from La Penca] and I explained the situation to them, that at any moment they would kill us. Ten hours later it was happening.'

Pastora seemed to have been more aware than I had realised – or, at least, he now claimed to have been. I was becoming thoroughly sceptical of this man, whose massive ego I suspected would not be capable of admitting a mistake. Like everything else I was told during the investigation, I didn't believe or disbelieve it. I just stored the information in my mind, to be checked and double-checked.

One piece of information Pastora gave me during that interview didn't tally with this anticipation of danger, although it might have made us journalists rather less enthusiastic about making the journey to the press conference. According to him, on 29 May he had been visited in San José no fewer than nine times by a senior Costa Rican security official, Colonel Paniagua, and ordered to hold a press conference the next day. He had left the Costa Rican capital just as we had, scrambling to arrive before the press corps, to create the illusion that he had been in the Nicaraguan jungle all the time. 'I had nothing to say, Susana,' he said, with a despairing gesture of his hands. 'But I was told I had to hold a press conference immediately and inside Nicaragua. Of course it all seems sinister now, but then I couldn't understand why.'

Now I asked him why he thought it was that after three years we hadn't found the people who organised La Penca. 'In your opinion, in your judgment, has there been a deep or real investigation carried out by the Costa Rican authorities, or any other authority?'

'That is one of the proofs, one proof more, that the act of terrorism came from the CIA. The man most targeted, most photographed, most filmed, whose voice was most recorded – no one has been able to find him. Not the CIA, not the FBI, not Mossad, or Scotland Yard, or the intelligence corps of France, or Costa Rica, or Venezuela – no one in the world has been able to find him. And this is because no one has done anything to find him. There is not the political will. Only that couple Martha and Tony

Avirgan have tried, and what happens? They have been in Costa Rica for years and years, but as soon as they begin to carry out the investigation, all the bodies, all these ultra-right organisations at the service of the CIA, turn against them and want to expel them.'

I asked him where, in his view, John Hull fitted into the picture, and put to him Hull's theory – that Pastora himself had planted the bomb and was secretly working for the Sandinistas.

Pastora responded quickly and fiercely. 'That statement of John Hull's shows me that he is himself involved there. Only someone engaged in the attack can state such a crazy thing, because he wants to show the contrary. John Hull's role was as representative of the CIA for the north of Costa Rica, according to what Joe Fernandez [the CIA Station Chief for Costa Rica] said to me. I even dare to think that he was one of those who conceived the plan . . . He once lent his house for a meeting with Alfonso Robelo when Robelo was manoeuvring with the CIA to divide ARDE.

'Another thing that strongly attracts my attention to John Hull is that he is an untouchable man in Costa Rica. They can expel everyone for insignificant things, but not John Hull, who can do everything in Costa Rica and is untouchable. That convinces me of the power that he has because of the support of the CIA or his work with them.'

He was convinced that the three men waiting that long night in the CIA safe-house were all involved. 'Until these three little angels, Hull, Owen and Clarridge, can give me a satisfactory explanation as to what they were doing meeting until three o'clock in the morning while the bomber reached the hospital at around two-thirty – until they can explain that I shall continue to believe the La Penca attack was carried out by the CIA together with Oliver North's men.'

Pastora would not be shaken in his belief that the CIA had carried out the attempt to kill him. But he did admit that there had been an attempt on his life in June 1983, made not by the CIA but by the Sandinistas. Two of their agents had been sitting in their car in a San José car-park, preparing to infiltrate a Contra meeting. Unfortunately for them, they had parked opposite a police station. Police radios, which had the same frequency as the rather crude two-way walkie-talkie detonating device, accidentally set off the bomb they were carrying, killing one of them and seriously wounding his colleague. I had been told by one of my informants, a Western diplomat with intelligence connections, that both the bomb at La Penca and its detonating device were 'identical' to this bomb – proof, he concluded, that the Sandinistas had been responsible. 'Anyway,' he went on, 'if the CIA had wanted Pastora dead they could have killed him anywhere. They wouldn't have blown him up at a press conference.'

Pastora had outlined what he thought were the motives of the CIA, and these, cynical as they were, certainly tallied with other explanations I had heard as to why the Americans might be prepared to number journalists, including American journalists, among the victims of one of their assassination attempts. But there were also numerous allegations that the Sandinistas were responsible for La Penca. They had a motive, they had tried before, and they had means of access. It seemed quite likely to me that Pastora was blinded to this possibility by his arrogance.

One explanation for Pastora's dismal military performance lay in the extraordinary level of penetration of his forces by Sandinista agents. Even Pastora's nineteen-year-old mistress, Marielos Serrano, turned out to have been secretly working for the enemy. In August 1984, she wrote an article for the official Sandinista newspaper *Barricada* describing how she had lived for two years with Pastora's forces, passing on all his radio codes and troop movements. Pastora had a training camp at Sarapiquí, run by Gustavo Peterson, where she heard the men chant, 'What do you drink? The blood of the people.' This, Peterson said, was aimed at keeping morale high. On one occasion, she had had to make contact with another spy in Costa Rica, but instead came face to face with one of Pastora's personal assistants. She was certain she had been betrayed, but to her astonishment discovered that he too was working with the Sandinistas. She described how she used to keep her fists clenched at night for fear of betraying herself while asleep. She also described Pastora's overweening vanity and egotism. He used, she said, to call up his commanders late at night simply to have an audience, and would then submit them to rambling monologues into the small hours, even though they were totally exhausted. Typically, Pastora could not believe that Marielos was really a double agent, but thought she was 'confused and unhappy' because he had been neglecting her.

Marielos's story was corroborated by a young Sandinista defector, David Moíses, who also described how Pastora's group had been infiltrated right from the start. One double agent was Pastora's personal assistant, another the head of the La Penca base, and a third, known as 'Oscar' (apparently the same man as was working for Hull), was head of security for a large zone around the San Juan river. (Curiously, 'Oscar' reported to his real bosses, the Sandinistas, his strange tale about the bomber being apprehended and then released on Pastora's orders, which he had earlier told Benigno and Hull. I still can't understand this story, unless he was a triple agent, working for the CIA.) David Moíses, who had worked as a diplomat for the Nicaraguan Embassy in Costa Rica, said all the Sandinista agents remained in place after the bombing. Had their government been responsible for the attack, he explained, normal practice would have been to rotate them.

In the face of all this, it seemed extremely unlikely that Pastora could have been acting as a fifth columnist, or double agent, as Hull had suggested. On the other hand, it was clearly doubly important, if I were to carry out a proper investigation, that I should check out the Left as thoroughly as the Right, and that I should never accept anything at face value. However suspicious I might feel of Americans like John Hull, I must have no *a priori* views on my findings.

# 8

# THE SCENE OF THE CRIME

The name of Nicaragua's most famous folk-hero and martyr, guerrilla leader Augusto César Sandino, who took up the struggle against the government and US Marines in the 1920s and 1930s, was later adopted (or 'hijacked', according to critics) by the Sandinistas. (The critics included Edén Pastora, who saw himself as Sandino's true heir.) The controversy arose because Sandino, despite being labelled 'communist' by the US government, was in fact a rather maverick anti-communist nationalist. He had, after a conventional military career, taken to the hills to lead a peasant revolt. His followers were decimated by US dive-bombings – probably the first example of organised counter-insurgency. Sandino himself was ambushed and murdered in 1934 by the National Guard, on the orders of future dictator Anastasio Somoza, the founder of the dynasty.

So potent was the Sandino legend – the little man who defied impossible odds – that graffiti throughout Nicaragua consisted simply of a scribble of Sandino's enduring trademark, the high-crowned, wide-brimmed, tilted hat he always wore.

His legend lived on. By the 1970s opposition to the corrupt dictatorship of Anastasio Somoza was growing, spearheaded by the Sandinistas in the hills. A number of Central and South American nations, particularly Costa Rica, Panama and Venezuela, provided the revolutionaries with support in the form of money, arms and even sanctuary. But Nicaragua's neighbours and former supporters had not expected the Sandinistas to gain an outright military victory.

As for the US – had they invaded the country three times in a century and imposed the dynasty of Somozas (the first of which was summed up in the immortal words, 'He may be a son of a bitch, but he's our son of a bitch') only to have to suffer a left-wing backlash?

The US had encouraged attempts in exile to cultivate a more liberal-democratic group that would govern Nicaragua in accordance with US values, but because of the legacy of corruption and brutality (encouraged by the US itself), and especially after the earthquake that devastated the country in 1978, this kind of 'moderate' solution was no longer possible. The Sandinistas who emerged as leaders were both the strategists and the heroes of the revolution: Nicaragua was theirs.

With the Sandinista leadership openly defying them and proudly declaring its independence, the US secret services racked their brains for a way to harass the government. They were worried by the 'threat of a good example' that could encourage other revolutionaries in Central America, such as El Salvador and Guatemala and even, closer to home, Mexico. They were also concerned that Nicaragua could become a Soviet bridgehead – a fear that had more to do with paranoia than reality. The Sandinista leadership was left-wing and did indeed obtain arms and advisors from the Soviet bloc, but given US hostility they had little alternative.

Then the US came up with its trump card in the form of support for those remnants of Somoza's National Guard who had managed to escape across the border to Honduras. A number had made their way to Guatemala, where they were welcomed by the right-wing military regime. 'Support' came in the shape of an initial $19 million, and later much more, as well as weapons, training, supplies and intelligence. Gradually, from fewer than 100 disaffected Nicaraguans, a right-wing guerrilla army of many thousands (most young peasants) was built up, with the express aim of attacking, and if possible eventually overthrowing, the Sandinista regime. The official justification, solemnly trotted out, was that this force – known as 'contrarevolucionarios', or 'Contras' for short – was to intercept arms shipments from Nicaragua to left-wing rebels in El Salvador. As the Sandinistas struggled to rebuild their bankrupt, war-ravaged nation, trying to make good their pledges to bring education, health-care and justice to the poor, they found themselves having to devote the lion's share of their meagre income to defending their country from attacks that concentrated on 'soft' civilian targets, such as rural health centres and schools.

Even the US military advisors in El Salvador, who presumably would have known about such arms transfers, denied when I asked in our weekly briefings that arms reached the Salvadorean guerrillas from Nicaragua: 'Too far, too difficult and unnecessary,' they said, explaining that the 'Gs', as they dubbed the rebels, were able to overrun Salvadorean army positions and capture nearly all the arms they needed. There were also transactions involving Salvadorean army supplies being unloaded by corrupt colonels and sold to the guerrillas.

The most ironic aspect of the situation was the way the thoroughly corrupt Honduran army sold weapons destined for the Contras to Salvadorean guerrillas. But few of these devious routes involved Nicaraguan-Salvadorean transshipments. A further irony was that when Edén Pastora, by then no longer the Sandinista hero, started up his Southern Front, based in Costa Rica, the CIA was worried that this would blow its cover story.

Most of the initial US funding for training the Contras was secretly given to Argentina, a country with its own dirty war and ample experience of dealing with terrorism. This cosy arrangement lasted until December 1982, when US support for Britain over the Falklands caused General Galtieri to withdraw the training force. This role was then taken over by the US.*

* In 1983 I met a Honduran left-wing woman who had been kidnapped from the busy shopping centre of Tegucigalpa, horribly tortured but released alive after international pressure was brought to bear. She told me that in Honduras, under General Gustavo Alvarez, the Contras were used as an unofficial death squad, to 'disappear' Honduran opponents of his regime.

Within Nicaragua itself, there were some who were unhappy with the Sandinistas' left-wing policies, not having anticipated such a regime and finding little tolerance for political dissent. As Tomás Borge, Minister for the Interior, said to me in 1983, 'You're either with us or against us; there's no middle ground.' Even before the US sanctions had made their full impact and the Contra war had begun to affect the country's economy, the expectations of the Nicaraguans, raised by the revolution to wholly unrealistic levels, were not being realised. The new Nicaragua was a bankrupt country with an inexperienced and doctrinaire government. What was surprising was the Contras' inability to capitalise on this popular discontent. In August 1983 I wrote an analysis of that failure for the American magazine *US News and World Report*:

> The Contras' campaign is bogged down, and after more than a year of strikes into Nicaragua they have failed to win any significant victories or to hold populated areas. Support from the Nicaraguan people, the litmus test of guerrilla warfare, is visibly lacking, the rebels unable to overcome the widespread suspicion that they have links with the deposed dictator Somoza – seen as a worse alternative to the Sandinistas. 'Not only have the Contras failed to achieve what they were designed for, but they have lost all credibility. This reflects very badly on the US,' said a diplomat in Honduras.

The main FDN group operating out of Honduras had made ineffective strikes into Nicaragua, jabs usually contained by local militia, leaving regular army units unscathed; the few thousand who found a foothold inside the country were confined to the mountainous and thinly populated provinces of Jinotega and Nueva Segovia in northern Nicaragua. The insurgents were clearly not strong enough to take on or defeat the Nicaraguan army:

> As the Contras have become bogged down, morale has plummeted and friction and infighting within the political and military wings has increased. Field commanders complain political

leaders based in the capital Tegucigalpa and in Miami are living extravagantly while combat troops suffer. Many of the Contras I met in the camps along the Honduran–Nicaraguan border didn't even know the names of their supposed leaders. Politicians complain they have little control over the men. And while political leaders talk of winning popular support, the rebel soldiers ignore these objectives. The FDN leadership admits 'excesses' occur. Only last week a truck was ambushed in Jinotega province and 15 unarmed peasants were killed by 60 Contras. Inside Nicaragua I have heard horrifying stories of atrocities from eye witnesses – corpses found with eyes gouged out; severed heads displayed on poles as warnings; babies bayonetted; women raped and killed . . .

The Contras' problems are compounded as the Sandinistas build up the army: there are now 50,000 government regulars and reservists backed up by some 80,000 local militiamen. Conscription is planned to boost their numbers and could bring a further 200,000 men under arms. One response being studied by the Americans is to increase the number of Contras to around 15,000 from an estimated 8000, but the consensus among military experts is that this would do little to alter the balance of power.

The Achilles' heel of the movement is the forces of former Sandinista leader Edén Pastora. The most popular leader of all, he believed that if he turned on the regime to lead armed opposition against it, many former comrades would follow him. Pastora hoped to split the Sandinista army with thousands deserting to join him. Unfortunately such a plan had much to do with Pastora's massive ego – and simply didn't happen. Raids mounted by his guerrillas inflicted little damage and the word is Pastora is conducting his own one-man show, reflecting his own volatile personality. Lacking direct support, he also has severe supply and money problems.

Pastora, moreover, has contributed to the disunity of the anti-Sandinistas by openly insisting that FDN operations are nothing more than an effort by the Somocistas to regain power. And he has refused pleas to join the Northern Contras to give the movement more acceptability as his lieutenants have urged. The activities of the Misquito Indians – the smallest of all the Contra forces who are fighting on the Caribbean – have been equally ineffective. Desertions have diminished their ranks and factionalism has weakened them.

There is no sign that the divisions among the various guerrilla groups will be healed. The coordinated Contra attacks that were once envisaged as a real threat to the Sandinistas no longer seem even remotely possible. US officials had once hoped for a merger between the two main forces, whereby the Northern Contras would provide the military muscle, and Pastora's Southern Front the political respectability. They also envisaged a coordinated attack from north and south that would trap Sandinista forces in the middle. Such hopes have now been replaced by doubts about the entire future of the Contra movement. Unless their military performance dramatically improves, they will have only a marginal impact on the course of events in Central America.

I find this article depressing reading. One year, and many, many lost lives, after writing off the Contras as no-hopers, the situation was unchanged. God knows, if I, a reporter, could make this analysis, so could people in charge.

Predictably, given the need of the Americans and their allies to counter the Contras' failure, most of the first 'explanations' for La Penca pointed not, as most of my investigations seemed to, to the Right, but to left-wing organisations, especially the Sandinistas. The very day after the bombing Adolfo Calero, a top Contra leader, had appeared on prime-time US television to insist that the Sandinistas had carried out the attack. Looking even more thuggish than usual, and sounding yet more inarticulate, he declared, 'There is no doubt about it; the Sandinistas have done what they have been doing.' 'You mean they were responsible in this attack?' queried the American reporter. 'Yes, there's no doubt about it,' Calero had replied.

At the same time, the International and Costa Rican press carried stories that those responsible for the atrocity were, depending on the source, Fidel Castro's Cubans, Libyans, Basque terrorists, left-wing Uruguayans, the Italian Red Army faction, the German Baader Meinhof group, Italian neo-fascists and the CIA. The beleaguered Costa Rican Interior Minister, Angel Solano, said that two weeks after the bombing he received no fewer than six different versions about the identity of those responsible for the bombing: 'each version varied according to the ideology of the person telling the story,' he said wearily.

One curious story, which went out only hours after the bombing, had an American news-agency reporter in Miami quoting Havana Radio saying that the bomb was planted by 'a couple posing as journalists'. Oddly, this story appeared some ten days before the Costa Ricans found out that the photographer was indeed the bomber. Havana Radio subsequently denied having made such a broadcast. This story emerged after a number of reports that Pastora was planning to go to Cuba. He was not; nor could the source of the story be easily identified. It appears to have been a deliberate plant to demonstrate Pastora's left-wing bias at a time of crisis within his organisation.

One of the most widely circulated reports had the bombing carried out by Basque ETA terrorists on behalf of the Sandinistas. Curiously, the reports were based on leaks – phone-calls to major newspapers in Washington and the US from Intelligence sources, including the State Department's Office of Public Diplomacy. The Pentagon correspondent of the US television network ABC said he received the information from 'reliable CIA sources'. But two other spokesmen, whose opinions and reports were widely circulated, said they heard the news 'from sources close to Pastora'. Pastora's aides denied having provided this information. The *New York Times* correspondent, Stephen Kinzer, quoted Pastora as saying he blames the Sandinista government, but later admitted he had not talked to Pastora. Even worse, Arturo Cruz Jr, the son of a Contra leader, went so far as to accuse Linda Frazier, the woman who died in the explosion, alleging that, according to ARDE sources, 'Frazier was very close to ETA and other leftist groups'. In fact, Linda's views were conservative.

The 'ETA terrorist' network stood up no better to close scrutiny. First, there is little evidence that Basques (who have admittedly sought and been given asylum in Central America, notably Nicaragua and Panama) carried out terrorist acts outside Spain or in Latin America. I had already checked out the Basque named Lujua Gorostiola, who was supposed to be the terrorist responsible, and had discovered that not only was the source of the story extremely murky, leading to the suspicion that it could have been planted, but that this cobbler and former militant had been under house arrest in Hendaye, southern France, at the time of the bombing, forbidden to leave the area. I learnt too that he was much shorter and older than the bomber.

Even more mysterious was the tale told by Edgar Chamorro, at the time a leading Contra in charge of Public Relations for the Northern rebels. He later defected, appalled and disgusted by what he had learnt of CIA-inspired atrocities. I had met him in Washington in May, and he had said that three years earlier, just before La Penca, he had been handed a number of posters by his CIA sponsors and ordered to display them. They bore the letters ETA and a gun superimposed on a map of Central America. 'At the time I didn't understand the purpose of the posters,' he told me. 'But then, after allegations that Basques were responsible for La Penca, I put two and two together and realised that the posters were part of a propaganda campaign to provide a legitimate "background" to the Basque terrorist theory.'

As I delved further into the murky, amoral world of espionage, counter-espionage and 'dirty tricks', where nothing and no one were what they seemed, and where it was often hard to know who was working on which side, I came upon an intriguing tale, one I have never satisfactorily resolved. It concerned one Leonel Prevato. Of Italian background, and holding dual Italian–Australian nationality, Prevato had, while still a teenager, become deeply involved with the left-wing group the Red Brigades (the urban terrorist group responsible, among other attacks, for the murder of Aldo Moro). After one escapade too many, and on the run from the police, Prevato escaped to Nicaragua. There, according to a sworn statement he made from jail in Managua after he fell foul of the authorities, he started working for the Sandinista Security services. At first he said he had relatively low-level jobs to carry out, but in early 1983 he was ordered by his boss, Lenin Cerna, to carry out a far more important task. Together with a commando group of Nicaraguan and international operatives, selected for their experience in terrorism, he was to arrange the assassination of the 'traitor' Edén Pastora.

In his statement, Prevato says he and others were issued with Danish passports in preparation for the attack. Such a detail is astonishing, because the man who planted the bomb was travelling on a stolen Danish passport. Prevato was disappointingly short on details of how and when the actual assassination was to be carried out, because he refused to go along with the plans. In his deposition he says, 'I didn't mind being a courier, but I didn't want to kill anyone.' As a result of his defection, and because he knew about the plot, he was thrown into jail near Managua on what he alleges was a trumped-up murder charge. He was never brought to trial, but continued to languish in captivity until his Australian mother arrived in Managua to publicise his case and demand his release. As the result of the unwelcome publicity – and threats of an aid cut-off by Australia unless the Prevato case was resolved – he was quietly released in 1985, no charges ever having been lodged, and is now back in Australia.

Western reporters in Nicaragua as well as diplomats assured me that Prevato did indeed make these allegations, but I have not been able to contact Prevato in Australia, and I do not know if his allegations are true, or if there really was a Sandinista plan to kill Pastora, let alone what happened to the plot. Was this more disinformation? One experienced American reporter then based in Managua, John Lantigua, said he became suspicious because Prevato insisted on telling him all the details of his case while he was in jail, instead of waiting until he was released. 'Had I published the story,' John pointed out, 'he might not have been released. I kept saying to him, "Why are you telling me this now? Why don't you wait until you are safely back in

Australia before spilling the beans?"' John admitted he found Prevato's explanation – that he just wanted the truth to come out – 'fairly plausible', but explained, 'I felt the whole story was so controversial I needed more back-up. So, on balance, I decided not to print it. I've never made up my mind about the whole thing.'

I had few illusions that finding anything out in Nicaragua, where security was notoriously tight, would be any easier than in Costa Rica. But I had to try. Apart from revisiting La Penca with Peter Torbiornsson, I wanted to ask Interior Minister Tomás Borge, whom Pastora had so obligingly released from jail back in 1978, whether his Security forces had picked up any new information about the bombing. I also wanted to ask him directly whether the Sandinistas were involved. I realised, of course, that he might not tell me that, but it was a question that had to be put.

I found Managua, which I had not visited for three years, visibly more run-down, the city streets more potholed, the supermarket shelves even emptier, the people even poorer. There was a tangible sense of war-weariness, exhaustion and despair at the shortages, at the endlessness of it all. The inflation rate was now running at around 20,000 per cent, and queues of patient and not so patient Nicaraguans stood for hours in the blazing sun outside banks where money was now handled in sackfuls. They queued for food, for buses. The pharmacies had run out even of aspirins. The talk was of the war, of whether the Americans would invade, of the death of a neighbour's son in the fighting, of the difficulties of making ends meet. 'Even the bananas were bigger in Somoza's day,' commented one elderly woman, clearly not a staunch supporter of the revolution.

But it was above all in the hospitals that I saw the real price of the war. The wards were full of young men whose legs had been blown off when they stepped on Contra mines; there were men covered in dreadful burns, others with terrible bullet wounds fighting for their lives. Most were teenage peasants. Their morale was absurdly high. One who had lost a leg and an eye had lain in his own blood for three days before he was taken to hospital.

God knows how he survived. He told me, 'I want to get back and fight.' The wounded did not seem bitter, but extraordinarily and heartbreakingly courageous. Some were soldiers and many were civilians, the preferred 'soft' targets of the Contras. I wondered, once again, whether the men in Washington, who from the comfort of their plush air-conditioned offices thousands of miles away had dreamt up the Contra programme, had any idea of the suffering caused to both sides by their policies in this futile and evil war.

When I asked Tomás Borge, a tiny man who resembles a wizened frog and who had been fearfully tortured under Somoza, about the La Penca bombing, he flatly denied that the Sandinistas had played any part in it, insisting his country would never be involved in an attack in which innocent people were hurt. 'We do not use those methods,' he told me firmly. I asked him if he had any idea who had carried out the attack, and he said thoughtfully, 'It's possible it was the CIA. That is to say, what happened is similar to other actions the CIA has carried out. But Nicaraguan Security has no proof that the CIA was responsible.'

He went on to explain that the site of the crime, just inside the Nicaraguan border, consisted of impenetrable virgin jungle and was a place to which neither the Nicaraguans nor the Costa Ricans had access. This made it extremely difficult, almost impossible, for either side to carry out an investigation. 'The attack at La Penca,' Borge concluded, raising his hand and then letting it fall back on his thigh with a theatrical slap, 'was conceived as the perfect crime.'

Borge was adamant that his country had not been involved, but he also denied the Sandinistas had made any previous attempts on Pastora's life, something I knew to be a lie, or that his country had any training camps for left-wing sympathisers, let alone the armed guerrillas who, according to other reliable sources, mostly came from Latin American countries such as Guatemala and El Salvador, but also from Chile and Uruguay. I myself had met foreign guerrilla fighters, who all said they were 'resting'.

The crew, Peter and I met up at the little town of Juigalpa in the centre of Nicaragua, from where the helicopters that would take us to La Penca were due to leave the following morning. It was the first opportunity I'd had to see Peter, but he looked much the same as when I'd last seen him: tall, slim, tanned, seemingly relaxed, apart from his constant smoking. Both of us felt awkward at first. 'It's strange to see you,' he said. 'Strange because it's been such a long time and because I didn't know if I would like to see you. I had expected something really awful – much, much worse.'

He talked about the sense of guilt he had carried with him for bringing the man who turned out to be the bomber to the press conference, and of the time they had all spent on the river in the previous weeks, filming and looking for Pastora. 'It was a very strange world where Pastora lived, a little bit like *Apocalypse Now*,' he recalled. 'There were speed-boats on the river, a lot of armed people racing up and down . . . There was optimism. Pastora was in charge. But then, a few months later, when we returned just before the bombing, there was complete disorder and people were demoralised. No one knew where Pastora was, he was hiding, and some commanders didn't like him, kept saying he was an obstacle to unity. I got the feeling then Pastora was the most persecuted person in Central America.'

Peter's views were important because he was closer to that scene than anyone else. He described the intense discussions about how the Northern-based Contras and the CIA were urging unity; how many infiltrators there were in Pastora's movement; how many of his commanders were swayed; how Pastora was aware of what was happening and feared for his life; how all this was coming to a head at the time of the bombing. 'His position was very insecure inside the organisation. There were people from the north who wanted to get rid of him . . . There were rumours in Miami they planned to assassinate him, and I got that feeling very strongly when I was on the river looking for him.'

Peter said he felt 'about 80 per cent sure' that the 'pretend Dane' was the bomber, but added, 'I wish there was another explanation.' I asked him if he had ever suspected the man, something that had long been on my mind. But Peter said, 'No. Of course, you always take some risks; you always meet strangers. I never check them. I just thought he was one of the many photographers who come to Central America because there's a lot happening to get a break, make a name for themselves. The idea that someone should attach himself to you to try and kill you and has a bomb in his bag is just too far-fetched . . . Thinking about it gives me a nightmarish feeling.'

I pressed him: surely there must have been something about the man that stuck in his mind. 'He was very interested in military matters,' said Peter finally. 'Always asking the Contras questions. And seemed very knowledgeable.'

Peter and his crew had noted that the man seemed uninterested in the politics of what he was doing – that he kept saying he didn't care about the intense, desperate power-struggle going on, the crisis involving the whole Contra movement and the CIA; he just wanted to get his pictures. Most photojournalists I knew were at least as interested as we writers; often more so. Otherwise, as they pointed out, why do this most dangerous of jobs? Being a photographer – as I well knew from the toll of my dead and wounded colleagues – was far more dangerous than being a writer: they had to capture images of war.

The only time Peter saw his fake Danish assistant really animated was when the assassination of Anastasio Somoza came up. Apparently he kept asking Peter to describe everything known about the assassination. He also told Peter bits about his past. He had, for instance, said the time and place he loved best in the world was sunset in Montevideo; he was quite knowledgeable about Latin culture, but he also appeared to know Europe well – 'including Belgium, not a country that many ordinary tourists know'. He said he had a wife and child in Paris and had spent a period in London working in film archives. Before coming to Costa Rica he had travelled to New York City, Miami, Mexico and Honduras. Immigration records showed he had been in Costa Rica a year before the bombing, in February and September 1983, staying in the run-down Hotel Talamanca, a favourite of Cubans such as Felipe Vidal. When he was in Costa Rica the month before the bombing, he sent picture postcards to Uruguay and Chile. But there were strange discrepancies. Although the bomber said he was Danish, he did not know the name of that country's most famous beer – Carlsberg; nor, so far as Peter recalls, did the man ever speak Danish.

It seemed odd to me that Peter hadn't smelled a rat, but when I asked him about this he said he didn't really think about it. 'It didn't strike me as strange because the photographer had told me he was only half Danish and so I assumed he was one of the many Latin American political exiles living in Scandinavia in the 1960s and 70s who wouldn't know much about local customs.'

Peter's off-hand reply and the fact that he had taken him on as an assistant without checking seemed bizarre, particularly as Peter's crew often remarked how useless the man was. He would never carry anything; he was always obsessed with lugging his camera-case with him as they searched for Pastora at the Contra base-camps along the river near La Penca. They remonstrated with him about this, but he insisted he 'had to have the case as he needed his things with him'. Peter's team noticed the camera-case held an array of Nikon, Olympia and Polaroid cameras. They never suspected it had a false bottom – let alone that it contained a quantity of powerful plastic explosive. But the man's behaviour was strange. No professional photographer I know ever took more than a couple of cameras on location, particularly to a dangerous area, and they would always leave their cases back at base. He was not an 'aggressive photographer', commented Peter, who had noted with surprise that he took his film to be developed at local camera shops: professional photographers either develop their pictures themselves or send the film back to their agencies. (When I watched a video taken by Pastora's public-relations man of the Swedish crew at work I was astonished to see 'Hansen' taking photographs without removing his dark-glasses.)

Peter was extremely reluctant to believe the 'fake Dane' was really the bomber – even though this has always been the one aspect of this maddening story on which there has never been any doubt. He kept insisting that not enough research had been done, that the man was more likely just a spy. 'He seemed very normal, rather square, a bit boring maybe. He had his breakfast, he had his lunch. He speaks Spanish better than me: I think he thinks in Spanish; he's a bit younger than me; between 28 and 35 I would say . . . He didn't have anything about him that stuck out. He was a bit impersonal – he spoke if you spoke to him but not otherwise. He was discreet. He was a good companion. He didn't mess things up, helped with contacts, didn't go out much.'

I accused Peter of not having done anything, either to help investigate the bombing or to clear his name, and said that I had heard the suggestion that he had been an accomplice. He replied, 'I don't want to get killed,' and told me about all his difficulties, financial and political, how he had been jailed in Central America, but that he was working on it, would do something to find out how the bombing happened. Perhaps not surprisingly, he became very defensive. I was questioning him aggressively, and he said I was being unfair. I felt that, even if inadvertently, he bore some of the responsibility for what happened to us, and had done less than anyone to atone for this. I still feel angry, although I try hard to remind myself that he has suffered considerably since.

In May 1985, following an explosion in a Tegucigalpa nightclub frequented by US servicemen and Nicaraguan Contras, Peter Torbiornsson, his daughter Helena and his Spanish assistant – who were actually filming in neighbouring El Salvador – were all arrested on suspicion of involvement in that bombing, and also in that of La Penca. Peter was held naked and blindfolded in a cell in El Salvador for two days before being moved to jail in Honduras. Once there, the authorities released a stream of misleading and conflicting reports about him that were grotesquely reminiscent of the farrago of lies directed at innocent victims just after La Penca. The involvement of a CIA-funded Contra radio as instrument of the campaign against Peter was interesting, to say the least.

The campaign even continued after a local guerrilla organisation claimed responsibility for the bombing.

The Costa Rican and Honduran press accused Peter's 11-year-old daughter of being the bomber's accomplice in the Pastora bombing, alleged the Honduran authorities had charged and then released a Swedish journalist named 'Bert Anker Hansen',* and even insisted Peter had links to ETA and other international terrorist groups. To their credit, the Costa Rican authorities later said there was no evidence connecting Peter to La Penca. Not surprisingly, he was devastated and extremely angry. He said at the time, 'I'm a journalist, not a terrorist, but I'm in the middle of some kind of Central American police conspiracy against me.' Given this experience, perhaps Torbiornsson's reluctance to be involved in any way in the investigation is understandable.

Guiding the conversation back to my real concern, I played Peter the tape-recording we had of the bomber's voice. Posing as a victim, he had had the unbelievable nerve to give an interview in Spanish to a local reporter from his wheelchair in hospital.

The recording is a little scratchy, but according to Peter it was definitely the bomber's voice. I found it thoroughly unnerving to listen to the man who planted the bomb speaking haltingly, as though suffering from shock, mixing his tenses, describing in impassioned detail how it felt to be a victim of such an outrage. He talked of how everything went dark after the explosion; how he heard shooting afterwards. He got rattled when asked if he had thought the explosion was caused by a grenade or a bomb. '*La verdad no podría saber*' roughly translates as 'How could I know?' but is an odd expression. He glossed over how he came to be outside and unhurt. His performance was totally convincing. What nerves of steel, and what unbelievable cynicism to continue his charade in the very midst of those he had maimed. Peter's reaction to the tape was revealing. Listening carefully, he said this was not the assassin's normal way of speaking.

* In fact the name Galil had been using when he was arrested with Vidal in 1983 was Peter Jensen.

He was far more fluent; didn't search for words; even his accent was different. Peter believed 'Hansen' had deliberately disguised his voice, either to avoid detection or to sound more authentically like a shocked victim. If true, that could account for the conclusions of voice experts hired by Martha Honey, who had a number of different theories (European background, cadence not Latin, 'r' sounds too soft for a Spanish-speaking German and so on) but concurred that the man was not a native Spanish speaker and had spent some time in Spain as well as Latin America.

Sleep in the modest pension we found in a cobbled side-street in Juigalpa was impossible. Judy and I shared a narrow room off the courtyard; the four men another room. It was infernally hot; mosquitoes bit us; the roosters started to crow at about four in the morning. Even the rum we had drunk over dinner the evening before didn't help. I tossed and turned, going over and over in my mind what it would be like to go back to La Penca, the place where it had all happened. How would I feel?

We had breakfast at six the next morning, but I was too nervous, even with the support of our little team, to do more than drink sweet black coffee, leaving the beans, rice and eggs. Then, following our Sandinista pilots and crew, we drove to an airstrip in the middle of a field where two Soviet helicopters were waiting. We clambered aboard one; a second followed. After flying north for over an hour they stopped to refuel, and we got out to stretch our legs and look for something to drink. A cow had just been shot, but it wouldn't die, so the locals made it run round in circles until it collapsed. It was rather horrible. Then we climbed back for the final leg of our trip.

We couldn't hear ourselves speak in the helicopter because of the noise of the wind. Peter kept shouting in my ear, 'This is very dangerous, the area is full of Contras.' We were having to fly very low so as not to give them time to aim their 'red-eye' missiles. A soldier stood in the open door, his submachine gun pointing outwards. It was like films I had seen of Vietnam. Near La Penca, the trees had wonderful flowers – blue, white and yellow

– fifty feet from the ground. The whole scene – the helicopters, the scenery, the danger – was strangely exhilarating, and dramatically different from my last visit, when we had chugged slowly upriver by canoe.

Looking for La Penca was an anticlimax. Now we'd arrived, we couldn't find the hut. We plunged down through thick, tall grass that kept tripping us up, aiming for a spot on the river where the Sandinistas believed the hut had been. They admitted they had cannibalised all the Contra buildings they could find for their new military camp, higher up on the ridge, and warned us we wouldn't find much hut left. 'It's over there by the coconut trees,' one young man in fatigues told us, pointing. But Peter, who obviously had a far better sense of direction than I, immediately shook his head when we got there, after about half an hour, pointing out that the one guideline we had was the '*muelle*' – the mooring place – where our two long canoes had tied up that damp evening, and insisting we strike off again several hundred yards upstream.

Struggling with the dense undergrowth and the tall grass with its saw-edged blades was exhausting even though a Sandinista soldier walked ahead, hacking a trail with his machete. I was tempted to give up and fudge it, but having come this far, we had to find the right spot (despite mutterings from the camera-crew), if only for symbolic reasons; it was a bit like finding the exact position of the North Pole.

Then Peter saw the mooring jetty, the river. We found blackened pieces of wood and corrugated iron, all engulfed by the jungle. 'It was here,' he said with finality. 'The kitchen was back here' – he gestured – 'and the press conference was where we're standing.'

We stood in the burning sun with insects buzzing and dancing around us. I felt numb, empty, disoriented. I couldn't equate this scene – the grass that had obliterated everything; the dreadful heat and the shimmering light; the birds singing – with that terrible night three years earlier. The two experiences had nothing, but nothing, in common.

The Nicaraguans were already telling us, even before we started filming, that we must hurry and return to base before an expected thunderstorm; on no account could we spend the night here. We had only a few hours of light left – 'It's too dangerous,' they kept repeating, looking impatient. Meanwhile the film-crew – tactfully standing at a distance, preparing their equipment, sorting out the best camera angle, miking me up – were obviously expecting me to feel overwhelming emotions.

Peter and I started talking in a desultory way. This charred beam must have been part of the floor, this buckled corrugated iron the roof. Peter, already familiar with La Penca, had gone back into the kitchen to have a cup of coffee with the Contras before the press conference started. The journalists had been milling around Pastora, pushing and asking questions. I reminded him how he'd been with the 'Dane', whom I'd mistaken in the gloom for a Contra until Peter had interrupted me, saying, 'You're wrong, Susie, he's one of us.' 'I wish he had been,' I said bitterly. 'Yes, he had been, for some weeks,' replied Peter laconically. But then he launched into an eloquent and extraordinarily moving evocation of what he remembered of that night, of its grotesque horror – only to be stopped abruptly in mid-flow by the cameraman shouting, 'Cut,' and needing to reload his film. Peter, immediately asking if he could light a cigarette, looked upset and rattled, and was not again able to drag up from his heart with the same passion those terrible memories – memories undoubtedly all the more painful because of his sense of guilt.

First he had heard a noise 'like pressure going out of the air'; then 'this light – and pieces of things coming towards me. Time went very, very fast.' At the moment of the explosion 'you, like, go with it . . . You don't even know the outcome. I thought I was going to die, but going with this tremendous speed was kind of nice; and then you come back and still don't feel anything. You don't understand anything. You see this mess, you're coming back into this room and everything is different. This is how it must be to die. There's Linda the other side of a hole in the floor with a hole in her stomach; here's the Costa Rican cameraman dying; you're lying crying, "I can't see, I can't see, help me." People are screaming. There's no floor any more. A lot of people have disappeared and the moon is coming out and everything is completely white and the hut completely open. You're starting to feel the heat and the pain, and we stood, you and I, like this at first, we hadn't yet felt the impact – you were like you had been before it happened, so we stood there, we didn't know what to do with ourselves – and then you suddenly collapsed completely.'

'It seems so strange to be talking about death,' I said to Peter, 'but not to be dead, and to be talking about it afterwards.'

'Yes, I think people who haven't been close to death would find it hard to believe,' he replied.

But my memory of things is much more blurred than Peter's. Of course, unlike Peter, I had been so badly hurt that many sensations had been blotted out, and of course I couldn't see anything or anybody. All I knew was that it was like nothing I had ever known in my life, but at the same time terribly familiar. But I can't find the words or thoughts or feelings to do justice to any of it. I just know I'm feeling dizzy and slightly sick from the heat and suppressed emotion.

I'm supposed to talk about it and I can't. I feel such turmoil, panic, inside myself, I no longer know anything. Of course, because I'm a professional, I will give a performance. But not one that can approach what I feel – disintegration. I must pull myself together. Take a deep breath. Yes, I do remember, far, far more than I have ever wanted to: that I had blotted out until now. (I've needed three-quarters of a bottle of wine and paced around my flat for two days to bring myself to write even this. It's simply too unbearable to remember.)

Peter and I talk about the evacuation, how the worst wounded were brought out last because they couldn't walk. 'That's terrible,' I comment. 'Yes,' agreed Peter, adding bitterly, 'I think we learnt about many terrible things here in this place.' He says he wasn't suspicious about the fact the bomber put pressure on him to leave hospital early the next morning – 'just irritated because I wanted to stay with my injured cameraman'. He went because he was still in shock, because money had been stolen from him in hospital and because there was nothing for him to do there. He also wanted to send a dispatch to Sweden about the bombing. In retrospect, now, he wasn't that astonished to learn about the 'Dane's' real identity, and admits to 'perhaps having had subconscious suspicions, particularly about his dyed hair and deep interest in military matters'.

But the Nicaraguans are saying we must go *now*; no more filming, not even five minutes. We race back through the thick grass, crossing the muddy streams, climbing the steep, slippery banks to the Sandinista base and our waiting helicopters. A guide, seeing I'm lagging behind, gives me his hand, takes my bag, helps me across the streams. We board our waiting helicopter about two hours after arriving. With a tremendous whirring noise from the rotors, wind flattening grass, we take off, heading back to safety. Peter and I are subdued, lost in our private thoughts, thinking of that awful night, of our friends, of those who didn't make it.

# 9

# MIAMI VICE

A century ago, Miami was an ordinary kind of swamp, infested only by alligators. Today, it is a different and more dangerous type of swamp, the alligators replaced by drug-dealers, arms-traders and mafiosi. When I had gone there earlier in the year it had been to interview people I feared might be killed because they knew too much. For myself, I had been warned that finding anything out would be very difficult, and possibly dangerous.

Miami's fast-growing population has been swelled by successive waves of Latin and Caribbean immigrants – a volatile mix of Cubans, Haitians and, most recently, Nicaraguans, many of them 'retired' Contra fighters and their families. Most share a visceral hatred of communism, and harbour a complex blend of resentment, desire for revenge and patriotism that makes a breeding ground for political activism, a murderous heritage passed down from father to son.

By the early 1980s, these 'Hispanics' had, through their shared culture, language and attitudes, transformed Miami, a dozy vacation spot catering mainly for elderly Jews from the Northern US and inhabited in the main by redneck Southerners, into a city with the exotic, vital and thoroughly alien feel of Latin America. Most Central American and Caribbean capitals are actually closer to Miami than many American cities; Miami's lingua franca is more Spanish than English; and the gulf between rich and poor is just as wide as in Latin America. Some of the enterprises are legal: Cuban immigrants, who arrived penniless, are now the dominant economic and political force, a tribute to their remarkable energy and entrepreneurial skills. But coexisting with these is the dangerous underworld of 'hot' money, derived largely from drugs and inevitably accompanied by internecine killings as rival gangs, dominated by Cubans and Colombians, fight over enormous spoils.

It was in Miami, I had been told, that Cuban Americans had held dozens of secret meetings to discuss and plan the bombing, some in the down-town bars and hotels frequented by drug-smugglers, others in private homes in Cuban ghettoes like Hialeah. It was in Miami, according to other sources, that the camera-case bomb had been built. And the fake Danish cameraman was said to have been in Miami both before and after La Penca. One source even had him lodged with a bodyguard of Pablo Escobar, a leading member of Colombia's Medellín drug cartel.

The Miami Cubans I wanted to investigate were fanatically right-wing and operated a closed society that did not take kindly to outsiders, let alone prying reporters. These men, all exiles from Fidel Castro's regime, were so right-wing they considered even Edén Pastora a traitor to the 'cause' – even, many muttered, a closet communist. As one contact, once a CIA agent, now a 'journalist', told me over several beers in the plush Hotel Omni (allegedly a drug-smugglers' haunt), 'Many people who could help you and know about the bombing are loyal to their friends and to their cause; helping you would betray all that. Others know that if they want to stay alive they have to keep quiet.'

I already knew that the Miami Cuban/American connection with the La Penca bombing had long antecedents. Cuban exiles have been used and trained by the CIA ever since the early 1960s, when the Agency put together the Bay of Pigs invasion force for their unsuccessful attempt to overthrow Fidel Castro; these close links continued over the years with the assassination programme 'J.M. Wave' (the euphemism for a secret CIA training school built in

Miami University) and then the hit-and-run programme of 'Operation Mongoose', both involving attempts – all failed, and some, such as the 'exploding cigar', astoundingly stupid – to eliminate Fidel Castro. Cubans have been linked to local Mafia gang bosses of the 1960s like Santos Trafficante and Meyer Lansky and to other elements of the violent Mafia underworld, including prostitution, gambling, protection rackets, extortion – and assassins for hire. Some of the same names cropped up in connection with local Cuban terrorist groups (Coru, Omega 66, Alpha 7), with the CIA, and with major crimes ranging from the assassination of President Kennedy to the killing of Orlando Letelier and to the Watergate break-ins. The tentacles of this criminal underworld reach out to Latin America, to the Middle East, and to Europe: the Miami-based terrorist group Coru was founded in the Dominican Republic; Miami is a major centre for cocaine-smuggling from Medellín, Colombia; further afield, I found principal characters known to be based in Miami involved in the Italian neo-fascist terrorist network, then on trial for the Bologna train bombing. CIA/Miami Cuban 'ops' had been carried out in Latin America, where local-looking 'latinos', rather than 'gringos', have been required: of course, most of these secret operations involving Cuban 'assets' have 'deniability' attached – that is, no link to the US can be traced – and have never been uncovered.

It was terribly difficult to know how many of these links – arms, drugs, European, Middle Eastern, American – to pursue. The search looked endless, but I had limited funds and time. How and where, if at all, would these links overlap with my sole concern, the La Penca bombing? How could I equate, for instance, the persistent rumours that the bomber was a US 'asset' but apparently had links with the Colombian Medellín cartel? Hardest of all, perhaps, in a place like Miami, how would I know if I ever came upon the truth?

I had lived in Miami on and off for two years in the early 1980s, with my photojournalist boyfriend – mostly on 'rest and recreation' visits from Central America, although I found 'no go' parts of the city more desperate and frightening than much of what I was 'resting' from. My two visits during the La Penca investigation reinforced for me the depressing seediness behind the macho image. Most of the Cuban ghettoes I had to visit were light-years away from the ersatz glitz and glamour depicted in TV series like *Miami Vice*. In contrast to the hot colours, light reflected off sleek white powerboats cruising along shadowy waterways, elegant mansions, palm-fronds, fast cars and improbably beautiful men and women, my Miami was pinched, monotonous, irredeemably ugly and mean.

Judy and I spent hours driving nose-to-tail along crowded, dusty streets bordered by interminable down-market stores; hamburger and pizza joints lit by brash neon signs; the same shopping centres extending for mile upon dusty mile with the shimmering, muggy heat beating relentlessly down.

Most of my Cuban and Nicaraguan contacts lived up to 40 miles out of the centre, in drab bungalows (a safeguard against hurricanes), each bordered by a strip of balding brown lawn, usually littered with rusting automobile hulks, and with a motley assortment of mongrel guard-dogs scratching listlessly or lying panting in what shade they could find. The streets were organised on a grid system; neither they nor the houses seemed to boast any distinguishing features. This anonymity, coupled with my inadequacy at map-reading, meant that we were frequently lost.

As usual, we started on all fronts at once – using contacts we had already been given, new names suggested by the contacts we met, even the telephone directory, in the belief that if we tried every possible avenue we would get a break. One focus was the secret societies so beloved of Miami Cubans – the Bay of Pigs Veterans' group; the 2506 Brigade (named after the first combatant to die in the fighting); and the more violent and sinister Coru, Alpha 66 and Omega 7. I had been told that members of these shadowy organisations – responsible for much of the wave of bombings and terrorism in Miami in the 1970s – knew about La Penca. But I found them extremely hard to penetrate.

I did manage to meet a charming old leader of the 2506 Brigade, and drank Cuban rum with him in a bar in 'Little Havana', the Cuban area centred on Calle Ocho (Eighth Street), while all around other old men read Spanish-language newspapers and reminisced about their past. He, like John Hull, told me, his liver-spotted hands shaking as he sipped his rum, that none of his members offered more than 'humanitarian' support to Contra rebels. And I learnt about a paramilitary wing of young activists that sent fighters down to Central America and who trained in the Miami Everglades – just as their fathers had done two decades earlier. Conducted mostly at weekends with screaming children enjoying picnics in the grass and Cuban women with high heels and immaculate make-up gossiping to their friends while their paunchy middle-aged husbands shakily aimed rifles at bull's eyes, it was a far cry from the serious operation I had been hoping to uncover. I managed to interview Cubans involved in raising funds for the Contras – doctors who had flown down to Central America to treat wounded Contras, Nicaraguan Contra leaders living the life of Riley in Miami – but they all disclaimed any knowledge of La Penca. And I could find no one who would admit to belonging to the more extreme Cuban political groups or tell me of their activities.

In Miami, as in Costa Rica and Nicaragua, I fell victim to sickening weariness and frustration. Wherever I turned I caught only glimpses of half-truths, the sense of a hall of mirrors. Fear, secrecy and patriotism were potent blocks. After all, these men were fanatically loyal to what they called 'the cause' – fighting communism wherever their sometimes paranoid imaginations saw it rear its head. They wanted above all to overthrow the Sandinista government in Nicaragua, and saw that fight as a precursor to their own fight against Fidel Castro. 'Cuba, Nicaragua, the same fight' proclaimed posters soliciting cash for the Nicaraguan 'freedom fighters'.

Another major obstacle in tracing suspects was the CIA's velvet-gloved handling of its long-standing Cuban allies. These, now dubbed 'Unilaterally Controlled Latino Assets' for the purposes of the Contra war, were systematically distanced from their real sponsors to give the impression they operated independently. These Latin 'cut-outs' have contact with only one figure, identified by a *nom de guerre*, and are deliberately kept in the dark about the real purpose of the operation, its scope, who else is involved, and the identity of the sponsor. This 'cell' system – in which the asset knows only a single link in the command chain – has long proved effective in left- and right-wing terrorist groups worldwide; it has proved impervious, even under threat of torture or betrayal, to unravelling, and preserves that leitmotif, 'deniability'.

In the Contra supply operation the public was long fooled by what appeared to be private operators emphasising the down-home 'good-ole-boy' aspect of over-zealous private individuals operating a seat-of-the-pants operation with money raised at local get-togethers. When operatives had the bad luck to be killed, US officials at once stressed they were private individuals. Grisly rumours even went around about 'body washing' – the corpses of Americans killed in the secret war in Central America being clandestinely shipped back to the States, where fake accidents (car-crashes were a favourite) were given to grieving relatives as the cause of death.

The truth about the private network was revealed partly by carelessness and arrogance on the part of senior operators like Oliver North and his assistant Rob Owen. Their actions infuriated supporters like my ex-CIA contact in Miami, who felt personally betrayed by such unprofessional 'preppy idiots'. I was particularly interested in this part of the Contragate scandal, as I had been told that the same system of cut-outs was used for the La Penca bombing.

One man I needed to see was Rolando Martínez, jailed for his role in breaking into the Watergate Headquarters of the Democratic National Centre, and promptly hailed by fellow Cubans as a '*martir de la lucha*'. My interest in this important CIA 'asset' was that he had been named in the Christic lawsuit as one of the twenty-nine defendants allegedly involved in La Penca. He was supposed to have contacted and helped recruit the bomber.

After a few false starts I tracked Martínez down at the firm

A genial John Hull standing by one of his light planes at his ranch in the north of Costa Rica, almost on the Nicaraguan border. *(Tico Times)*

Brian Moser, our producer, wearing a black plastic bag to keep off the driving rain. *(Brian Moser)*

Hull (middle right) giving a speech to local citrus farmers. *(Brian Moser)*

Interviewing Hull at his ranch the day after the rally. *(Brian Moser)*

Interviewing Hull's 'David' at a distant part of the ranch in pouring rain. *(Brian Moser)*

The glorious scenery on the remote west coast of Costa Rica *en route* to Pastora's shark-fishing cooperative. *(Brian Moser)*

Interviewing Pastora, now a shark fisherman and retired from the fighting; he claimed the CIA was behind the bombing. *(Brian Moser)*

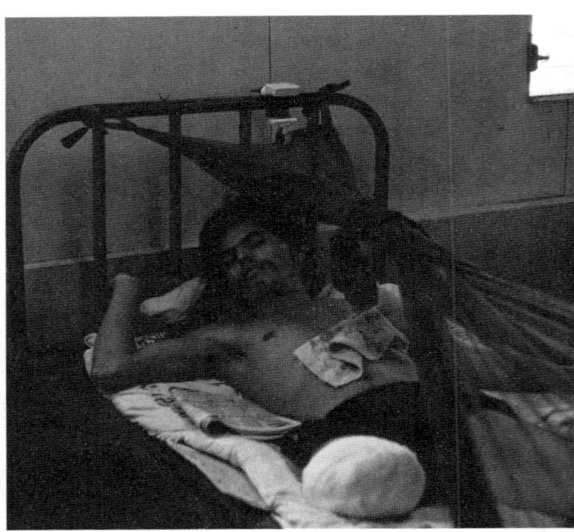

*(Top left)* Mel and Noel standing under a huge Sandino mural in Managua, Nicaragua. *(Brian Moser)*

*(Top right)* Young Sandinista soldier in hospital in Juigalpa. *(Brian Moser)*

*(Above)* The armed Russian helicopters that took us back to La Penca. *(Brian Moser)*

*(Left)* Noel filming from inside the helicopter. *(Brian Moser)*

With TV team and Sandinista soldiers overlooking the San Juan river as we searched for the site of La Penca – a very different experience from my last visit. *(Brian Moser)*

Standing talking to Peter Torbiornsson in the tall grass where the La Penca hut once stood. *(Brian Moser)*

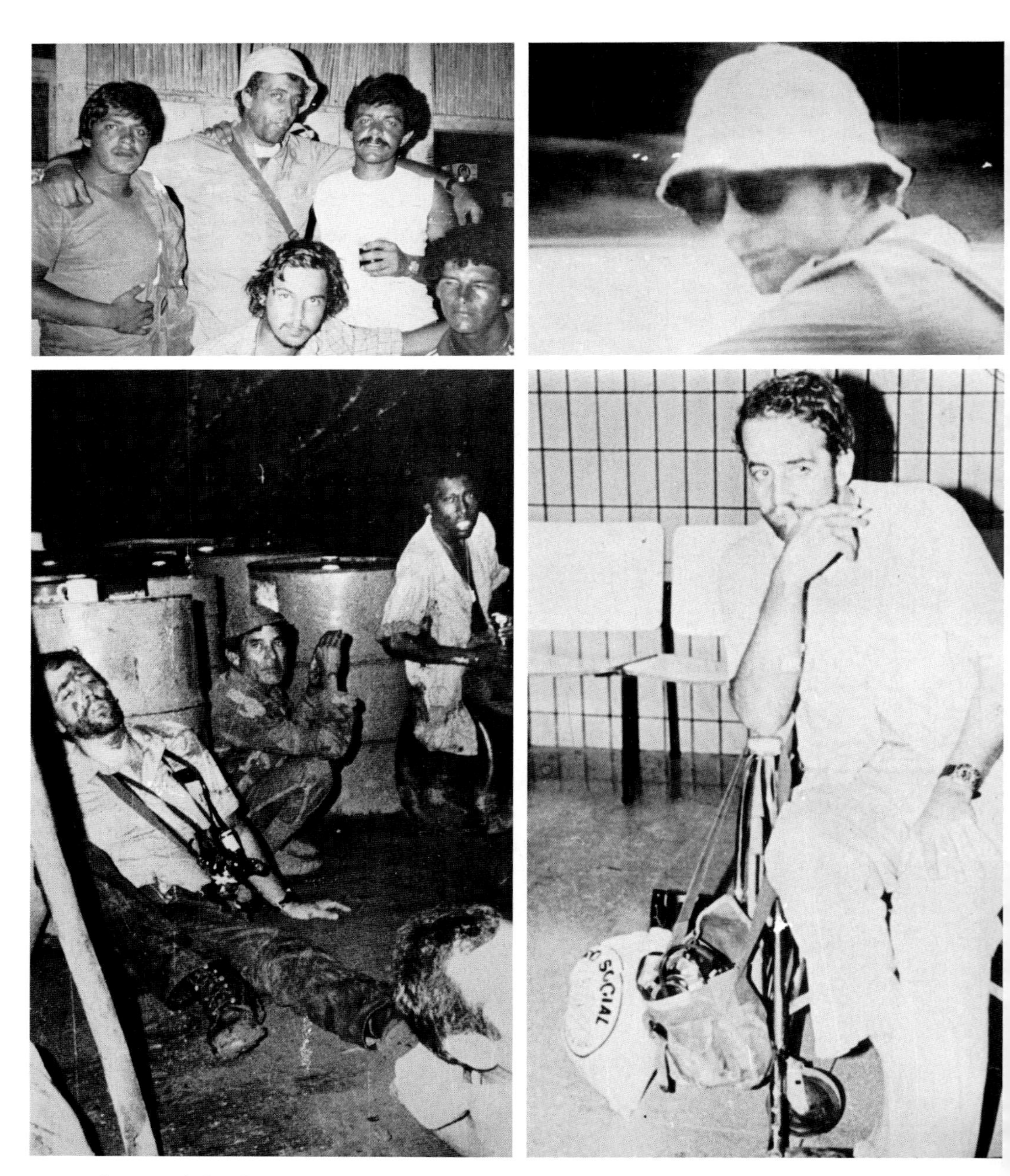


'No lower-echelon hit-man.' These are four faces of the bomber: *(top left)* as the 'photographer', his arms chummily around rebels; *(top right)* in dark glasses looking for Pastora in the weeks before the attack; *(bottom left)* lying 'in pain' outside the hut after the bombing (this picture was flashed around the world by news agencies); *(bottom right)* in hospital, where he was treated for an apparently self-inflicted wound – no one ever checked the contents of his bags, let alone questioned him. *(Costa Rican police)*

Ex-US President Ronald Reagan (right) meets Contra leaders at his hotel in Los Angeles: facing the camera are, left, Enrique Bermudez, military leader of the Northern-based Contras, the FDN; right, with back to camera, Adolfo Calero, political leader of the FDN, who hosted meetings that were allegedly attended by the bomber himself. *(Popperfoto/Reuter)*

Colonel Oliver North being sworn in for the Iran-Contra hearings in July 1987. *(Popperfoto/Reuter)*

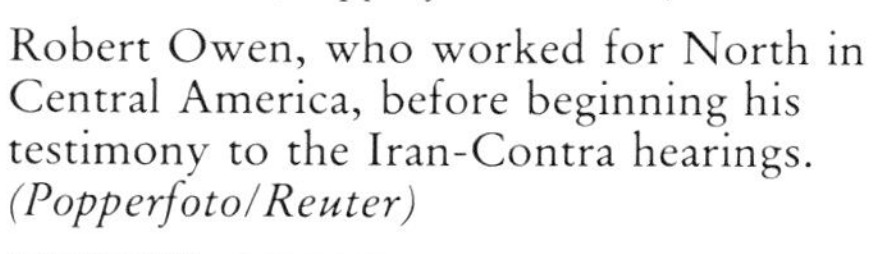

Robert Owen, who worked for North in Central America, before beginning his testimony to the Iran-Contra hearings. *(Popperfoto/Reuter)*

Danny Sheehan, head of the Christic Institute. *(Julio Lainez, Tico Times)*

MINISTERIO DE SEGURIDAD PUBLICA
CENTRO DE COMPUTO

C E R T I F I C A N

JE EL SEÑOR (A): KHALIL AHMED CONOCIDO: GALIL AMAC
NACIONALIDAD: EGIPCIA PORTADOR DEL PASAPORTE No. Z6099028
ESTUDIADO DEL AÑO 01-83 AL 04-89 ; Y DE CONFORMIDAD CON NUESTROS REGISTROS DE
ADAS Y SALIDAS LE APARECEN LOS SIGUIENTES MOVIMIENTOS MIGRATORIOS:

| NTRADAS | SALIDAS | ENTRADAS | SALIDAS | ENTRADAS | SALIDAS | ENTRADAS | SAL |
| --- | --- | --- | --- | --- | --- | --- | --- |
| -04-83 | 10-04-83 | 03-10-83 | 00 00 00 | 28-10-83 | 06-11-83 | 04-03-87 | 07-0 |
| -02-88 | 00-00-00 | 00-00-00 | 00-00-00 | 00-00-00 | 00-00-00 | 00-00-00 | 00-0 |

Ultima linea

MINISTERIO DE SEGURIDAD PUBLICA

EXTIENDE LA PRESENTE CERTIFICACION EN LA CIUDAD DE SAN JOSE A LOS VEINTE
S DEL MES DE JULIO DE MIL NOVECIENTOS OCHENTA Y NUEVE A SOLICITUD DEL INTERE
PARA EFECTOS DE: LEGALES

AGREGA Y CANCELA TIMBRES DE LEY

89-07-04647

ILLY ZUNIGA SALAS
DIRECTORA GENERAL

HERNAN BORGE CARVAJAL
SUB—DIRECTOR

CENTENARIO DE LA DEMOCRACIA COSTARRICENSE
"EL CAMINO DEL FUTURO"

Print-out from Costa Rican security with passport and immigration details of one Ahmed Khalil, 'known as' Amac Galil, who travelled in and out of Costa Rica between 1983 and 1988.

Two views of Pie de la Cuesta: Mexican terrorist camp, or just an airforce base? *(Judy Jackson)*

where he worked, a sprawling outfit covering four blocks and selling new and second-hand cars and trucks of all descriptions. I had been told that car-dealers are often fronts for laundering drug money. I persuaded the affable Martínez to have lunch with me, but this didn't get me very far. As we sat on banquettes in a Pizza Hut, I tried to get him to relax, to at least tell me why he thought he had been accused of involvement in murder. Martínez replied the charge was 'utterly absurd' and flatly denied having had anything whatever to do with the bombing. Even if he wasn't personally involved (which was possible), I was sure that as a former, and probably current, CIA asset, he had to know who was involved. If he did, though, he wasn't telling me.

Some of the most notorious Miami Cuban terrorists were now being used by the US in the secret Contra network. One of the most shocking cases was that of a Cuban exile named Luis Posada Carriles, who was jailed in Venezuela after he planted a bomb in 1976 aboard a Cubana airliner leaving the Bahamas. It crashed, killing all passengers aboard, including the entire Cuban basketball team. Posada Carriles later 'escaped' from his Venezuelan jail, allegedly with CIA help. The involvement of Posada Carriles with the Contras came to light when Eugene Hasenfus was shot down. Sandinista Intelligence then named Posada Carriles as Hasenfus's 'controller' operating out of a safe-house in a wealthy San Salvador suburb.

Enterprising reporters in El Salvador succeeded in obtaining the telephone records of the safe-house from the sympathetic Union of Salvadorean Telegraphic Workers. By calling the numbers listed, they stumbled upon links to the heart of the secret supply network. At the end of one phone-line was the voice of Richard Secord, an arms-dealer and a key figure in Iran-Contra; on another, they reached a private line in the White House for Oliver North. So much for Hasenfus, Posada Carriles and Co. being 'independent'.

By this time Posada Carriles was operating under the pseudonym of 'Ramón Medina'. He has since gone to ground, but is said still to be operating out of Miami, under another assumed name, and to be enjoying the protection of the Cuban underworld.

The photographs of two Miami Cubans who, I felt certain, knew about the La Penca bombing – René Corvo (nicknamed 'the Maniacal Dwarf') and Hull's 'evil bulldog' Felipe Vidal ('Morgan'), leaders of the 'Cuban brigade' that had been sent to fight with Edén Pastora – were on one of the Cuban posters plastered around the city. Surrounded by fierce-looking and heavily bearded men wearing camouflage fatigues and armed with M-16 rifles, they knelt in a stagey pose in what purported to be the thick undergrowth of Nicaragua but was more likely Florida. The caption 'Sponsor a Freedom Fighter' was followed by a Miami box number, where donations could be sent.

I had managed to find out the Miami address of Corvo and on my earlier visit, after driving for several hours through a sprawling working-class Cuban suburb, had located his home. When I knocked on the door and gushingly enquired about Corvo's 'wonderful work with the Contras', I was greeted by a hugely overweight woman in an apron and curlers who spoke English with a halting Latin accent. She introduced herself as Corvo's wife. Behind her, several small children eyed me with suspicion. Was René at home, I asked. 'No, he's out of the country.' She had no idea when he'd be back. Yes, she would pass on the message that I wanted to see him.

It turned out that this abandoned wife had been set up to provide a respectable front for René Corvo. She told me she had to work night shifts as a nurse to keep herself and her family and then look after the children during the day. She said she was completely exhausted. I'd already learnt that her absent 'husband' was living it up with prostitutes in Costa Rica – and spending a lot of Contra money on himself. He was in serious trouble with the rebel leadership as a result. Now, six months later, the house was deserted. Evidently, too many people had come looking for Corvo.

Felipe Vidal was an even more unsavoury character. He was notorious in Miami as a small-time hit-man, but had now gone on to bigger things; he had once boasted to a man posing as a drug-smuggler but actually working for the US government that 'they' had already tried unsuccessfully to get rid of Pastora, and would try again. Vidal had also said he had attended a meeting at the Miami house of Adolfo Calero, where plans to assassinate the 'traitor' were discussed.

I was unable to track Vidal down either. Eventually I heard he was hiding out in the jungles of Costa Rica. 'But if you found him,' warned my contact, 'he'd kill you.'

We were growing desperate. So far we'd found no one who would even talk to me, let alone go on camera for us. I started contacting other right-wing Cubans on my list, but as, for the most part, I had only telephone numbers, no addresses, the person on the other end of the line could simply hang up if they didn't want to talk. I'd call back to hear a recorded message telling me the number was now unobtainable. Occasionally I got a break, as when I tracked down through his estranged wife one Raúl de la Milera, who I had been told knew about the bombing. I was also told he was a middleman and 'fixer' involved in arms and drug enterprises, and, unusually, a heavy cocaine user, which, his ex-wife said, had totally changed his personality: he had become paranoid and violent and had abused her and their daughter. I had met the daughter. She was only seventeen, but was grotesquely overweight and reclusive, spending her time watching television and eating.

When I knocked on de la Milera's front door one Sunday morning, asking about the bombing, he reacted aggressively, threatening to call his lawyer and the police before banging the door shut in my face. I returned on two other occasions but I couldn't get him even to open the door again. Perhaps it was just as well. When I told people in Miami about the encounter they said I was crazy to go anywhere near Milera, that he was highly dangerous and that his nickname was 'Shooter' because of his readiness with a gun.

I was constantly being warned by my friends that finding out about the bombing was not worth the damage I was doing to my health, that I should have more concern for my safety – ultimately, for my life. But it was no good. I was determined to find one piece of hard evidence. Occasionally my desperate attempts ended up in farce. One man I was looking for was Ramón Cecilio Palacios, who was said to work for the drug baron Pablo Escobar and to have harboured the La Penca bomber. Leafing through the phone-book, I found a Ramón C. Palacios and decided to try the number.

The man who answered sounded extremely suspicious when I claimed to want insurance (this was given as his profession in the phone-book) – so suspicious, in fact, that he put the Miami police on to me and I had to spend several hours explaining to a thoroughly sceptical sergeant what I was really doing. Not only had I got the wrong man (even to me it had seemed a long shot); I had called a part-time cop specialising in drug busts who was afraid I was an angry trafficker trying to lure him to a meeting in order to kill him.

It is a measure of my desperation that I finally turned to a private detective, Jack Kasovits, a thin, nervous man with a straggling grey beard who shared his house with five German shepherd dogs he claimed were descended from the brutes kept by Somoza and which, Jack boasted, were trained to kill on command. Most of the time, I was relieved to find, these dogs were kept in a small dirt yard at the back, but there was a further assortment of sickly mongrels that wandered all over the house scratching and urinating. Jack lived with a young woman who said she was a 'cocktail hostess'. On one wall there was a large sign reading, in six-inch capitals, 'PROSTITUTES ARE SATAN'S PEOPLE'. The 'cocktail hostess' wore stiletto heels, extremely tight jeans, and her long fingernails were painted in black and red stripes.

On entering the gloom of the house, with its suffocating, sickly-sweet odour of dog, dope, stale air and urine, I nearly stumbled over several life-size waxwork models of men and women in period costume, involved in rituals of killing, rape and torture. The surreal atmosphere continued. Lying about the place were well-thumbed pornographic and mercenary magazines including *Soldier of Fortune*, and a small arsenal of submachine guns, pistols and handguns.

The whole scene was creepy in the extreme, but Jack came recommended, and at least he was energetic and enthusiastic, rushing about, expounding on his extraordinary theories, telling me about his past as a game-warden (I wondered if any of the animals survived), making me print-outs from his computer of names he said could help me, checking names I gave him to see if they came up in any other context. I showed him the pictures I had of the bomber to see if he or anyone he knew recognised the man. First, Jack told me he was certain he'd seen the bomber in a jewellery store in down-town Miami. Our man, he said, was usually hiding out at the back, and the store was actually a cover for a big drug operation. We visited the store, and dozens of others, but nowhere could we find our assassin. 'He's probably hiding in the store-room,' said Jack, with a conviction I didn't share. He then scrutinised one of the photographs again and insisted the bomber was wearing a black necklace (it looked to me like a shadow on my rather grainy picture). This, said Jack, proved the bomber was a member of the Cuba-based Voodoo cult, the Santeria, which was very big in Miami. It represented an important clue to the bomber's identity: it showed he was Cuban. (When I checked the existence of this cult with the Cuban community I discovered to my surprise that it does exist, having come over from Cuba via West Africa; it is quite significant and very secret.)

Jack never gave me any hard information, but he was always full of new ideas, angles, tips, contacts and theories. He even enlisted the support of a friend of his, a Miami police investigator, and we all solemnly met to discuss new approaches to the investigation. These, too, came to nothing. Absurdly, I was loath to give Jack up, even though I knew in my heart he was no good, crazy. In retrospect, I think it was his enthusiasm I needed. It supplied something I was finding harder and harder to summon in myself.

Finally, as a last resort, I went to see people who couldn't get away because they were in jail. One, Jesús García, in prison on what he said was a trumped-up charge, had been deeply involved in the illegal supply of weapons and supplies to the Contras. He was about to be paroled, and I had been told he might be killed on his release: there had already been bomb attacks on his home, and the day before I saw him his wife had tried to kill herself. The fact that he was talking to his US lawyer, John Mattes, about the clandestine support network to Central America meant that the Miami Cuban community, of which García was a leading member, regarded him as a traitor. And the Cubans had a habit of dealing harshly with traitors.

John Mattes, a seemingly frank and forthright man in his late thirties, had been assigned to García's case in his capacity as a public attorney. Assuming he was dealing with a routine case of illegal arms dealing, he heard instead a bizarre account of law-breaking; of a web of conspiracies; of illegal, secret, arms shipments; of attempts to murder the US Ambassador to Costa Rica, Lewis Tambs; of the La Penca bombing – and more. As a lawyer and an upright American citizen, Mattes felt it his duty to investigate what lay behind his client's extraordinary revelations, and, if they were true, to bring justice to bear. Instead, he said, he was abruptly pulled off the case on 'orders from Washington'.

To his even greater surprise, Mattes was warned that if he continued his investigations he and his Cuban prosecutor, Ralph Maestri, would themselves face prosecution. Maestri was a Bay of Pigs veteran of extreme right-wing persuasion and he hated communism. Like many exiles, he embraced American values more than many native-born. His outrage, therefore, at these attempts to stop an important investigation in its tracks, was all the greater. Since then, according to John Mattes, evidence had started to emerge of a massive cover-up of all the murky goings-on in Central America, including interference with Grand Juries dealing with cases of violation of US neutrality.*

* In 1985, Jeffrey Feldman, assistant US attorney for Miami, who was sent to Costa Rica to investigate possible violations of US neutrality there – including CIA involvement in Central America and the activities of US citizens such as John Hull – went on the record to protest that he was obstructed in his investigations, then ordered not to pursue them further and recalled to Miami.

The cover-up originated at the very top of the US administration. It was designed to keep the secret network in place and illegal American supplies flowing to the Contras at whatever cost after Congress had banned that aid.

It was a very long drive to the jail on the Florida–Georgia border. Judy and I drove for sixteen hours, stopping periodically for snacks of greasy chips and hamburgers and spending the night in a cheap motel with sagging beds. The jail was discreetly tucked away on a side road, approached by a long tree-lined avenue. A functional building, of uniform grey, it was surrounded by row upon row of lethal-looking barbed wire. In the entrance – where I had to leave all my possessions save my notebook and tape-recorder, sign several forms pledging I had no weapons on me and go through a metal detector – I was met by a female warder, a thin, pinched, youngish woman wearing an incongruously pretty floral dress. She managed to be both slightly spooky and thoroughly unhelpful, telling me I could not spend my allotted time with the prisoner before reluctantly escorting me through a complex combination of huge, heavy doors.

Jesús was a soft-spoken man with spaniel eyes and prematurely grey hair. He was in bad shape the day of my visit because of his wife's attempted suicide and because he appeared to be on drugs (something other journalists who interviewed him confirmed). His eyes looked glazed, his mouth very dry (he constantly licked his lips) and his speech was slightly slurred. Another reporter later told me she believed the drugs were an attempt to stop Jesús García from being clear-headed, to limit the damage of what he might say. I don't know if this is true.

'I am down, I am arrested, I'm doing time. I can't help contribute to the cause, but some do believe in the cause,' Jesús said, looking as though he was about to burst into tears.

'Look, I was at La Penca, Jesús,' I said, to try and draw him out. 'I was very nearly killed; some of my friends were killed. What do you know about it? Just tell me the truth.'

Jesús, looking nervous and shifty, said, with admirable understatement, 'Yes; that was a sad incident. If I told you that a lot of us in the Latin community knew about it, I would not be lying.' He said that several planning meetings had been secretly held in Miami just before May 1984.

'Who was at those meetings?'

'I can't name them, but many of our leaders, many people that were prominent – they discussed, planned the La Penca bombing.'

'Who, Jesús?' I pushed. 'Members of the 2506 Brigade?'

'To us, the Brigade is sacred. I will not betray them,' replied Jesús.

He admitted he was afraid of more revenge attacks on him and his family, so his reticence was understandable. He was more forthcoming about the identity of the assassin. 'He was a Libyan named Amac Galil, trained by DINA [the notorious secret police] in Chile. He was recruited from Chile by Miami Cubans.' But Jesús would say no more than that. 'When I get out, I'll ask around, I'll try to help you,' he said. But when, much later, he was released (and contrary to my fears, he has not so far been harmed), he went into hiding, and I have been unable to contact him again.

What seems to add further credibility to García's testimony is that he has been the target of a major smear campaign by US intelligence services, including the FBI. A secret US report that came to light during the Iran-Contra hearings brands him as 'unreliable, a total liar'. If what García said was untrue, why go to such lengths to discredit him?

Despite my alternately pleading and hectoring, Jesús García would not give me any names of people involved in La Penca, but he did give me the name of another prisoner who might be prepared to talk. George Morales, the Colombian drug cartel's man in Miami and a very big drug-smuggler indeed, was in the Metropolitan Correctional Center together with several of his pilots.

The Metropolitan Correctional Center is known as the 'Country Club' because of the relative comfort of life there; its amenities include extensive landscaped grounds with beautifully manicured lawns, flowering shrubs and even an ornamental lake. I came to know the long road there by heart, making five trips in all. Obtaining access to the prisoners involved first talking to their lawyers to request the prisoner's consent, and then making a formal request to the prison authorities. It seems to me indicative of real political openness in the United States that I was allowed to interview men whose information could prove damaging to the administration.

I would be escorted by a warder through automatic interlocking doors, opened by pressing a coded switch, which led eventually to the prisoners' recreation room. Outside I could see the perimeter fence, consisting of rows of lethal-looking barbed wire with honed edges that glittered ominously in the bright sunshine; not for nothing was this known as razor wire – it would literally cut to shreds anyone attempting to climb it. From here I would be ushered towards a tiny, windowless, virtually airless cubbyhole to interview my prisoner.

George Morales was a good-looking man with an olive complexion, shrewd eyes and a thick, dark beard. Before his arrest he had been a billionaire. He owned a fleet of aircraft in Miami, several islands in the Caribbean, and had held the world speedboat record for several years. Rather pathetically, he showed me photographs recording his former sporting successes as well as of his stunningly beautiful wife Susan, who had dumped him on his arrest for an extremely rich Arab. The couple had once been surrounded by the most powerful in the land; now the same people shunned him.

The champagne. The women. Wearing out adding machines from having to count millions of dollar bills. Buying half a dozen houses in Miami simply to stash the dosh. This was the stuff of legends. It was also an incredible and joyous relief from my normal diet of agonising, dourly serious effort for no reward – of staying by the telephone for hours, sometimes days, as I paced up and down, daydreamed, chainsmoked, went stir-crazy, waiting and waiting in my hotel room for people to call me back.

George said his first act on being indicted was to send his lawyers to the then US Vice-President, George Bush, the man he claims he was working for. The connection failed to secure his release, a fact that Morales used to explain his readiness to talk. He claimed he was originally approached by the CIA and told that if he 'cooperated' with the Contras by flying down arms to Central America and providing money for the rebels, the drug charges pending against him would be 'taken care of'; he and others like him were believed to be in jail as a result of interagency rivalry between the CIA, the Drug Enforcement Administration and US Customs.*

On a personal level, I found George to be a convincing witness, both through a 'gut' feeling and because when he didn't know something, or had only hearsay information, he would say so. He told me he had ferried down arms, explosives and millions of dollars to the Contra rebels. The planes were then reloaded with Colombian cocaine and flown back to the States under CIA protection.

'Where did the arms to Central America go?'

'To this particular ranch in the north of Costa Rica, almost on the Nicaraguan border.'

'Who owned the ranch?'

'John Hull.'

Having identified John Hull as the key Costa Rican figure in the operation, George told me the American rancher had been the Colombian Medellín cartel's main liaison in Central America long before the Contras became an issue. Drug planes, including George's own, regularly refuelled at secret landing strips on Hull's ranch, paying a hefty tax for the privilege.

When I asked Morales who he thought had been responsible for La Penca, he looked me straight in the eye and said, 'The CIA,' going on, 'I mean, not just me but everybody knew about it.'

'Do we know this or do we think this?'

* The 1988 Kerry report on drugs and terrorism argues that convicted traffickers like Morales, by claiming to work for the CIA, were involved in what is known as 'ticket-punching' – that is, trying to obtain a reduced sentence in return for providing information or for extenuating circumstances. Morales testified that he thought by assisting the Contra cause his indictment would be dropped because of the Contras' connections with the CIA. Not only are the details George provides convincing; they have been exhaustively and independently checked and found to be correct. George himself underwent a lengthy lie-detector (polygraph) examination and was found to be truthful.

George paused. 'It's very hard. We know it, but it's very hard to prove it.'

'Who was actually involved on the ground in organising La Penca?'

'Well, the street talk is the whole thing was planned on John Hull's ranch. It was, it is, common knowledge.'

When pressed, George seemed to have quite a lot of information about La Penca, although he stressed that none of it was first-hand. He had heard that the man involved 'went down from Miami' and that Miami Cubans were involved. 'They used some of the Cubans and some of the Contras. It's got to be an inside job, definitely – they knew what they were doing.' Furthermore, he stated categorically that the Contras – or the Costa Ricans – had been given the expertise and technology to acquire, make and detonate the bomb.

'I mean, a remote-control bomb is highly sophisticated. They had to have help from the Americans, technical expertise. That is what I understand . . . You can't get proof. People are afraid. The Costa Ricans are afraid to investigate, to go too deep inside. They're afraid they're going to come out with one answer, and they'll have a lot of people behind bars. It involves people from Washington.'

'Do the Costa Rican authorities know this?'

'Yes. From the US point of view, it had to be done out of the country and then they were going to blame the Sandinistas.'

When I showed George a photograph of the bomber – a by now rather dog-eared three-by-five black and white snap that went everywhere with me – he looked at it long and hard. He then said he thought he had seen the same picture in a pile of Costa Rican diplomatic passports in a CIA safe-house in San José. 'We all had those passports,' he commented. 'I remember noticing that one because the bomber had a beard like mine but strange eyes.'

Although George appears to have been the biggest figure in the notorious 'drugs for guns' operation that helped finance the Southern Front, he also gave me the names and telephone numbers of others involved. One of them, Popo Chamorro, who was Pastora's right-hand man at the time of the bombing, was also operating as a narcotics trafficker. This may help explain how he came to buy his own bank in Miami.

On the one occasion I managed to talk to him on the phone, the day after my interview with Morales, Popo immediately asked, 'How did you get my number?' I told him a Contra support group in Miami had provided it, and this seemed to satisfy him. He then told me he was financially ruined and had never made a cent out of his involvement in the war. 'I lost everything. I don't want to think about the past ever again.' Then he hung up. Next time I tried to contact him a recorded message told me his number was no longer in service. I was particularly sorry, as I had hoped to confirm the story I had been told that Popo, one of Pastora's most trusted leaders, had actually been working against him for the CIA.

The operations Morales had outlined to me were important for three reasons. First, because they demonstrated how convicted drug-smugglers and other criminals were working directly with the CIA, and were certainly known by Oliver North and Rob Owen to be doing so. Second, far from stopping the scourge of narcotics from reaching the States, US government officials and the CIA were secretly encouraging it. Third, and most important for my investigation, the network of men involved in these transactions, notably John Hull, were widely considered to have been involved in the La Penca bomb plot.

George told me he used up to a dozen of his own pilots for the drug and gun runs to the Southern Front. I interviewed two of them in jail. Gary Betzner, a thin, hunched man with auburn hair and glittering green eyes, referred to Morales simply as 'El Jefe' – 'The Boss'. He began by telling me that he used to take enormous amounts of cocaine 'for medicinal purposes' and that coke had given him a new lease of life. I had to admit he looked well enough, albeit a little crazy. He knew less of the 'guns for drugs' operation than Morales, but had first-hand experience of landing his plane at John Hull's ranch, showing me on the large-scale map I had brought with me exactly where. He had been an eye witness to

John Hull personally overseeing the loading of cocaine on to the planes. On one occasion, in 1984, he said he and Hull watched while weapons were unloaded and approximately 500 kilos of cocaine in seventeen duffel-bags were loaded for the return flight to Florida. (According to Morales, each plane-load was worth $11 million – much more at street value. Profits from the drugs sold in the US were spent on buying more illegal supplies for the Contras. 'That was the only purpose,' said Morales, although I and others suspect that the bulk of the profits stayed in the smugglers' hands.) Once the plane was loaded with cocaine, Betzner would fly back to the States, usually to the area around Miami, but sometimes even landing at US air-bases with his illegal cargo. He always received CIA protection.

The testimonies of George Morales and his pilots made it impossible for the CIA to implement 'damage limitation'. The prisoners were so angry, and felt so betrayed by their sponsors, that they were prepared to spill the beans about everything they knew. They played a crucial part in bringing to light the existence of the illegal Contra pipeline and US involvement. It was from them that, despite official denials, the public first learnt of the scope of the operation and of illegal American activity. It emerged that what had been going on, under the nose of Congress, spearheaded by William Casey, the former head of the CIA, and Oliver North of the National Security Council, was nothing less than an alternative, illegal, US foreign policy.

They suffered for telling the truth. Gary Betzner was once very nearly strangled by a fellow prisoner, an ardent Cuban nationalist who considered him a 'traitor to the cause'. Both Morales and Betzner had been put repeatedly in 'the hole', local slang for solitary confinement, after fighting with other prisoners. George certainly believed his troubles increased after he talked to reporters and documentary films were aired to a shocked public on American television.

I finally obtained direct proof concerning the Miami end of the La Penca operation from a former US mercenary called Jack Terrell, a middle-aged man with blond hair, blue eyes, a paunch and a Southern twang you could cut with a knife. He had worked closely with the Contras as a military advisor and explosives expert before he defected, disgusted, he said, at how the CIA mismanaged the war and sent thousands of Contras to unnecessary deaths. He told me he had attended a meeting in the Miami home of Contra leader Adolfo Calero nine months after the bombing. At that meeting were present, apart from Contra leaders, Robert Owen and John Hull, as well as several CIA operatives.

'At one point during a discussion focusing on the problem of Pastora and the Southern Front and what to do about it, a Miami Cuban named Felipe Vidal stood up and recounted how the attack against Pastora the previous May had failed because of what he called "bad timing", so the rest of the meeting was devoted to planning a second attempt to assassinate Pastora. That was the first time I had heard about the La Penca bombing.'

Terrell had kept a diary and had made scrupulous notes about key meetings he attended. When I asked if he was sure about the details of the La Penca plot and who was at the meeting at Calero's house that December, he picked up a notebook from a back pocket and read out the following notes on a new plot to kill Pastora – one that sounded remarkably similar to La Penca:

> The termination of Zero [Pastora] discussed with Adolfo, Arístides, John Hull, Donald Lacayo and a man not identified but told he was 'with company'. Many people involved, some look like Cubans, some Nicaraguans, some Argentinians. Adolfo Calero very upset with statements made by Pastora. Says he too Sandinista. Must die. Big problem. Asks me to put it together and not tell them how it will be done. Just do it. Will have complete cooperation of all Costa Rican officials. Have several safehouses in C.R. under control of John Hull and Bruce Jones. Seems Rob Owen in on most of this . . . am told he is private consultant and liaison man for US (Company). Must appear that Sandinistas did it. Discussions on capturing Zero and having men dress in captured uniforms. Am told this must be very visible

> hit and people must believe the Sandinistas did it. Am told to let Hull know when ready to move. A.C. [Adolfo Calero] open to anything. He desperate. Wants and needs Southern Front.

He had another startling piece of information. He said that for the entire meeting two men were sitting on the back patio of Calero's house. One, he thought, looked Cuban, the other Middle Eastern. He swore he had never seen the 'Middle Eastern' man before but that subsequently he had been able to pick his face out of some sixty photographs shown him by Costa Rican authorities who had taken advantage of his presence as a witness at Hull's libel trial to interrogate him about any knowledge he might have of the bombing.*

After the meeting, worried by the security risk of having these two unknown men overhear assassination plots, he had taken Felipe Vidal aside. 'I asked him, who are these men – who is the tall one with auburn hair? And I was told that was the La Penca bomber. I was told his name was Amac Galil.'

* His testimony was completely disregarded, even though he was the only witness able to provide a first-hand account of a meeting of those involved in the bombing. See p. 202.

# 10

# THERE MUST BE MORE

Washington, the final leg of our film-trip, was staid and a bit dull. It was already September. The hectic pace had caught up with us; we were tired; and time and money were running out fast. We were in Washington to tie up a few loose ends, and duty rather than enthusiasm was now driving us. Our schedule was still hectic, but the constant whirl at least kept my mind off the depression which threatened to envelop me, the result of the sheer awfulness of the people and events I had been involved with in Central America.

First, we needed an intellectual heavyweight who could draw together the complex strands of the US–Central American network and make sense of the wider picture. This person also needed to have impeccable credentials, the authority to counterbalance the dubious impression given by our assortment of witnesses – jail-birds, ex-mercenaries and the like, necessary on the principle of 'set a thief to catch a thief', but we knew from past experience that efforts would be made to smear them as 'untrustworthy liars'. Also, most of them knew only their own bit of the jigsaw, but nothing beyond that.

No one could write off a former US Ambassador to El Salvador who had resigned in disgust at US 'diplomacy', making the scathing comment that, 'We don't have a foreign policy in Central America but a crusade in which anything goes, even breaking the law, in order to defeat communism.' Robert White, we decided, was our man. Intelligent, principled, sardonic and highly articulate, he also bore a striking resemblance to Steve McQueen. We met him at his Washington-based Commission on US–Central American relations, finding him perturbed and uneasy after a break-in at his offices. Sensitive files had been stolen, but the authorities, he said, were showing a marked reluctance to investigate, having ignored his earlier phone-calls alerting them to the presence of unauthorised men in uniform on the roof. White told us he believed the break-in was the work of Oliver North's Security Chief, Glenn Robinette. Robinette had already admitted at the Iran-Contra hearings to having been sent down to Costa Rica with large sums of money to spy on Martha and Tony, bribe people and 'bring back any dirt' for his other boss, General Secord, the arms dealer, who was part of North's cabal. He had also tried to bribe Jack Terrell to change his story, and, when that failed, to smear him. Confidential North memos produced at the Iran-Contra hearings describe Terrell as 'very dangerous' and 'possibly working for the Sandinistas'. What is significant is that these notes were not just sent from North to his National Security boss, Admiral John Poindexter, but also from Poindexter to President Reagan himself. Indicative of the extraordinary level of concern Terrell's defection and revelations were causing was the bizarre allegation that Terrell had been involved in an attempt to assassinate the President. (The charge had later to be withdrawn.) Later still, Terrell was charged with 'violating US neutrality', even though such charges were levelled at none of the men he was working for.

White argued that the attempts to smear and bribe Terrell were 'both desperate and criminal', made 'because they feared his testimony would implicate Oliver North and Robert Owen in criminal activities.

'I hope,' he went on, 'that people at the top of the Justice Department will be indicted for obstruction of justice because . . . they were trying to impede a key witness.' So far White's hope has not been realised.

It was strange to be conducting an interview in a civilised office, with book-lined walls and no rows of razor-wire glinting outside. Even I, feeling a bit odd, was wearing a frock. I plunged straight in with my usual questions.

'Do you think, as Edén Pastora does, that the CIA was responsible for La Penca?'

White said he thought it was possible, given that 'anything goes when you're out to destroy communism'. Then he added, ever the diplomat, 'I'm not saying that the CIA carried out that plot at La Penca; we don't yet have enough evidence to know that. I'm saying that, given the other plots we now know the CIA was responsible for, this would not have been such a great leap . . . even though to indulge in an assassination attempt is against our law . . .' Given the professionalism of the 'operation', he said, and 'our close relationship with Costa Rica', it seemed 'inconceivable' that senior figures in the administration weren't involved.

I was particularly anxious to try and demonstrate a link between the men who had carried out the bombing and the secret network involved in Iran-Contra. White couldn't supply this, although he did give me an intriguing analysis of the key figures in the US end of the Central American 'crusade' – an operation run by former CIA boss William Casey that was 'like something out of a John Le Carré novel'. He explained that Casey had taken over the National Security Council, 'and used it as a private vehicle to advance the Contra supply operation that Congress had said was outlawed . . . They set up a shadow organisation called Project Democracy to carry out this illegal policy.' He singled out John Poindexter as the man 'who protected them and made sure they had the high-level clout required to keep this [network] going'.

According to White, there were two wider issues thrown up by the Central American shenanigans. One was the way the CIA had been 'quite simply hijacked' by the swashbuckling Casey (who had died of a brain tumour earlier in the summer, before he could testify to Congress), in order to carry out this illegal alternative foreign policy. The second was that some CIA 'liberals' had been so angry on discovering what was happening under their noses that they had leaked its details. White was bitingly critical of the Reagan administration's moves to blur accountability and encourage deniability: 'When you blur the distinction between active-duty CIA officers and retired CIA officers, and active and retired military men – when you bring in men like General Secord and you don't know if he has an official position or is, as is claimed, an independent contractor but is receiving funding – you're undermining accountable government.' (Significantly, General Secord had spent about $100,000 of his own money to fight the criminal suit brought by the Christic Institute on behalf of Martha and Tony, in which he was listed as a defendant, even though he publicly dismissed it as a 'fairy tale'.)

Next, we drove north to the Christic Institute, whose case Secord had so scathingly dismissed. My feelings about what might come out of the meeting were mixed. I knew that Martha and Tony were privately worried that Danny Sheehan, head of the Institute, had cast his net too wide. The Institute was something of a media circus, depending on private donations, many given by rich, radical-chic Hollywood stars. Danny would dash around the country giving rousing talks about the evils of US government, its connections with drugs and organised crime. People flocked to hear him: Danny confirmed their worst suspicions about 'what was really going down'. Some friends on the Left were concerned by the demagoguery – and the inaccuracy. 'It's as though Danny wants to fulfil radical-thinking Americans' desires for myths, not facts,' one friend tried to explain. 'It's hard to put it into words, but I think the danger is people are having this great emotional void filled by a sort of half-truth. I think it's dangerous.' On the other hand, only the Christic had taken up the La Penca case, and they did, undoubtedly, deserve credit for publicising it.

I asked Danny who he thought was responsible for La Penca. His reply ran to over two pages of transcript, and I can't see a full stop anywhere. I already knew a lot of what he was telling me

– and rather more to boot. I couldn't help interrupting him, but Judy intervened, pointing out that we would have no interview if I didn't let him talk. I felt if this was an example we wouldn't have anything usable anyway. It was also very important to me to show that we were independent. As I saw it, the strength of our investigation lay in the fact that we had done it all ourselves. Worse, on a personal note, I found myself becoming annoyed with him. In the end, with Danny irritated in turn by my none too tactful insistence that he should try to give direct answers, we began to argue like a couple of six-year-olds and the tape was unusable. Judy was cross; the camera-crew took my side. It was a lousy interview, a waste of an opportunity, and a lot of it was my fault.

Only when, instead of arguing, I tried to find out specific things, was our exchange at all fruitful. I was interested in his assessment of Guevara – the man Martha had met at the petrol station. Danny said Guevara had given testimony under oath that at the very beginning of May 1984, about thirty days before the bombing, 'Hansen' had come to his office with a letter signed by Carlos Monge, head of DIS, instructing him to provide a vehicle for Hansen and his woman associate (he identified Hansen from a photo). They had left along the road that leads to La Penca. Guevara also talked about a second visit, about three weeks before the bombing, when Hansen, the same woman and John Hull came with another letter from Carlos Monge ordering them to provide a boat and a motor; they loaded this on the top of their Landrover, and again drove up in the direction of La Penca. 'This is a direct, eyewitness account,' said Danny. On the second visit Guevara said Hansen had with him an aluminium case with a yellow sticker on the side saying 'US mail'. Guevara said that later on in the month of May he saw the same aluminium case sitting in the office of Carlos Monge. I was fascinated, but then I remembered Peter Torbiornsson saying that the Danish photographer had had the case with him on the river during May, when they were looking for Pastora. I also told Danny that Monge had vehemently denied having the case, but Danny replied that of course he wouldn't admit to that, implying I was very naïve.

I asked Danny to explain the link between the private network and La Penca, which formed the basis of his suit. He explained that he had learnt about the guns and drugs network to Central America, and that it was centred on John Hull's ranch, long before he was approached by Martha and Tony. Only in March 1985, however, after the defector David had linked Hull directly to La Penca, claiming the bomb-plot originated on Hull's ranch, could he definitively link the two parts of the plot. A year later, after Hull's libel trial against Martha and Tony, Danny said he was contacted by a former high-ranking military officer in the US who told him not just that Hull and associates in the Civilian Military Assistance (a group of supposedly private individuals providing money for the Central American operation) were involved in Central America, but that its participants were far more important and were in fact high-ranking officers in the CIA and the Pentagon who had been selling weapons and explosives around the world. Danny said Martha and Tony had no knowledge about this racket, but that he had gone on acquiring information, bringing in a team of professional investigators. It was on the basis of their information about the 'enterprise' that he brought the criminal racketeering charges.

Danny had other pieces and snippets of information. He confirmed that the bomb detonator was very sophisticated – a radio long-distance detonator, not a simple clock device. He said it was hard to determine whether the people who organised La Penca were acting on direct orders from superiors or had made their own decision or 'interpretation' to carry out the bombing in that particular fashion. He insisted Pastora had been given a thirty-day ultimatum by the CIA – even though I had told him Pastora's story that he was never given a direct ultimatum. Pastora's denial was wrong, he said.

I felt guilty after the interview for wasting Judy's and the crew's time, but I was also worried about the future of the suit, which represented a unique chance to force out the truth and to obtain justice for the victims. So much of what Danny was saying seemed to be all over the place, interspersed with claims that he and he alone could solve the case.*

One of our other pursuits in Washington was to find the CIA headquarters at Langley, Virginia, and, if possible, film it. The only time we had available was at night, and our approach via wooded, unmarked back roads to a rear entrance made good cops and robbers stuff. Unfortunately, we couldn't see anything inside because of massive security – fifteen-foot walls, search-lights etc. Our cameraman, Noel, said there was no way we could get a decent picture of me standing outside: I could have been anywhere. We persevered, edging our car along the wall surrounding the complex, trying to find another way around, when we suddenly found ourselves addressed by a disembodied 'Big Brother' voice from above, telling us to get the hell out and that we were in a restricted zone. It was a bit spooky, but I'm afraid we found it funny rather than frightening. Since we'd (a) been spotted and (b) couldn't film anyway, we gave up.

Our other activities were more mundane. We had applied for permission to film in the room in Congress where the Irangate hearings had been held earlier that summer. I was supposed to walk thoughtfully through the room delivering my carefully rehearsed but impassioned speech about 'the man Edén Pastora blames, Oliver North, who worked for the National Security Council', but the whole thing was a fiasco. It may sound absurd,

* In fact the suit was thrown out by a Federal Judge in Miami in June 1988; a follow-up ruling ordered the Christic to pay defendants nearly $1 million in costs and damages, describing their suit as 'an abuse of the legal system'. The suit accused the twenty-nine defendants – among them Adolfo Calero, John Hull, ex-CIA chief of operations Theodore Shackley, Iran-Contra figures Albert Hakim and Richard Secord, and the conservative activist Major-General John Singlaub – of setting up the bombing, as well as working with drug-traffickers in a thirty-year conspiracy that included anti-communist activities in South East Asia, Central America and elsewhere. The Christic bitterly criticised the ruling and are trying to get the case resubmitted. The case has become a *cause célèbre* in the US.

but I just couldn't walk naturally and talk at the same time: I looked like a penguin. After about fifteen takes we gave up. I was rather relieved. This was the camera-crew's last day, and Judy said it was traditional to get very, very drunk. We went out, had a slap-up meal and then proceeded to drink . . . At about three in the morning, I left them all to it – and to my best Nicaraguan rum. We all felt utterly dreadful the next morning, when we had to check out and the poor crew had to pack. I hadn't realised what a performance it was to lug quantities of heavy camera equipment and dozens of cans of film in and out of hotel rooms and taxis and through Customs. It was even worse with a hangover.

For some time I had felt frustrated that we had not been able to get further in our search. I had not been able to devote as much time as I wanted to uncover the assassin, first because I had simply been too ill; then because I had been working full-time for the BBC. Now, having been reluctant to start the investigation, I found I couldn't stop. I wanted to follow up all the leads we never had time for.

A couple of nights before the crew left, Judy and I, nearly dropping from exhaustion, had looked at what parts of the La Penca jigsaw we knew – and what would make a return trip worthwhile. It was difficult. We had all along been working simultaneously at different parts of the plot: the bomber himself; the men who organised the bombing; everyone else involved, however tangentially; the situation before the attack and after. Our knowledge of all these important areas was incomplete. Above all, we lacked eyewitnesses, circumstantial evidence and hard facts. What made it harder was that our search was international. Finally, after a lot of discussion and several cups of strong, black coffee, we wrote up a chronology called 'Countdown to the Bombing', hoping that if we looked at the facts, dates and places we knew, we could more easily spot the gaps. We were especially concerned with the months leading up to the bombing. We came up with the following:

*1982:* A man travelling on a passport stolen from (or maybe given away by) a Danish architect and using the name Per Anker Hansen spends some time in Panama, probably under the protection of Noriega (then Intelligence chief and working for the CIA). For part of this time he has a woman accomplice who is travelling on a stolen French passport in the name of Patricia Anne Boone de Mariscot.

*1983–4:* Immigration records show Hansen travelling widely throughout Central America, as well as to Peru and Mexico. He made one trip to Holland. He went in and out of Costa Rica, entering on 1 October 1983; leaving Peru for Costa Rica on 4 November; entering Costa Rica from Panama by land on 29 February 1984; leaving Costa Rica for Mexico on 2 March. On 3 March he is in Honduras and on 26 March he flies from Honduras to Costa Rica, having hired cars in Honduras from 9 to 26 March. In December 1983, moreover, two men wearing military-style clothing are arrested near the Hotel Costa Rica when they are overheard talking about terrorism and bombs. One is armed with a 45 calibre pistol; he says he is a Cuban American and has an American passport and journalist's credentials in the name of Peter Jensen; he gives an address in Tibas, a working-class suburb of San José. He is later identified as the bomber. The other man is apparently Felipe Vidal. Both men are quickly released by Colonel Alvaro Arias after a phone-call from a superior.

*7 May 1984:* The bomber, carrying identification and press credentials in the name of Per Anker Hansen, checks into the Hotel Gran Via, San José. He is travelling on a 28-year-old's passport. He is tall (1 metre 86), has green eyes and reddish hair and is clean-shaven. He speaks fluent but not native Spanish as well as English and French. At the hotel he links up with fellow guests Peter Torbiornsson and his Bolivian camera assistant, who are making a documentary film about Edén Pastora. He tells them that he has come from Mexico, where he lost all his luggage. Everything he has is Mexican and brand new.

*14–22 May:* The Swedish film-team, Hansen and a few other journalists visit the string of Pastora camps along the San Juan river, including La Penca. They fail to find Pastora, later discovering that for part of the time he is far inside Nicaragua, hiding from his troops, as pressure against him mounts and the crisis within ARDE deepens. While they are still looking for him Pastora leaves for Panama. There, again trying to obtain support and money, Pastora gives radio and television broadcasts about mounting CIA pressure and his fears for his life. The film-team return to San José and make frantic efforts to get Pastora. The normally phlegmatic Hansen is perturbed for the first time, note the crew, that he may be unable to meet Pastora.

*29 May:* The film-team plead with ARDE officials and see Orion, Pastora's cousin, who calls them late that night to say there will be a press conference early the next day.

*30 May:* Having blown us up and posed as a victim, Hansen spends the night in hospital.

*31 May:* At 7 a.m. he takes a taxi with Peter Torbiornsson back to his hotel, the Gran Via, arriving at around noon. Muttering he is going to Miami, he pays his bill in cash and checks out in twenty minutes flat, sauntering outside wearing dark glasses, jeans, a dark shirt and light jacket and with a bag over his shoulder. He hesitates, then walks away.

There are several theories about where and how the bomber gets out, the most popular being to Panama with John Hull's help – but no proof.

What else do we know about the bomber?

Apparently a right-winger hired by Miami Cubans, the CIA or possibly a drug cartel. Known as Amac Galil, but we don't know whether this is the name he is now using. George Morales told us he'd been hired in Chile but trained in Libya and was going back to Libya now. Jack Terrell had been told he was a former Israeli Intelligence officer. Man's real name/nationality/identity/putdown unknown . . .

So far, so good. But from this point our notes grow less clear. Should we concentrate on the drugs network? The 'secret team' run by North? The arcane details of Iran-Contra? The Iran end of the operation? The fact that, according to Danny Sheehan, the US was secretly paying Vietnamese and Cambodian warlords and trafficking in heroin to finance CIA 'black operations'? How much of all this is relevant to that split-second on 30 May 1984 when my life nearly ended? And how can I ever know? I find myself torn between wanting to cover everything and trying to be practical. I have to husband my dwindling mental and above all my emotional resources. I know, rather like a terminal cancer patient, that I can only do so much; have only so much time.

Eventually we decide, given my limited funds and time, I should concentrate on Costa Rica, the rear-base of the plot, and, if time permits, take in Panama (which we had not visited on the filming trip), because we knew the bomber had spent time there before the bombing and apparently afterwards as well, and because there was some evidence that General Noriega, the country's strongman, had worked closely with Oliver North.

We decide we want (if possible) to find out more about the Cuban-led 'gang' on Hull's ranch that David and 'Sebastian' talk about. We decide too that I must pursue the Costa Rican involvement: it was the Costa Ricans who ordered Pastora to hold the press conference inside Nicaragua; either this was used by the bomber or the whole thing was set up for him. The man who ordered the press conference is dead of a heart attack, but I have names of others he was close to. Then there are Pastora's fellow commanders who turned traitor. Peter Torbiornsson was convinced some, particularly Peterson, whom Marielos, Pastora's ex-mistress, remembered meeting, were close to Northern-based Contras. Linked with this is the double- or triple-agent 'Oscar'. Other connections with the Southern Front were the drug pilots, who might know who flew the bomber out of the country and who might confirm the rumour that the attempt on Pastora was partly to do with his being anti-drugs.

The list of 'dos' was steadily growing, and I was beginning to doubt whether I could cope. Worse – and this was something I couldn't confess to the indomitable Judy – I was growing frightfully bored with the whole story. I didn't think I could face more discussion with self-absorbed, earnest Contras and ex-Contras who thought their fight and region were the centre of the world. To them, of course, it was; for myself, I had other, more mundane, ambitions – to have fun, see friends, go to the beach, the ballet, anywhere so long as it was a million miles from the relentless, blinkered, overheated scene that was Central America.

Perhaps what finally decided me was a desire to see the American film consultant, Brian Barger, with whom I had unwisely begun a relationship at the start of our filming. Everything had seemed fine until he left half-way through the filming in late August to carry on with his work in Washington. Now, whenever we spoke (and it usually seemed to be me calling him), I sensed a distance, a hesitation in his responses. Something was wrong. I knew Brian was returning to Costa Rica as he was working on a US documentary on La Penca – taking all our information with him. Judy and the film-crew were outraged, but my own loyalties were torn. Now I found myself hoping that perhaps things were really all right between us.

In fact, Brian was the very first person I saw when I walked through Customs into San José airport, having just realised I'd lost my return ticket. Instantly, my worst suspicions were confirmed. He said (without too much enthusiasm) that he 'hadn't expected to see me back so soon'. Old pro that I am, I reacted with magnificent if extremely forced nonchalance. I then disappeared to my cheap, down-town hotel. I remember lying there, unable to sleep because of the noise of the traffic and the night revellers, feeling stupid to be so upset. I tried to tell myself it didn't matter – but it did. I did manage not to contact him, though, and after three days he called me. We decided, very casually, to have a drink. Of course, I blew the whole 'cool' thing by bursting into tears as he explained he couldn't cope with life, couldn't cope with a relationship, didn't want anyone in his life, felt so bad, so ashamed because he couldn't cope while I who had been injured was so terribly strong. In a way, I felt it was a relief to find out where I stood. I also felt bereft.

Having a relationship had meant to me, on some very deep level, that I was now 'normal' – a proper paid-up member of the human race. And now here I was, alone again, and being told, yet again, how brave I was, when all I wanted was just for once to give up, to be allowed to drop the image of the brave, coping little blonde, and collapse.

I'd come back to do the investigation, and Judy and everyone at Central Television was counting on me. But all I could do was lie on my back in that sordid room gazing at the ceiling. Sometimes I would have lunch in a nice restaurant to cheer myself up, only to feel the world fall in upon me. I remember one day in the Balcón de Europa, a delightful, old-fashioned Italian restaurant, with wonderful daguerreotypes on the wall of turn of the century Costa Rica, all painted ox-carts and men with moustaches. I was eating pasta with a glass of wine when suddenly I wanted to die.

I've never been able to work out why I felt so bad. Maybe the whole investigation was more of a strain than I could ever admit. Maybe dredging up all those buried memories of the explosion was the reason. Maybe having a 'relationship' had meant too much to me after having subconsciously written myself off so far as men and romance and fulfilment were concerned. Whatever the case, Brian's going off was the last straw, and it threw me straight back into the self-punishing depression I had known in hospital. I had been right, I told myself. Something in me had died when I was blown up. Nothing would ever be right again.

I didn't have a TV budget now, which was why I was in a cheap hotel. But it was on a main street and unbelievably noisy, and after a few days I moved to the office of a good friend of mine, which was less noisy – and free. I tried to do the work, but I missed the comforting network of the crew and the support of Judy.

Everything was more difficult. Many of the contacts I wanted to follow up were out of town, and I couldn't afford to hire a car. But taking a taxi twenty miles out of town was also very dear. I cut down on meals, thinking I'd save money that way, but I don't think it was very good for me.

I started by trying to track down Contras who I thought might have turned against Pastora, and I managed to find Peterson, who Torbiornsson thought was actually secretly working against Pastora, and might know something about the La Penca plot. He was involved in a Contra public relations exercise, providing political asylum to 'former Sandinistas', and this involved flying them from somewhere inside Nicaragua to an airstrip close to the border with Costa Rica. Peterson, a skinny little man with a face like a weasel, was shocked that I knew who he was. He couldn't talk to me there, he said, but he'd give me a number and I could call him any time. Needless to say, when I did call I was told he was '*fuera del país*' – 'out of the country'. I never managed to reach him again.

Every day I made plans and schedules of people I had to see, places I must visit. I returned almost daily to the office of Allan Solano and tried to persuade him to tell me more. I tried to track down the contacts given me by the renegade Contra 'Sebastian'. I tried to get further with Rudy Sinclair's story. Tried . . . and nearly always failed.

After about ten days I found I'd got no more out of people I'd already seen than I had on my rushed earlier trip. No one wanted to tell me any more. I got no more out of Pastora and his aide Carol Prado than I had in my earlier interviews, and found myself starting to take the rejection terribly personally, to brood on it. I kept trying to force myself on, to push myself to the limit, but the adrenalin was all used up. Finally, I decided I would go on to Panama. There, in a new country, perhaps I would find out something really significant.

It was to Panama, according to several reports, that the bomber had skipped, aboard a crop-dusting plane belonging to friends of

John Hull, just after La Penca. One version had him sauntering out of the Hotel Gran Via – the last time anyone had seen him – and getting into one of John Hull's vehicles, which was waiting round the corner. He was warned that commercial flights out were being watched and told that he must take the second route; he was then driven to a distant rice-farm in Alajuela province and flown across the Panama border. Another version had him leaving by taxi for Guanacaste province, from where he was flown by drug pilot Gerardo Durán to Puerto Quepos in Costa Rica, put on a yacht to Golfito and then taken to Puerto Armuelles in Panama. He then flew from Paitilla airport to Miami, to the home of Adolfo Calero. It wasn't possible to prove any of this.

I saw a lot of Panama City, with its crumbling, teeming tenement buildings (the worst slums I had seen in Central America), its pretty colonial centre and ultra-modern banking centre (for laundering drug money), and caught occasional, hazy glimpses of the sea as I sped by. Taxi-drivers all solemnly warned me I would be knifed or raped if I tried walking instead of paying them fortunes, and indeed I heard many tales of muggings. But my caution came expensive.

Panama was in political ferment at this time – although on nothing like the same scale as countries like El Salvador or Guatemala. Here the opposition was mounted by right-wing businessmen from the Chamber of Commerce building (with, I was sure, a little help from the US, although they denied this). Protests took the form of wearing white, waving handkerchiefs from cars and twice-daily horn honking. Daringly, shredded papers were thrown from office blocks, and candle-lit rallies and vigils were held by rich, middle-class Panamanians almost daily, although these usually broke up at the sight of the 'Dobermen': government thugs armed with metal bars and weapons. I took care to avoid wearing white. I'm not sure if the disruption made my search harder. It was, as usual, both difficult and, on the whole, fruitless. I wasn't helped by the refusal of Allan Solano – who had urged me to come to Panama to 'advance the investigation' – to give me any of his contacts.

Many of Panama's disparate ethnic groups – Lebanese, Chinese, Jewish – were impenetrable to outsiders, and would have provided the perfect cover for the bomber. Certainly, if he had been here, someone had covered his tracks pretty effectively. There were also sound political reasons why he would have been welcome here. Under General Manuel Noriega, Panama had played a vital role in the secret US pipeline to the Contras, channelling funds and equipment to them, creating a complex network of phony 'front' companies to fund Contra projects (such as the Contra airstrip at St Elena in Costa Rica) and providing free accommodation and tickets to Contra fighters, many of whom described Panama to me as 'our second home', where 'we were totally protected'. Then, I was told, under a secret deal between Noriega and North, Noriega's cronies used Costa Rica to smuggle arms, and drugs, back into the US. It was because of his usefulness, which went back several decades, that the US had waited for so long before acting on the 'Noriega problem'; he was, after all, a US creation. It was only when he got out of control that they felt they had to ditch him.

Now, in 1987, the US was belatedly distancing itself from this one-time ally, prompted by a remarkable accusation against 'Pineapple Face', as Noriega was known (a reference to his acne-pitted face), made by his former second-in-command, Colonel Diaz Herrera. Herrera, who had recently found God, was an unimpeachable source. Furious at being forcibly retired, he had accused Noriega of corruption, election-rigging and murder.

A colleague had told me of a source, known to me as 'Tomás', with good intelligence connections. I met 'Tomás' in the elegant surroundings of the yacht club (he paid for the drinks). He was a voluble, super-smooth, heavily built man who told me that from house arrest Diaz Herrera had held a series of press conferences. At one, according to 'Tomás', a man who said he was a Spanish journalist had carried a briefcase with him which he guarded throughout the conference but then left behind. Herrera, alarmed to see this man leaving so abruptly, ran after him and directed his taxi, which had been waiting for him, to stop. He then handed the reporter his property, which was grudgingly accepted. 'Tomás' was convinced the case contained a bomb, although he gave no evidence to back this up, and was certain the Spanish reporter was my bomber.

I checked out this story, only to be told it had been found to be full of holes. I was told that the Spanish Ambassador himself confirmed the reporter was just what he seemed to be, and had not even been carrying a case. Unfortunately, I couldn't get to Diaz Herrera to ask him directly.*

I then tried the US Embassy – pockmarked with bullets from recent skirmishes with Noriega supporters – with no better results. The CIA denied any knowledge of the man; so did Southern Command, where I spent two successive mornings, getting the standard, outmoded commie-bashing lecture I had heard on earlier trips. I tried to contact the Panamanian accountant whom 'Per Anker Hansen' had allegedly hit with his hired car in 1982, and the car-hire firm itself, without success. The accountant's firm, 'Forestales CA', was not listed in the phone-book. I tried to get access to immigration to find if 'Per Anker Hansen' had entered or left the country. I was shown the door.

I made repeated visits to the 'Las Vegas' apartment block I had been told was 'Hansen's' base. The building was whitewashed, quite smart, with potted plants and lots of pine. The rather basic flatlets I asked to see – fitted carpets, unimaginative furnishings – were self-catering and cost $45 a night. I was offered a room, but declined because of the price. No one there had heard of 'Per Anker Hansen', and I was told the records before 1984 had been destroyed as the building had changed hands. But I should come back, I was told, as the personnel knew someone who had been there at the time and would be able to identify my man. I kept coming back. I was fobbed off with different

* In July 1990 a Christic investigator who had been to Panama to check out the bomber's movements, including this story, told me he believed this incident had in fact taken place. He had spoken to witnesses but didn't have a positive identification. The incident remains a mystery.

stories. I entrusted a photograph of the assassin to a pleasant young Hungarian working in the building, who promised to show it to the former owner; she 'would certainly recognise him if he had been there'. A few days later my young Hungarian, shaking his head, said the owner hadn't recognised the man in the picture. Or said she hadn't. Still I persisted, although by this stage I was becoming so depressed that I could scarcely force myself to go on, to leave my grotty hotel room (the only one I could afford) with its sagging bed and patches of mould on the walls, to try one more phone-call. I used to lie on my back for hours trying to summon my reserves of energy and strength, fighting the morbid thoughts that kept crowding into my mind.

Something kept driving me on – or, more accurately, preventing me from giving up. I was obsessed by my search. If I tried just one more time, one more day, I kept telling myself, maybe I could crack this story, find the bomber. Then, one day as I was climbing another hot, stinking stairwell, an unbidden thought flashed into my mind: 'I wish I was dead.' The thought terrified me. Why should I, the lucky survivor, feel that? A day later, it happened again. And again. Soon after this, after two months back in Central America getting nowhere and down to my last $50, I gave up and flew back home to England.

# 11

# The World's Most Unlikely Hero

At home I faced a half-renovated basement flat, mounting debts, and Judy, who was going crazy trying to piece together a film that seemed unmakable. She didn't need my help, she told me: that would only make matters worse. I understood, but felt shut out.

In the end I did work on the film, travelling to Birmingham every Monday, where we wrote and rewrote the script and did the voice-overs, trying to get the right mix of professionalism and passion to make the story come alive. I also continued making phone-calls all over the world, sending letters to anyone I hoped might know something. I was determined to find something more to say about the bomber himself.

One day I got a phone-call from a reporter from Spain, Guillermo, who worked for the investigative magazine *Interviú*. He told me he had learnt from a detective contact that the bomber had gone, not to Panama, or even Miami, as I had been told, but straight to Spain. He had travelled under the name Ahmed Khalil (remarkably similar to Amac Galil), on either a Syrian or a Libyan passport, on the Spanish national airline Iberia; he then changed planes and flew out on a Royal Air Maroc flight bound for Casablanca, where he disappeared into thin air. My colleague said that shortly afterwards his contact had clammed up completely and would say no more. He suspected the CIA had ordered him to shut up, because that had happened in a similar case recently.

Was this true? And how could I check it? I attempted to obtain Iberia's passenger lists for the first days of June 1984, only to be told that in this most bureaucratic of countries I'd need a judge's approval. I could not obtain it. Guillermo tried to get back to his police contacts for further information. They refused to help. I then tried the Moroccan link, calling a journalist friend in Rabat to see if he could find out where our man had gone once he reached Casablanca – if indeed he had – and giving him the latest alias.

I was not optimistic, until a week later I suddenly received a phone-call from him. My friend had been as good as his word. He had managed via a French contact to sneak a look at the French Embassy's computer, and found a name remarkably similar to my missing bomber's. Ehmed Khalil 'El Arabe' was apparently 'not permitted to enter France'. His nationality was Moroccan and he was born in 1952 at a village between Rabat and Casablanca. I contacted Interpol, but they said our quarry did not appear on any international 'wanted' list. Through another journalist friend in Paris we gained access to the foreign editor of *Le Monde*, who in turn contacted the number two in the French Secret Service, only to be told the Secret Service had never heard of 'Ehmed Khalil'. Another dead end.

We heard at about this time that Amac Galil had been monitored by Cuban Intelligence in Miami a year after the bombing. We were not allowed to reveal our source, although we knew it to be reliable, and once again were unable to verify the information. But then we received another phone-call from someone who had traced the name 'Ahmed Khalil' on the Costa Rican computer: he had found a man named 'Khalil Ahmed' who was 'known as Amac Galil' and who had been travelling on an Egyptian passport: no. Z6399323. Astoundingly, they had him entering and leaving the country *en route* for Panama, Holland and Miami in 1983, 1987 and even 1988. No one in Costa Rica had even thought to check or question the man. Sadly, even though this was such an extraordinary find and it seems likely this was indeed our man, we still had no way of contacting him.

One lead we could follow was that involving a man named Arturo Figari. His name came to light just after the bombing through an ex-Uruguayan guerrilla fighter named Bruno Menghetti. In a newspaper for exiles published in Sweden, Bruno had claimed that Figari, whom he had known when they were both Tupamaru guerrillas back in Uruguay in the 1960s, bore an extraordinary resemblance to the bomber. He told eager reporters that Figari was now, just after La Penca, in Venezuela, having returned from Central America. Several reporters interviewed him there but they concluded the man was innocent. On the other hand, there were some quite remarkable similarities between the bomber's identity and background and those of Figari.

The bomber had said he worked for a photographic organisation called 'Europe 7'; Figari was employed by a French-based organisation called 'Paris 7' (according to Menghetti, a front for recruiting mercenaries for South Africa). The bomber said he worked for a photographic agency in Paris, but it turned out not to exist; Figari had said he had a photographic studio in Amsterdam, but when reporters checked they couldn't find it. The bomber had told Peter Torbiornsson that his father was in Venezuela; Arturo Figari's father had been forced to leave Uruguay because of his son's guerrilla activities, and was now living in Venezuela. I knew that, rather than invent an identity, terrorists usually base their identities and background on real people, and this, I strongly suspected, was the case with Figari. I had also been told that Figari was a former leftist who had become a right-wing mercenary and police informer.

Judy, both directly and through intermediaries, pestered Figari's family until they finally gave us his current address and phone number in Amsterdam. Then we went to see him.

Amsterdam was cold, damp and misty, a welcome change from the hot places of my other encounters. We had made a rendezvous with Figari at an elegant hotel, all dark-panelled wood, soft lights and deep-pile carpet. I waited nervously, thinking I saw Figari a dozen times, until a tall, rumpled man dressed in jeans and a black duffel coat, with a long sad face and a dark beard, came and greeted me.

We drank coffee and he told me a bit about his background. He was, he said, the black sheep of a distinguished Jewish family, and in his teens had become politically active and joined the Tupamarus, an armed left-wing guerrilla group trying to overthrow the government. His speciality was explosives, and he had skipped to Argentina when things got too hot, and then to Chile. Eventually he moved to Europe and joined the Spanish Foreign Legion, serving in the Spanish Sahara until he deserted, unable to face his fellow officers, the flies and the heat. He also sympathised with the enemy, Saharan guerrillas from the Polisario Front who were fighting for independence.

Arturo had a disconcerting habit of making everything appear a huge joke, whether in a deliberate attempt to make light of his rather hairy exploits, to deflect attention, or caused by nerves, I'm not sure. His manic giggle punctuated a confusing tale of plots and counter-plots, which I had to interrupt in order to bring him back to my main concern: his links with the bomber. I brought out my photos. Did Arturo recognise this man? Arturo composed his features and concentrated: he thought he might have met him after he had escaped from Uruguay, but that he hadn't seen him for years and had absolutely no idea where he was. Arturo admitted that, by sheer coincidence, he was in Venezuela just after the bombing: he had suddenly felt the urge to see his father. This led to more stories about Figari's past. My head was beginning to spin. He told me at one point that he had driven round Scandinavia as a penniless hippy, siphoning petrol out of cars until he mistakenly took some from a police car and was arrested. He laughed hysterically at this. He said he had worked for a fanatical (and crazy) right-wing political group, La Rouche, based in the US. (I don't use 'crazy' lightly: among other charges, the group's leader Lyndon La Rouche has claimed the Queen of England is a drug-smuggler.) One of this group's subterfuges is to set up press and photographic agencies with names almost identical to existing left-wing publications, in order to confuse people.

What about 'Paris 7' and 'Europe 7', I wondered. Figari said he worked for the organisation 'for a laugh', stumbling into the job by accident, but was sacked for incompetence. Then the laugh. It was beginning to affect me a bit like Munch's *The Scream*.

We took Arturo out to dinner, eating extremely spicy but mediocre Indonesian food with red wine and then drinking quantities of Irish coffee in a bid to get him to relax and reveal what he was really up to. We played the 'tough and tender' routine, with Judy shouting at Arturo that he was lying and that he did know the bomber and was involved, and me making soothing noises and offering him cigarettes. The routine was not successful – although he got very nervous when we mentioned the CIA – and we never did work out what Figari really knew, or even what he did or who he really was: comic, informant or hitman. I wondered whether he himself knew. We visited the address Figari had given us for his photographic studio – in a cobbled street just off one of Amsterdam's many picturesque canals. But it was a lock-up garage: peering through the letter-box flap we could see a big white truck with advertisements for Italian ice-cream painted all over. No, neighbours told us, it had never been a photographic studio. Arturo himself had claimed the place had burned down, presumably not expecting us to bother to check.

Bruno had gone to great lengths to tell me that Figari looked just like the bomber. Figari was certainly not the man who blew me up. ('Are you sure, are you absolutely sure, Susie?' Judy kept asking hopefully.) But although Bruno himself was a strange, paranoid, rather mad fellow, according to those who knew him, I still found it impossible to explain away the coincidences between Figari and the bomber.

We returned to England and the film realising that in this story there were no 'quick fixes', no lead that would suddenly, miraculously, 'solve' La Penca; just stories that led back into other stories, all of which had to be exhaustively checked.

Then, amazingly, just when I had thought there was nowhere else I could turn, my luck changed. Through a mutual journalist friend who believed he could help me, I met 'Hank'.

I joined 'Hank' and my friend Paul in a Soho bar, where they sat surrounded by glasses of gin and bottles of beer that they were drinking as chasers, Dutch fashion. 'Hank', a short, very powerfully built man, blond, with an expressionless flat face and cold blue eyes, was introduced as a deputy sheriff from Austin, Texas. He worked in Intelligence and was well connected. He apparently knew a lot about the American end of the Central American operation.

We talked. I explained my obsession with finding the bomber. 'Hank' listened and asked questions. We continued to chat, although I feared, as the awesome drinking continued, that the finer points of my pursuit might escape them. At the end of the evening, 'Hank' promised to do what he could to help when he returned to Texas.

I didn't honestly expect anything – so many people had promised but not delivered – so I was really astonished when, a few weeks later, the phone rang and I heard a voice with an exaggerated Texan twang. 'Hank' was stuttering with indignation. He said he had made enquiries: 'I asked for permission to go after the man, you know, just routine stuff. I was told, "Don't touch him, he's one of ours."

'I had always assumed,' he explained, 'that he was one of the Left, working for the Cubans and Nicaraguans.' Instead he discovered that his own government was responsible for the La Penca bombing. 'It's outrageous,' he kept saying. 'My own government. Killing Pastora is one thing, but killing journalists . . . it's definitely not in the Constitution.' He wouldn't talk much over the phone and wouldn't promise to say any of this on camera. There was nothing else for it. I took a plane to Texas.

Austin, the capital and 'Hank's' base, is a small, pretty town surrounded by wooded, hilly country and lakes. Everyone was at least six foot six. Even on the plane men wore cowboy boots, big stetsons and said things like 'howdy' to each other. The weather was perfect: hot but breezy. There were baby turtles in the river by my hotel. Blackbirds swooped down to pick toast crumbs off my balcony. It was perfect for a holiday – but I had to work. 'Hank' was coming over that evening.

I had brought a bottle of duty-free Johnny Walker Black Label as a present for him. It was a mistake. I hadn't realised until 'Hank' arrived that he was a gun freak. Later in the evening I saw he had no fewer than three pistols in his briefcase. We talked. And drank. 'Hank' expanded on what he knew.

'I've been told the CIA Southern Desk was responsible. I've been told the United States government was responsible.'

Finally, after all the run-around of scared sources, people who clammed up at the sight of the camera, who explained they couldn't talk because they had families, someone was coming out baldly with what certainly seemed like the truth. It is extraordinary that of all the panoply of people – from government employees to mercenaries, from drug-smugglers to spies – 'Hank', no angel, was the only one who had the guts to tell me what he knew. What he was saying was dangerous stuff. It could make his life very difficult. I was immensely grateful, and slightly wary. I knew he had fallen foul of the US authorities on a number of occasions, and I hoped he wasn't just trying to get back at them. I set the tape-recorder running.

'How many sources have you got? Is it just one person who's told you this?'

'No, three separate sources.'

'And would you place a great deal of trust in what they told you?'

'Total.'

'So you believe that, to the best of your knowledge, what they said was true?'

'Yes. They were telling me for my own benefit. Don't go looking for this guy because you'll wind up dead. I also have information from William Northrop, who is an Israeli Intelligence officer, and I have a tape-recording of him.'

Then 'Hank', the all-American thug with the perfectly manicured fingernails, switched on his machine.

'La Penca's big-time, pal. I'm telling you, it's a dangerous situation. I know you want to be a good American and I don't know exactly where your mandate comes from or where your agenda goes, but I'll tell you this, you've got to be real careful of these people.'

'Did you ever come up with the guy's real name?'

'Galil.'

'But you said you thought you had his real name.'

'That is his real name. Galil is it.'

'And he is Lebanese?'

'Well, no. Our records show he's Libyan.'

'Do you have a put-down as to where he might be?'

'Mexico or Panama, travelling to and fro. A guy like that can't survive without a sponsor.'

'I was told Panama and Mexico. I was told he was freelance and that he's our asset.'

'That would mean the Americans were responsible for the La Penca bombing,' said Northrop slowly in his North Carolina drawl, so exaggerated it appeared an affectation.

'Hank' added, 'Northrop also told me in an earlier conversation that he'd heard the Southern Desk of the CIA was responsible for La Penca.'

The material was the most damning testimony I had heard so far – and far, far more than I had ever dared hope.

Where was the bomber now, I wondered.

'Being moved between Panama and Mexico, under US protection.' This latest information tied in with our earlier information. But I had spent weeks in Panama, failing to find any trace of him. Well, clearly, no one wanted me to find him. And Mexico? I remembered he told Peter Torbiornsson he had lost all his belongings and had got completely kitted out in Mexico; even his rucksack was Mexican. I also remembered how Joaquín Vargas, who had paid a private detective to find the assassin way back in 1984, had come back, all that time ago, with the information the man he wanted was in Mexico. But then, either because the detective was warned off, or because the Vargas brothers were nervous on hearing of a CIA connection, that trail had been dropped.

I was intrigued by 'Hank's' information that the man's appearance might be changed. I needed to know, if I was ever to find him, exactly what that meant or how I would recognise him. And what did 'being under our protection' mean?

'If he's under deep cover, will he be hidden or disguised or something like that?'

'A new identity goes without saying,' explained 'Hank'. 'Money, plastic surgery to alter his appearance if it is required. Eliminating any threat. If this guy's compromised at all, they'll eliminate whoever's coming after him.'

'Do you think the bombing was planned so that journalists would die in it?'

'There's not a doubt in my mind. If someone with a devious enough mind has decided they're going to kill Edén Pastora and blame it on the Sandinistas and the Cubans, then it will only enhance the impact and the impression when a bunch of innocent people die, because the Americans are immediately going to stand up and say: "We don't kill employees of *Newsweek* magazine; we don't blow up journalists."'

I kept saying, 'This is great, wonderful, but none of it's any use unless you'll say it on camera.' Finally he agreed. But later in the evening he got amorous – and, as he put it, 'a little authoritarian' – by which I mean he threatened me with a gun unless I slept with him. I have a calm disposition, but even I was a little shaken. I told him, in my best nanny voice, not to be silly, that he wouldn't really want me to do something I didn't want, and eventually I persuaded him to go with what I thought was a great line: 'Put that thing away; put both those things away.' Only one was a gun.

God only knows how 'Hank' drove home. He returned at eleven the next morning, sheepish and pale, to collect the sheriff's badge he had left behind with his jacket; he also agreed to go on camera. He had arranged for a friend of his, an ex-Special Forces officer, to see me. This man had interesting information, 'Hank' told me conspiratorially, adding, 'He's killed a lot of people,' much as I might say, 'He's a terrific tennis-player.'

'Pierre' – he didn't want his name known or his voice or face to be recognised, as he still worked for the US government – had made his own enquiries about La Penca because, he explained, an acquaintance of his, General Singlaub, had been accused of involvement by the Christic Institute, charges he vehemently denied. He had agreed to see me, he said, because he was angry about it and about US operations in Central America. 'I didn't object to Pastora being terminated "with extreme prejudice", but it shouldn't have been done in that way, killing journalists. They allowed too many of these so-called *Soldier of Fortune* types to become involved. Hull, for example, and many of the people he surrounded himself with: they became the cutting edge; they were the guys who were out front and they were mishandled, they were allowed to go out of control.'

'Could this group have been responsible for La Penca?' I asked.

'I think it was American instigated. That group could have been responsible for anything, and had an American involvement become public that would have been it for the Contras, so they had to cover it up.'

'Pierre' had started his investigations by calling a Costa Rican law-enforcement agent he knew from the time they worked on a joint drug-interdiction programme. 'I knew he'd been involved in the La Penca investigation, so he'd know what really went down,' Pierre said. 'But when I called and asked him what he knew my colleague got very angry, replied it was none of my business and hung up. I couldn't understand his reaction. We were, after all, old buddies who'd worked together for years. So I called him back and said I didn't understand. He then explained that the Americans – either the CIA or someone from our Justice Department – had come and taken away all the physical evidence of the bombing for examination. They were asked to – the Costa Ricans don't have any experts. But, what, it's been four years now, and the material has never been returned, nor have the results of the analysis ever been made public. What the Costa Ricans are very sore and resentful about is that this smacks of a cover-up, pure and simple. But they can't say any of this. So while it looks as if the Costa Ricans are dragging their feet – it's not them, it's the Americans.'

'Where was the material taken?' I asked.

'CIA headquarters in Langley, Virginia,' was the prompt reply.

'Is it still there?'

'So far as I know.'

We did get Hank on camera, and he delivered the goods. Then, the second we finished shooting, we packed our bags and raced for the next plane back to England. We had only three days to incorporate our extraordinary new material. Central had been patient with us, but we were way over budget and they had already, after some persuasion, financed the extra trip to Amsterdam, only to decide the Figari episode didn't 'fit'. We had been told to find six more minutes for the film, and Gary's information certainly broke new ground. But when we arrived in Central's London office with our cans of film, worn out but ecstatic, we were bluntly told that in the four days we had been away in Texas our extra six minutes had been taken away.

To anyone outside the industry, six minutes may not sound important; to us, they were crucial. Eventually, we succeeded in clawing back four and a half of them. We were in business.

The film was twenty-two weeks in the cutting room (almost a record), but finally, on 17 May 1988, it was aired. The preview was shown in an underground screening room in Wardour Street. As it ended, there was silence. I think even before the congratulations I realised that Judy had somehow – God knows how – out of the mess and ghastliness, the tragedy, the exhausting, unending, unresolvable search, made an extraordinary film; a film that would make a difference; a film, dedicated to the victims, that would do them justice.

I was overwhelmed by the reviews and by the letters pouring in: one, passed on by a friend and still stuck on my wall to encourage me when things look a bit bleak, reads: 'I must thank you for drawing my attention to last night's film *In Search of the Assassin*: it was a spell-binding and extraordinary film from a remarkable woman. It must have been truly traumatic for Susie Morgan to have gone back to the scene of the crime and she displayed great courage in doing so.' I was very moved by what most critics saw as a triumph of the human spirit, and flattered, because it often hadn't felt like that; at the same time, I was a tiny bit embarrassed to be seen as a heroine when I didn't feel I was one.

I also realised that there was much of the 'real' story that we hadn't been able to convey in the film: we were always having to pare down, to simplify. It wasn't the right medium to get across the psychological complexities, the richness and awfulness of the background, to make sense of the politics behind the story and bring the unbelievable characters to life. It didn't explain the personal struggle in the mind and heart of that 'gutsy little blonde' (me), or the gritty reality. In the film I hadn't been able to express, for instance, how I often hadn't felt brave at all – how being a journalist in Central America was hard and often discouraging work; how boring much of it was; how it was sometimes almost unendurable. It didn't say anything about how it was to work as a woman in that world. You had to be Wonderwoman. I wasn't. I was human.

As the euphoria wore off, and all the accolades – 'Best documentary for a decade or more', 'Gives a new meaning to investigative reporting' etc. – were filed away, this feeling grew stronger. The only way to do it, I realised, was to write a book.

I had reservations. I suspected I would find it terribly hard, and, being a gregarious person who loves fun, excitement and action, I wasn't too sure how well I'd adapt to spending months in my dark flat alone with a bad-tempered computer trying to avoid writing the word 'chilling'. And, of course, in some ways I'd had enough of reliving that awful story.

I think it was after being interviewed for the TV review programme *Open Air* that I finally made up my mind. I had been asked, 'Can other people benefit from your experience? What happened to you was so extraordinary, can other people relate to it?'

A serious question. I started to answer yes, that the important thing was to stop being a victim and fight back, that this was of benefit for anyone. I tried to explain that, even though my story was unique, there were lessons and morals that could apply to all sorts of people: that it is possible to go through awful experiences like mine and come out the other side – stronger; that you can take on the impossible. Even if you don't win, you can have a go. Later, I thought, perhaps I'd better write about it to show how.

# 12

# Sanctuary for an Assassin

I started on the book soon after the film was aired. I hoped more information might be teased out as a result, and that I might even find the bomber. As usual, it's all been far harder and less conclusive than I would have liked. All the documentary led to were break-ins of some of the men we interviewed, including 'Hank', but no new information. Then, again, 'Hank', or 'the thug who loves me', as my friends call him, came up with what seemed like a sensational new lead.

He had recently learnt from CIA contacts that the bomber was in Mexico, in what 'Hank' described as 'part concentration camp, part crematorium, part rest and recreation area'. It sounded grotesque. Before he would tell me where it was he made me solemnly promise not to go and check it out myself, as I would get killed. I promised.

He then phoned me late one night from Amsterdam. He said he could no longer come to England, as he would be arrested by MI6. He wanted me to come over. He would give me more details. I left first thing the next morning, but when I got there 'Hank' had already checked out of his hotel. No one knew where he was. The wife of Paul, the friend he had gone to meet, whom I now called from the airport, told me from deepest Oxfordshire that she believed he was flying back to Texas. I hung around the airport, hour after hour, checking the immigration line. Then I discovered there were two, so dashed between both. Then I had a better idea. I managed to persuade the remarkably sympathetic Dutch authorities to page 'Hank' every half-hour as I 'desperately' needed to speak to him. I'm sure the nice young woman to whom I confided my message assumed this was a lovers' tiff.

Finally Paul answered my paging. He said 'Hank' had thought I wasn't coming: 'I doubt you can persuade him to stay. He's very pissed off. I'll talk to him.' Then 'Hank' called. He was furious, and refused to change his flight. I hadn't called him back like I'd promised. I was unreliable. I grovelled. He hung up on me.

I decided I would not accept this rebuff after coming all the way from England. So I walked nonchalantly through Immigration and asked which gate the next flight to Texas was leaving from. With 'Do you have a boarding pass?' ringing in my ears, and my heart pounding, I swept up escalators to find a long, winding line of passengers. Among them was 'Hank', wearing his usual grubby T-shirt and jeans and carrying a lot of duty-free bottles. I rushed up and kissed him, the best disarming technique I could think of.

'How the hell did you get here?' he growled.

'Shushh,' I murmured as passengers turned round, conscious that people like me with no tickets were not supposed to be here.

'You're crazy,' he kept saying to me. 'What do you want?'

'I want to find the bomber, finish the investigation. You know that. That's all I want.'

'I keep telling you, you can't go after this man, you'll get yourself killed. I can go after him for you – but you can't do a damn thing. They'll waste your ass. What do I have to do to convince you? Look at you. You're a bundle of nerves. Do you want *me* to deal with it?'

'No, no, no,' I kept saying. 'I want justice, a trial.'

'It's not possible. Look at you. This thing will kill you. Don't you understand, you'll never get to the bottom of it, you can never find the man. They'll kill you first. You don't seem to understand a thing I'm telling you. I won't give you any more information. Let me deal with it.'

'No, no. Just tell me where he is.'

Finally, as the line snaked forward, he relented and told me the name of the bomber's hideaway. 'It's called Pie de la Cuesta,' he kept repeating. 'Got it? Pee-aye-dey-la-Cwesta. I'm sure of it, this guy just told me.'

I got it.

But what did I do with this tantalising new information? How did I find my man? Particularly as 'Hank' had warned me I'd wind up dead if I visited the place. In the end, I took a plane to Texas, but I felt so worried about seeing 'Hank' on my own that I persuaded Judy to come with me.

In the event, 'Hank', who even met me off the plane at Dallas, was charm itself. I had a splitting headache from the long flight, the unaccustomed heat and my apprehension. But there were no fights and the meeting went well. Judy nudged me on noticing that he had a pistol in the top of his boot, two submachine guns in his van, a pistol in his waistband and another, larger one, in its holster in his gunbelt. She admitted she'd thought I was exaggerating. As we left 'for a vacation' in Mexico we solemnly promised we would not go near Pie de la Cuesta. But I'm afraid to say we sneaked off and did just that.

I was told that the Mexican police – a byword for brutality and corruption – had been using places like Pie de la Cuesta for decades to deal with troublesome students, trades-union leaders and left-wing political activists. But I had no information on this particular place beyond 'Hank's'. We had a contact in Mexico City, where we stopped on the way down to Acapulco; he promised to get hold of a teacher who had been at Pie de la Cuesta and was one of the very few to survive. Unfortunately, it turned out he was now in Veracruz and we couldn't get hold of him in the short time we had left. We sent letters asking for details, but never received a reply.

Judy did, however, meet a man who was seeking political asylum in Canada and who said he had been a member of a Mexican death-squad and had taken prisoners to 'facilities' such as Pie de la Cuesta. Zacarías Osorio Cruz said he was part of a secret military unit (a death-squad) that executed at least sixty political prisoners in the late 1970s and early 1980s. He told her the killings of political opponents were ordered by senior Mexican Army and Air Force officials, some of them still on active duty. He said the prisoners were removed clandestinely from military prisons, killed, and their bodies disposed of. Hooded and handcuffed prisoners were taken to killing fields and riddled with gunfire until their bodies were 'practically torn apart'.

'Hank' had insisted there was a US link and that US Air Force personnel flew in and out of Pie de la Cuesta all the time. He claimed the US was interested in 'preventing the Left taking over in Mexico'; whether this was true or merely reflected his own extremely right-wing views, I'm not sure.

Pie de la Cuesta lies just behind Acapulco, that tarty and glittering tourist resort. We drove – with, I confess, some trepidation – until we reached the entrance to a long, thin spit of land with a rather wonderful, hazy lake on one side and sea on the other. On the sea side were some down-at-heel holiday houses, a single dirt track and a sign: 'ZONA MILITAR; PIE DE LA CUESTA'.

We turned and drove carefully down the street, debating whether to hire a boat and take snaps. Judy was protective of me, and terrified that, if the bomber was there, he might recognise me. I didn't feel nervous at all, although in this case – as indeed in many, many others – the risks were almost impossible to calculate. How could I know if anyone had been monitoring my movements, my phone-calls, my current trip? 'Hank' kept insisting everything was known. I doubted this. But then again, how many of these sleepy-looking Mexicans lolling in their hammocks were informers?

We stopped at a motel just before the barbed-wire complex for a Coke and peanuts, asking casual questions about the military facility, which was blocked off by armed guards and a big iron gate through which covered trucks and jeeps rumbled at intervals. According to the locals even the beach was patrolled at night; the place was very secret and invisible from the road, concealed by thickly planted palm trees; no one was allowed in. I tried not to ask leading questions and alert locals that we were not just tourists, but it was difficult and Judy, quite rightly, ticked me off for asking, 'How many people are in there? What goes on? Why is it secret?' and so on. Gazing at this idyllic spot, I couldn't really believe the assassin – the man I had hunted all these years – might be there. On the other hand, what better cover?

The day after we first explored near the site, Judy drove off alone along a dirt road that appeared to skirt the 'facility', to 'recce' and take photographs. She refused point blank to take me with her. After about three hours she returned saying she didn't think anyone had spotted her and that she had, while driving, managed to take snaps of the complex. Security looked pretty lax – just strands of barbed wire and a wall some distance inside it. She thought our photographer might be able to sneak inside. I thought it could be incredibly dangerous.

The next day we left for London via Dallas. Judy developed her photographs and sent them to Central with a note describing our latest trip. Central was interested – even though the photos, to be honest, were fuzzy and not very impressive – but said we were only in business if we could photograph the bomber inside Pie de la Cuesta.

We sent a questionnaire with basic questions like: what are the chances of a film-crew getting out alive from Pie de la Cuesta? We didn't get an answer. 'Hank' phoned a couple of times, reversing the charges, saying he'd found 'your guy' and reading out tantalising pieces of information from what he called a 'bio' of the bomber. He wouldn't answer any questions I put to him and had 'promised the other guys' (whoever they were) not to pass on any other material.

I complained to Paul, who said he was going to Texas and would talk to 'Hank'. Two weeks later he phoned back. 'Hank', it seemed, had now found 'a man who has had dealings with your guy'.

This intermediary was one of several people running a French restaurant in down-town Dallas. 'Only it's not really a bona fide restaurant,' confided Paul. 'It's a cover for other enterprises. And the waiters aren't really waiters, if you take my meaning.' I had visions of chunky, armed men with Don Johnson stubble, who spent their time dropping trays, snarling at customers who failed to appreciate the nuances of soufflés, and wrestling with their spelling.

'However,' said Paul, 'we've hit a snag . . . Your guy, the one who has regular dealings with the bomber, has taken off – with $150,000 belonging to the restaurant. I don't think he'll be coming back in a hurry.'

That, so far, is my latest lead. It's all rather in character, the black comedy of it – a metaphor for this appalling, unresolvable search. And because it is so absurd, it has made me realise that, although we got a long way, we would never reach the end. It was like chasing a rainbow: when you reach what you think is its end, it has moved on. I felt that, barring a miracle, even if we were to go on for ever, we would never find ourselves any closer. We simply didn't have the official backing we needed to crack the case and bring those responsible to justice. But now, at least, I feel I did as much as I realistically could. I have, finally, played out my obsession. Now, at last, I feel able to turn away from the bombing, and to get on with the rest of my life.

# The Official Version

Three years after the start of our investigation, we finally had official confirmation of our findings. In January 1990 a Costa Rican prosecutor, Jorge Chavarría, published the result of a 'preliminary' (six years after the event) investigation into La Penca. In his report he accuses John Hull and Felipe Vidal of first-degree murder for organising the attack, and recommends they be charged. Why, after so much prevarication, the Costa Ricans finally came up with a report is hard to explain. Perhaps the answer has to do with the fact that elections were looming, and the outgoing Arias administration wanted finally, at little risk, to set the record straight, and Costa Rica had *some* honest officials.

The report stops short of accusing the CIA of the bombing, but alleges that the two men – both CIA agents – were linked to the Iran-Contra conspiracy, which was run from the White House by Oliver North. It says La Penca was masterminded by Nicaraguan Contras, Cuban Americans, Costa Ricans and CIA collaborators, with links to international drug-traffickers. The aim was to circumvent the Congressional ban on aid to the Contras. The network was expanded after 1985 by means of a deal between North and Manuel Noriega, then the Panamanian leader, which paved the way for General Noriega's cronies to use Costa Rica to smuggle arms and drugs.

Former US officials, including Oliver North; John Poindexter, President Reagan's National Security advisor; Joe Fernandez, the former CIA Station Chief in Costa Rica; Lewis Tambs, the ex-Ambassador to Costa Rica; and the arms-dealer Richard Secord are severely criticised.* All except Mr Tambs have faced criminal charges in the US in connection with the Iran-Contra case, but this is the first time they have been accused by a government body of smuggling drugs from Central America to the US to fund the Contras. All five men have been declared *personae non gratae* in Costa Rica. The Chavarría report concludes there was a CIA cover-up to '*desorientar*' the investigation into the bombing and to protect the US network of support run by Oliver North.

Repeating well-known information, the Costa Ricans say the bomb was detonated by a man posing as a Danish photographer who infiltrated the press conference. After being treated overnight in hospital for an apparently self-inflicted wound, he was allowed to leave after a mysterious phone-call, without being questioned. He is named as Amac Galil or Ahmed Khalil. On the night of the bombing, John Hull, Rob Owen and Dewey Clarridge had met in a Costa Rican safe-house, and Mr Chavarría alleges that, despite his denials, Rob Owen was involved in the bombing and should be charged. Again confirming our information, the report also says that at a meeting in January 1985 at the Miami house of a Contra leader, which was attended by Rob Owen, John Hull and CIA officials, Felipe Vidal said, 'We planted the bomb: it failed because of bad timing.' The bomber was outside on the

* At the time of writing, Richard Secord is on probation after pleading guilty to lying to Congress about the Iran-Contra affair. On 21 August 1990 he was sued by Eugene Hasenfus, who accused Secord and the Miami-based Southern Air Transport of controlling the illegal network that supplied the Contras, and thus of being responsible for damages he suffered when his plane was shot down over Nicaragua in 1986. Jurors found there was a special relationship between the plaintiffs and defendants, and that there was evidence 'of a secret operation . . . but no proof'. No damages were awarded, Secord's attorney claiming that, 'These fellows were independent contractors. They took those risks.'

patio at the time. The prosecutor also says evidence, including the bomb's detonator, was taken by CIA officials and not returned.

The motive for the bombing was said to be partly political, just as we had believed, and partly drug-related. Pastora's refusal to permit Contra funding derived from drugs and his insistence on returning George Morales's aircraft when he learnt he was a major drug-trafficker were the final straw. 'From the evidence it is probable the assassin was contacted and contracted by a group of drug-traffickers who backed John Hull, Felipe Vidal and his Cuban movement,' says the report. Pastora was violently anti-drug because he believed involvement with narcotics 'would spell political death to his movement'.

The report links Colombia's Medellín cartel to the Contras and to Oliver North, and details how sovereign countries – including Costa Rica – were suborned and used by drug barons and the United States; their independence and their governments were undermined through external pressure, bribes and corruption. The 54-page, meticulously footnoted report exposes a murky conspiracy of espionage, drug-trafficking and murder carried out by US, Panamanian and Costa Rican officials working for the CIA.

Perhaps the most shocking part of the report is its exposure of the CIA's systematic infiltration of Costa Rica's Security and Police forces, including the takeover of the 'special affairs unit' supposed to be solving La Penca and run by Allan Solano; he had been on the CIA payroll all along. These units – whose officials were known as 'the Babies' – were apparently involved in aspects of the planning of La Penca as well as its cover-up.

The process of 'turning' the Costa Rican police had started back in 1982 when the Americans offered to train a fifteen-man Costa Rican team in counter-terrorism, in line with its policy of expanding Costa Rica's police forces to encourage the neutral nation to take an aggressively anti-Nicaraguan stance. Instead, the 'Babies' unit bypassed its Costa Rican bosses and actually spied on the Costa Rican government. 'The Costa Ricans lost total control of their men,' said the report. 'Instead the unit became totally loyal to the Americans.' CIA agent Dimitrius Papas (known as 'Papi') ran the unit from the American Embassy, providing offices, secretaries, wire-taps, cameras, vehicles and trips abroad – as well as large cash bonuses. This was, noted the report, 'totally against Costa Rican law'. 'The Babies' carried out break-ins, stole and forged documents and smeared and harassed left-wing opponents of the government.

The report details a series of crucial omissions and blunders in investigating La Penca, which, in the light of CIA control of the investigators, makes perfect sense. First, there was the inexplicable failure (described as a 'collapse of command') to question or detain the 'Danish' photographer, even though, as the report points out, 'he was under suspicion at an early stage'. Second, the key material evidence should not have been handed over to the Americans: 'at that stage the most likely suspects were either the Sandinistas or the CIA'. There was a failure to follow up vital leads provided by Martha Honey and Tony Avirgan, who handed investigators extensive photocopied notes. Investigators ignored the evidence of Jack Terrell, interviewed during the Hull–Honey libel trial in 1986, even though he was able to pick out the photograph of the bomber from sixty others. 'His testimony should not have been discounted,' comments the report drily, adding that smears then made against Terrell by Oliver North, Rob Owen and Adolfo Calero should themselves have been considered suspicious, 'given their interest in protecting their own role in the affair'.

The report details how Hull and others began to distrust Pastora to the point where they decided to kill him. It lists secret CIA meetings, including one hosted by Noriega in Panama, and gives names of fighters willing to form a new Front. An extraordinary new plan of Adolfo Calero's is outlined, in which Pastora was to be publicly hanged in Nicaragua by Contras dressed as Sandinistas; the Southern Front would then be taken over by Miami Cubans funded with drug money, and in a second phase

Cubans would use 'liberated' Nicaragua as a base to invade Cuba.

Mr Chavarría laments the lack of US cooperation: 'in the documentation examined both of the Iran-Contra Commission and the Commission on Terrorism and Drugs, all those passages referring to La Penca, and most of those referring to other activities of John Hull, Robert Owen, Oliver North, Joe Fernandez and others, have been blacked out'. It ends by saying: 'This report does not end the investigation into La Penca: much useful information is in the hands of the US authorities and it is up to the good will of the Americans to allow us access to the censured parts of the Senate reports. By the same token, it is impossible for us to interview American witnesses, which is why we consider it important for the Costa Rican Court's requests in this respect to be met.'

In addition to the murder charges brought against John Hull and Felipe Vidal, the report recommends charges of 'illicit enrichment' against members of the 'Babies' unit and dereliction of duty against the detectives who failed to investigate the La Penca bombing. It recommends charges be brought against Oliver North's 'messenger' Rob Owen, mercenary and Contra support organiser Tom Posey, and a number of Costa Ricans associated with the Nicaraguan Contras.

So far as Hull is concerned, he is, after twenty years, back on his ranch in Pakota, Indiana, having fled to the US in 1989 to avoid Costa Rican charges of drug-trafficking and terrorism. In February 1990 a Costa Rican judge, Maximo Esquivel, asked for Hull's extradition from the US. When telephoned at his ranch, Hull said he had no fear of the application's being successful, because 'The US government knows these charges are pure garbage.' It is interesting, however, to hear that he has recently applied to Amnesty International for help . . .

Oliver North's conviction of 1989 for his role in Iran-Contra was overthrown by a US appeal court in July 1990; a retrial may be ordered. North is currently on probation, earning his living on the right-wing lecture circuit and selling bullet-proof vests to Latin American armies.

Edén Pastora returned to Nicaragua just before the elections of February 1990, but failed to make his mark there. He has since returned to Costa Rica, and to his shark fishing.

According to unconfirmed reports, the latest sighting of Amac Galil was in Colombia.

# Appendix

## Oliver North's Diaries

In the summer of 1990 Oliver North's private diaries were released by Special Prosecutor Leonel Walsh. I obtained a copy, hoping to find clues about La Penca. Teasing them out – even *reading* North's indecipherable scribble – was hard going, and key portions were missing. Many entries are in code (Rob Owen, for instance, is 'the courier'); most reveal only the barest details and are clearly intended for North's own use as an *aide mémoire*. But there are interesting snippets. Key figures, including John Hull and Manuel Noriega, request protection; at one point North, supposedly in charge, writes, 'What the hell's going on?' Towards the end, in 1986, events spin increasingly out of control: there are phone-calls to and from the President; the shit is about to hit the fan; one entry in November 1986 reads starkly: 'No way out. Priorities: my country; my President; my family; those who helped us.'

There is one extraordinary item dated July 1984 which reads simply 'those who know', followed by a list of initials: 'RCM, JMP, OCN and John Neg'. I decoded these as follows: Robert McFarlane (National Security advisor), John Poindexter, Oliver North and John Negroponte (US Ambassador to Honduras). Then, 'those who suspect': 'Dewey, Casey' – CIA operative and chief Dewey Clarridge; William Casey. What do they suspect or know? Is it La Penca, or the whole of Iran-Contra?

Why should some know and others – the CIA – only suspect?

Only North himself can really fill in the details; I don't somehow think he will.

On La Penca I tried to deduce from the following entries the build-up to and aftermath of La Penca. Mysteriously, ten days of diary, from the day of the bombing onward, are missing. This is what I found:

*9 February 1984:* 'meeting Pastora: Coronel [Pastora's security man] won't leak.'
*23 April:* 'call from Grey "name is in net"; thing breaking over next 3–4 weeks.'
*30 April:* 'Clarridge will brief Calero.'
*3 May:* 'Rob Owen/Calero.'
*26 May:* 'call from Nestor Pino: Pastora arrives Costa Rica MONDAY from Panama and Venezuela. Call Clarridge: MON.'
*25 June:* 'call from Rob Owen: John Hull protection.'
*29 June:* 'get doctor to look at Pastora. Pastora dumping all over FDN commander. Why do we have to take this shit from Pastora? Pastora is totally confused, bitter, like a primitive animal.'
*23 July:* 'call from Utah; man named Wesley Smith [Hull's minder; Judy met him at the ranch] has video tape of Danish-Swedish journalist. Wants to help.' 'Hull feeling pressured by Pastora: may be under threat.'
*24 October 1985:* 'US trained plastic surgeon in Costa Rica willing to do each patient for US $3–5,000.'

I deduce that Nestor Pino, a Miami Cuban, who calls North direct with information about Pastora's imminent arrival in Costa Rica ten days before the bombing, must be a CIA plant. It's significant that North immediately calls his CIA man Clarridge: is this when the plan is finalised? The 'Hull protection' item must, I assume, refer to La Penca. The reference to the video of the 'Danish-Swedish journalist' must be to the bomber. But who needs the plastic surgery?

Some of the material is, to me, bizarre. Why does North want to get Pastora a doctor when they tried to kill him? (Pastora refuses.) Why are there scores of entries detailing Pastora's every movement? Does he still represent a threat? Even more confusing, why are there entries saying 'press conference: Pastora told to say Southern Front now controlled by Chamorro'? Why are there entries saying, 'Pastora must talk to CIA, Pastora has talked to CIA'? On whose side is Pastora – the man who told me he was sure the bombing was carried out by North and his men – and what game is he playing? Pastora is even referred to in one typewritten entry stuck on by Fawn Hall, North's secretary, as 'your problem child' – as though there is some strange collusion between him and North; as though Pastora (whom North at one point says 'is wandering miles off the reservation') has merely been 'disciplined' by La Penca but is actually still partly in the fold, or at least not totally outside it, and is still more influential than I had realised. And where does all this leave us, the real victims?

# A NOTE ON THE AUTHOR

Susie Morgan was born in Exeter, England. She has worked as a foreign correspondent in Africa, the Middle East and Latin America. From 1981 to 1984 she was based in Central America, reporting on the crisis for a variety of newspapers, news magazines and broadcasting networks including *Newsweek*, *The Economist* and the *Observer*. Following the bombing at La Penca, she made a documentary film, *In Search of the Assassin*, shown on ITV in 1988. This is her first book.